ABBREVIATIONS &
ACRONYMS

ABBREVIATIONS & ACRONYMS

A GUIDE FOR FAMILY HISTORIANS

COMPILED BY KIP SPERRY

Library of Congress Cataloging-in-Publication Data

Sperry, Kip.
  Abbreviations and Acronyms: A Guide for Family Historians/Compiled by Kip Sperry.
    p. cm.
  ISBN 0-916489-94-9
  1. Genealogy--Dictionaries. 2. Abbreviations. 3. Acronyms--Dictionaries. I. Title.
  CS6 .S64 2000
  929'.1'03--DC21

                                                                    00-021120

First printing 2000
10 9 8 7 6 5 4 3 2 1

Printed in the United States of America

INTRODUCTION

ALL FIELDS OF STUDY HAVE THEIR OWN UNIQUE abbreviations, acronyms, alphabetic symbols, initials, contractions, and shortenings of words. Genealogy and history are certainly no exception. Perhaps even more abbreviations are used in these two disciplines than one can imagine.

This book lists abbreviations and acronyms alphabetically as found in genealogical and historical sources—both in original records and in printed sources. Included is a brief explanation or description of the abbreviation, acronym, or initials.

This work is intended as a reference source for genealogists, historians, reference librarians, and others searching for the meaning of an abbreviation or acronym. Such references might be found in federal population census schedules, Soundex indexes, mortality schedules, court records, original records on microfilm or in archives or courthouses, or in printed sources, such as compiled genealogies, periodical articles, newspapers, and others. Abbreviations of many institutions, publishers, and organizations are also included, and some show their address. Internet addresses have not been included.

Most of the abbreviations refer to the United States and Canada, although others are found in British sources and sometimes other countries as well. Generally this guidebook does not include foreign language abbreviations, such as German, Greek, and so forth. Some basic computer terms are included; however, other manuals better explain computer terms in greater detail. A bibliography of reference titles and related Internet Web pages concludes this work.

One may question why medical and other abbreviations are identified here. Knowing the meaning of these abbreviations may be helpful when researching mortality schedules, death records, court records, and other similar records used by genealogists, historians, and reference librarians.

It is realized that not every abbreviation and acronym found in genealogical and historical sources is identified here. That would be an overwhelming task. Many county and local genealogical and historical organizations and libraries have their own unique abbreviations, as do compiled genealogies and other publications. Generally, periods have not been used in the abbreviations. Thus, C.G. is listed in this work as CG.

Appreciation is extended to the following individuals who assisted with typing the manuscript: Melissa E. Finlay, Robin Lewis, Amber Ostler, Angie Rasmussen, Marta M. Smith, and Marta E. Taylor. The following individuals served ably as research assistants: Misty C. Armstrong, Emily Carrie Hunter, Julie Kaufman, Echo King, Melissa Law, Amy J. McLane, Brandy Lynn Sago, and Jennifer Stoker. I am grateful to Brigham Young University, Provo, Utah, for its support.

-Kip Sperry

A

a   (1) about (2) abstract (3) acre(s) (4) administration (5) adultery (6) against (7) age (8) analysis (9) annual (10) *annus* (age[d]) (11) ante (before) (12) archives (13) aunt (14) sealing conversion

a.   after

A   (1) Agder-Aust'Agder (2) Alien (3) Aunt

AA   (1) Agricultural Adjustment (2) Associate of Arts (3) Australia (4) Automobile Association (British)

AAAL   American Academy and Institute of Arts & Letters

AAC   *Anno Ante Christum* (in the year before Christ)

AAC   Archives Advisory Commission (Massachusetts), Massachusetts Historical Records Advisory Board Massachusetts State Archives, 220 Morrissey Blvd Boston, MA 02125

AAC   Army Air Corps

AACR   *Anglo-American Cataloging Rules* (American Library Association)

AACR2   *Anglo-American Cataloging Rules* (American Library Association, 1990)

AAF   Army Air Force

A-Ag   Aust-Agder, Norway

AAG   Association of Accredited Genealogists, Utah, P.O. Box 4043, Salt Lake City, UT 84110-4043

AAG   Assistant Adjutant General

AAGG   African-American Genealogy Group, P.O. Box 1798, Philadelphia, PA 19105-1798

AAGHS   African-American Genealogical and Historical Society

AAGHSC   Afro-American Genealogical and Historical Society of Chicago

AAGHSTN   African American Genealogical and Historical Society of Tennessee

AAGRA   Australasian Association of Genealogists and Record Agents

AAGSC   African American Genealogical Society of Cleveland

AAGSNC   African-American Genealogical Society of Northern California, P.O. Box 27485, Oakland, CA 94602-0985

AAHGS   Afro-American Historical and Genealogical Society, P.O. Box 73086, Washington, DC 20056-3086

AAI   Automated Archives, Inc.

AAL   Aid Association for Lutherans

Aalb   Aalborg, Denmark

AAONMS   Ancient Order of Nobles of the Mystic Shrine

AAP   *Ancestors of American Presidents*, by Gary Boyd Roberts

AAP   Assessment of Achievement Programme (Scottish)

aar   against all risks

aar/Aarn   year

Aarhus   Aarhus, Denmark

AAS   American Antiquarian Society, 185 Salisbury Street, Worcester, MA 01609-1634

AASK — Adoption Answers Support Kinship, 8 Homestead Drive, South Glastonbury, CT 06073-2804

AASLH — American Association for State and Local History, 1717 Church Street, Nashville, TN 37203-2991

AASP — *American Antiquarian Society Proceedings*

AASR — Ancient Accepted Scottish Rite (Masonic)

AAUP — American Association of University Professors, 1012 14th Street NW, Suite 500, Washington, D.C. 20005-3465

ab — (1) abbey (2) about (3) abridgement (4) administrator's bond (5) appeal against bastardy

a & b — assault and battery

Ab/Abr/ Abrhm — Abraham

AB — *Artium Baccalaureus* (Bachelor of Arts)

AB/Alta — Alberta, Canada

ABA — American Bar Association, 750 N. Lakeshore Dr., Chicago, IL 60611

aban — abandoned

A Barb — Anna Barbara

A'Bard — Auster'Bardastrandarsysla

abba — an abbey

abbr/abbrev — (1) abbreviated (2) abbreviated form (3) abbreviation

ABC — Adoptee-Birthfamily Connection, P.O. Box 22611, Fort Lauderdale, FL 33335-2611

abd — abdicated

Abd/ABD/ Abdns — Aberdeenshire (Scotland)

ABE — American Board of Education

ABELL — *Annual Bibliography of English Language and Literature*

ABER — Anhalt Bernburg

Aberd/ ABER — Aberdeen, Scotland

Abg — Aldonberg

ABI — *American Biographical Index*

ab init — *ab initio* (from the beginning)

abl — ablative

ABMC — American Battle Monuments Commission, ABMC Courthouse Plaza II Ste. 500, 2300 Clarendon Blvd., Arlington, VA 22201

ab nepos — a great-great grandson

ab neptis — a great-great granddaughter

abot — abbot

Abou; Abu — literally, father; the first element in many Arabic proper names; sometimes abbreviated to Bu

Abp — Archbishop

abr — (1) abbreviation (2) abridged (3) abridgment

Abra^m — Abraham

abs — (1) abscond (2) absent (3) abstract

ABS — American Bible Society, 1865 Broadway, New York, NY 10023-7505

abst — absent

abstr — abstract(s)

abt — about

ABWE — Association of Baptists for World Evangelism, P.O. Box 8585, Harrisburg, PA 17705-8585

ac — (1) acres (2) adopted child (3) *anni currentis,* current year (4) archives case (5) attested copy

Ac — acres

AC	(1) Air Corps (United States) (2) Alsace Loraine (3) ancestor chart (4) *Ante Christum* (before Christ) (5) appellate court (6) Assumption College	ACGSI	Allen County Genealogical Society of Indiana, P.O. Box 12003, Fort Wayne, IN 46862
A/C	(1) according to (2) account (3) account of	achd	adopted child
ACA	American Congregational Association, Congregational Library and Archives, 14 Beacon Street, Boston, MA 02108	achiev	achievement
		ackd/ acknowled/ acknowd/ acknown	acknowledged
ACAD	academy, academies		
ACASA	Archives of Czechs and Slovaks Abroad, Regenstein Library, 1100 East 57th Street, Chicago, IL 60637-1502	ACLIN	Access Colorado Library and Information Network, Colorado State University, 201 East Colfax Ave., Denver, CO 80203
ACBLF	Association canadienne des bibliotécaires de langue française	ACLS	American Council of Learned Societies, 228 East 45th Street, New York, NY 10017-3398
acc	(1) accommodation (2) accompanied (3) according (to) (4) account (5) accusative	ACLU	American Civil Liberties Union, 125 Broad St., 18th Floor, New York, NY 10004-2400
ACC	American Computing Centers	acnt	account
ACC	Anglican Catholic Church	acpj	archives common pleas journal
accompt^t	(1) acomptant (2) account	ACPL	Allen County Public Library, 900 Webster Street, Fort Wayne, IN 46802
accon/ accot/acct/ acompt	account	act	(1) acting (2) active
		actg	acting
accord^g	according	ad	(1) administration docket (2) adopted (3) adopted daughter (4) adulterer, adultery (5) *ante diem* (before the day) (6) Archdeacon (7) archdeaconry
acco^t/acc^t	account or accompt		
acct	(1) account (2) accountant	ad/add	*addatur* (let there be added; addition)
accu	accurate	Ad	Adopted
ACD	Adams County Democrat, West Union, Adams Co.	AD	(1) *anno Domini* (in the year of the Lord) (2) Archdeaconry/ies
ACG	American College of Genealogy	Adau/AdD	adopted daughter
ACGS	American-Canadian Genealogical Society, 358 Notre Dame Ave., P.O. Box 668, Manchester, NH 03105-0668	ADC	Aide-de-Camp
		adcl/AdCl	adopted child
ACGS	Ashtabula County Genealogical Society, 860 Sherman St., Geneva, OH 44041-9101	adcon	archdeacon; archdeaconry
		AdD	adopted daughter

3

addl	additional
Add.MS	Additional Manuscripts (British Library, London)
addn	addition
ADE	Aden
Adelh	Adelheid, Adelheit
ADES	Anhalt Dessau
AdGcl	adopted grandchild
ADH	aus dem Hause (out of the house)
ADI	Area of Dominant Influence (such as newspaper or other media)
ad inf	*ad infinitum* (to infinity)
ad init	*ad initium* (at the beginning)
ad int	*ad interim* (in the meantime)
adj	(1) adjoining (2) adjourned (3) adjuster (4) adjunct
adj/adjt	adjutant
Adj Gen	Adjutant General
ad lib	*ad libitum* (at will)
ad loc	*ad locum* (at the place)
ad locum	*ad loc* (to or at the place)
adm	(1) administrator (2) Admiral (3) Admiralty (England) (4) admission (5) admitted (i.e., to church) (6) letters of administration
adm	admitted to communion (church)
adm/admin/ admin^ion/ adminism admon/ admn/adn	(1) administration (2) administrator
Adm	admiral
Ad M	adopted mother

Adm Co	Administrative county (British)
admin^r/ admn/admr(s) /admor/ adm'r/adnors	(1) administrative (2) administrator(s)
adminstr	administrator(s)
admix/ admin^x	administratrix
Admon	(1) administration (2) letter(s) of administration
admor	administrator (probate)
admr	administration
admrx/ admx/ adm'x	administratix
admstr	administers
adnors	administrators
a dnt	attendant
adop	adopted
ador	administrator (probate)
ADP	automatic data processing
ad patres	gathered to his father's; dead
adpt	adopted
Adr	Adrian
ads	(1) *adversus* (the opposite of versus) (2) advowson (3) autograph document signed
Ad S	adopted son
adtrix	administratrix
adv	(1) adverb (2) *adversus* (against) (3) advertising (4) advised (5) advisor (6) advisory
AdvGen	Advocate General
advr	(1) adviser (2) advisor (3) advisory

advt	advertisement	AFGE	American Federation of Government Employees, 80 F Street, NW, Washington, DC. 20001
ADY	Alderney		
æ/aet/aetat/ aetatis	(1) age (2) aged	AFHS	Alberta Family Histories Society, P.O. Box 30270, Station B, Calgary, Alberta, Canada T2M4P1
ae(t)/aeb	(1) at the age of; aged (2) each (3) one (4) one of several administrator's and executor's bonds	AFN	Ancestral File Number (FamilySearch)
aed	administrator's and executor's docket	aforsd/afsd aforesd/afors aforsd/forsd	aforesaid
AEF	*before ab initio* (before abate)	Afr	Africa
aegidius	Giles	AFr	Anglo-French
A El	Anna Elisabeth	AFR/ AFRI/Afric	Africa
Aelizia	Alice		
aeltester/ aelteste	oldest, eldest, elder	AFRA	American Family Records Association, P.O. Box 15505, Kansas City, MO 64106-0505
aet/aetat/ aetas	*aetatis, aetatis* (aged, generation, lifetime, of age)	AFRC	American History Research Center, University of Akron, OH 44325-1702
aetatula	very tender childhood	aft	(1) after (2) afternoon
af/aff'dt	affidavit	AFT	Ancestry Forum Trainee
Af/Afr	Africa	ag	age
AF	Africa	AG	Accredited Genealogist. One who has passed the rigorous tests administered by the Family History Library (FHL) in Salt Lake City, Utah
AF	Ancestral File™ (database in FamilySearch®)		
A-F	Anglo-French	AG	(1) Adjutant General (2) Attorney General (3) Attorney General's Office
AF & AM	Ancient Free and Accepted Order of Masons	AG/Arg	Argentina
afds	aforesaid	AG:ABC	"American Genealogy: A Basic Course," NGS' home-study course
Aff	(1) Affairs (2) Affidavit		
aff'dt/afft	affidavit	AGBI	*The American Genealogical-Biographical Index* (Middletown, Conn.: Godfrey Memorial Library). Formerly known as Rider's Index.
affin	(1) affinity (2) affinitive		
Aff/Liver	Affection of Liver	AGCIG	Arizona Genealogical Computer Interest Group, P.O. Box 51498, Phoenix, AZ 85076-1498
affl	affluent		
AFG	Afghanistan	agcy	agency

AGD   (1) Adjutant General's Department
(2) adopted granddaughter

AGE   (1) Assembly of Governmental Employees
(2) Association for Genealogical Education
(organization no longer meeting)

agee   aged

AGES   Accelerated Genealogical Endexing Schedules
(Salt Lake City, Utah)

AGI   Archivo General de Indias, Seville

Agl   Anglesey, Wales

Ag. Lab.   agricultural laborer

AGLL   American Genealogical Lending Library, P.O.
Box 329, 593 West 100 North, Bountiful, UT
84011-0329

AGM   *American Genealogy Magazine*, P.O. Box 1587,
Stephenville, TX 76401

AGM   annual general meeting

agncy   agency

agnt   agent

AGO   Adjutant General's Office

Agr   (1) agricultural laborer (2) agriculture

AGRA   Association of Genealogists and Record
Agents, 29 Badgers Close, Horsham, West
Sussex, England RH12 5RU

agric/agrl   agriculture

agrt   agreement

AGS   adopted grandson

AGS   Alabama Genealogical Society, P.O. Box 2296,
Samford University Library, 800 Lakeshore
Drive, Birmingham, AL 35229-0001

AGS   American Genealogical Society, Depository and
Headquarters, Samford University Library,
Box 2296, 800 Lakeshore Drive, Birmingham,
AL 35229

AGS   Anchorage Genealogical Society, P.O. Box
212265, Anchorage, AK 99521-2265

AGS   Arkansas Genealogical Society, P.O. Box 908,
Hot Springs, AR 71902-0908

AGS   Association for Gravestone Studies, 278 Main
Street, Suite 207, Greenfield, MA 01301

AGS   Augusta Genealogical Society, P.O. Box 3743,
Augusta, GA 30914-3743

agt   agent

agt/agst   against

agt brewry   agent for the union brew

agy   agency

AGY   Anglesey

AH   (1) *Anno Hebraico* (in the Hebrew year)
(2) *Anno Hegirae* (in the year of the Hegira)

AH   *Agricultural History*

AHA   American Historical Association, 400 A Street
SE, Washington, DC 20003-3889

A&HA   Ancient & Honorable Artillery Company of
Massachusetts

AHFA   Adam Hawks Family Association

AHH   Arthur H. Hughes

ahl   *ad hoc locum* (to this place)

AHN   Archivo Histórico Nacional, Madrid

Ahnentafel   literally means "ancestor table"

AHQ   *Alabama Historical Quarterly*

AHR   *American Historical Review*

AHS   Alaska Historical Society, P.O. Box 100299,
Anchorage, AK 99510-0299

AHS   Atlanta Historical Society, Atlanta History
Center, Library/Archives, 3101 Andrews Drive,
NW, Atlanta, Georgia 30305

AHSGR	American Historical Society of Germans from Russia, 631 D. Street, Lincoln, NE 68502-1199	Akhs	Akershus, Norway
A'Hun	Auster'Hunavatnssysla	al/AL	(1) alias (2) alien (not naturalized; citizen of another country; abbreviation often found in U.S. census schedules) (3) alley (4) aunt-in-law (5) autographed letter
AI	(1) *Annals of Iowa* (2) artificial intelligence		
aib	archives inventory book	Al	Aunt-in-law
AIC	Army Invalid's Certificate	AL	(1) Alberta LDS Temple (2) American Legion
AID	Adoptees Identity Discovery, P.O. Box 2159, Sunnyvale, CA 94087	A/L	Archives/Library
AIG	Adjutant-Inspector-General	AL/Ala	Alabama
AIGI	Amelia Island Genealogical Society	ALA	*ALA filing rules* (American Library Association)
AIHS	American Irish Historical Society, 991 Fifth Avenue, New York, NY 10028	ALA	American Library Association, 50 East Huron, Chicago, IL 60611
AIIM	Association for Information and Image Management	AlA&ML	Alabama Agricultural and Mechanical State University Library, P.O. Box 908, Normal, AL 35762
AIS	Accelerated Indexing Systems (publisher of printed census indexes and compiler of U.S. census indexes on microfiche)	Alab	agricultural laborer
AIS	Adoptees in Search, P.O. Box 41016, Bethesda, MD 20824	ALARM	Alliance of Libraries, Archives and Record Management
		Alas	Alaska
AISI	Accelerated Index Systems International (publisher of printed census indexes and compiler of U.S. census indexes or microfiche)	Alb	(1) Albert (2) Albier
		ALB	(1) Albania (2) Alberta, Canada
aj	(1) adjutant (2) associate judge	ALBER	Alberta LDS Temple
AJAG	Assistant Judge Advocate General	Albr	Albrecht
ajcc	associate judge county court	ALC	(1) Adult Learning Center (2) American Lutheran Church
AJGS	Association of Jewish Genealogical Societies		
AJHSQ	*American Jewish Historical Society Quarterly*	ALCTS	Association for Library Collections and Technical Services
AJLH	*American Journal of Legal History*	ald	alderman
AK/Ak	Alaska	Ald	Aldenberg
aka	also known as (often used before a name to indicate that the name is an alias)	AlDAR	Alabama Daughters of the American Revolution
AKC	Associate, King's College London	Aldern	Alderney, C. Island

aleg/alleg	allegation, allegiance
Alex	Alexander
Alf	Alfred
Alg	(1) Algiers (2) Algonquin dialect
ALG/ALGE	Algeria
ALHN	American Local History Network
ALIC	Archives Library Information Center (National Archives and Records Administration), 700 Pennsylvania Ave. NW, Washington, DC 20408
all	(1) alley (2) alliance (3) allow
ALL	Academy of Lifelong Learning, University of Delaware
Alld	Allied
ALMA	Adoptees Liberty Movement Association, P.O. Box 727, Radio City Station, New York, NY 10101-0727
alne	alone
ALOR	Alsace Lorraine (Elsass-Lothringen)
alph	alphabetically
ALPLI	Allen County Public Library, 600 Webster Street, Fort Wayne, IN 46802
als	alias
a.l.s.	autographed letter signed
als/alsoe	*alius* (the second, also)
ALS/al(s)s	autographed letter(s) signed
Als	Alsace/Alsem
ALS	Adult Learning Service
ALSA/Alsac	Alsace

AlSAr	Alabama Department of Archives and History, 624 Washington Ave., Montgomery, AL 36130-0100
AlsK	Alsies Kohem
als wt	alias writ
alt	(1) Alter, age (2) alternate (3) altitude
Alta	Alberta, Canada
altm	at liberty to marry
Alvsbg	Alvsborg, Sweden
aly	alley
Am	American
AM	(1) *anno mundi* (in the year of the world) (2) *ante meridian* (before noon) (3) *Artium Magister* (Master of Arts)
AM/AME/Amer	(1) America (2) American
AMA	American Medical Association (see especially Deceased Physician File, National Genealogical Society)
AMAE	Archives Du Ministère Des Affaires Étrangères, Paris
A Magd	Anna Magdalena
Aman	almsman
Am. Antiq.	American Antiquarian Society, 185 Salisbury Street, Worcester, MA 01609-1634
A Mar	Anna Maria
Amb	Ambassador
AMC	Anna Maria College
AME	African Methodist Episcopal Church
amend	amendment
Amer	(1) America (2) American
AMICUS	National Library of Canada online database

AMORC	Ancient Mystical Order Rosae Crucis (Rosicrucians) 1342 Neagles Ave., San Jose, CA 95191
AmRC	Amistad Research Center, New Orleans, LA, ARC, Tilton Hall, Tulane University, 6823 St. Charles Ave., New Orleans, LA 70118
Ams	Amsterdam
Amst	assistant master
Amste	Ger.-Amsterdam
amt	amount
AMtr	assistant matron
AMVETS	American Veterans of World War II, Korea and Vietnam, AMVETS National Headquarters, 4647 Forbes Blvd, Lanham, MD 20706-4380
an	*annus; anno* (in the year)
AN	(1) Anglo-Norman (2) Archives Nationales, Paris, France (3) Arapahoe Nation (4) Austria-Netherlands
Ana	Anna
ANB	*American National Biography*, 24 vols. (New York: Oxford University Press)
anc	(1) ancestor(s) (2) ancestral (3) ancestry
anc ch	ancestor chart
Anc Co	ancient county (British)
Anc File	Ancestral File™ (genealogical database in Family Search®)
Anc & Hon Artillery	Ancient and Honorable Artillery Company of Massachusetts
AND	Andorra
An Do/ AnoDom	*Anno Domini* (in the year of the Christian era)
Andr	Andreas
Andr^w/ And^w	Andrew

ANep	adopted nephew
Ang	(1) Angur (2) Angus, Scotland
ANG	American Newspaper Guild
Angl	(1) Anglican (2) Anglicized
Angl/ ANGL	Anglesey, Wales
ANGU	Angus, Great Britain
ANHA	Anhalt
anie	adopted niece
AniMap	AniMap locality software (The Goldbug)
Anl	Annual Report
ann	(1) annotated (2) annual (3) annum (4) annuity
Anniv.	Anniversary
annl	annual
annot	annotated
annu/ annuit	annuitant (has yearly fixed sum)
ano	(1) *annus* (year) (2) another
ano/an	year, as in "Ano 1683"
anon	anonymous
ANS	Angus (see Forfar)
ant	(1) antiquary (2) antonym
Ant	(1) Anthon (2) Anton (3) Antrim, Northern Ireland (4) Antsovlerberg
ANT	Antigua, West Indies
ante	(1) before, or prior to (2) in front, forward
anti	against
ANTI	Antigua

antiq	(1) antiquarian (2) antiquary (3) antiquities (4) antiquity
Antiq	Antiquarian
Ant°/Antª	Antonio/Antonia
anx	annex
ao	(1) *Anno* (year) (2) account of
AO	(1) Atlantic Ocean (2) Audit, Exchequer and Public Record Office, Kew
AO12, AO13	American Loyalists' Claims, 2 series, Public Record Office, Kew, Richmond, Surrey, England TW9 4DU
AOL	America OnLine (commercial computer online service)
AONS	Association of One-Name Studies
AOP	American Order of Pioneers
ap	(1) A prefix meaning "son of" (2) apprentice
Ap	Apprentice
Ap/Apr/ Aprill	April (month) Abrill
AP	(1) ancient parish (British) (2) Apia Samoa LDS Temple (3) Associated Press
apb	archbishop
APB	Archives de la Marine, Brest, France
apd	(1) appealed (2) appearance docket (3) appointed (4) attending places of division
APDU	Association of Public Data Users, Division of Business & Economic Research, University of New Orleans, New Orleans, LA 70148
APG	Association of Professional Genealogists, P.O. Box 40393, Denver, CO 80204-0393
APGQ	*Association of Professional Genealogists Quarterly*, P.O. Box 40393, Denver, CO 80204-0393
APH	Association of Personal Historians
API	Associated Press International
APIA	Apia Samoa LDS Temple
APJI	Association for Protection of Jewish Immigrants
apk	archives, packet
apl	Appeal
APL	Service historique de la Marine, Archives du Port de Lorient, Lorient, France
APLIC	Association of Parliamentary Librarians in Canada
APM	Assistant Provost Marshal
apmt	appointment
APO	Army Post Office
APOLROD	Association for the Preservation of Ontario's Land Registry Office Documents, 251 Second Street, Stouffville, Ontario L4A1B9
apoth	apothecary
app	(1) apparent (2) appendix (3) application (4) appointed (5) appraisement record (inventory) (6) apprentice (7) approach (8) approximately
app blksmt	apprentice blacksmith
app carptr	apprentice carpenter
app cbntmkr	apprentice to cabinet maker
appd	(1) appeared (2) appointed
App Div	Appellate Division
app'dt	appointed
append	appendix
appl/applic	(1) applied (2) application
appls/applls	appeals, as in law

Appop	Appoplectic
app prntr	apprentice printer
appr	(1) appearance (2) appellor (3) appraisement (4) appraisal (5) apprentice
apprd	(1) appeared (2) appraise
approx	approximately
apprs	appriser
appt	(1) apparently (2) appointed (3) appointment
app't	appointed
apptd/ appted	appointed
appur	appurtenances
appurts	appurtenances
appwagnmkr	apprentice to wagon maker
appx	appendix
Apr	April
APS	American Philosophical Society,105 South 5th Street, Philadelphia, PA
APSDS	Association de personnel de services documentaires scolaires
APSECS	Australasian and Pacific Society for Eighteenth-Century Studies
APSG	Association for the Promotion of Scholarship in Genealogy, Ltd., 255 North 200 West, Salt Lake City, UT 84103-4545
apt	appointed
apt(s)	apartment(s)
APVA	Association for the Preservation of Virginia Antiquities, 204 West Franklin Street, Richmond, VA 23220- 5012
AQ	Ancestral Quest genealogy software
AQMD	Assistant Quartermaster-General

aqs	autograph quotation signed. Usually a verse or statement or a few bars of music written out and signed.
a quo	from whom
ar	record of administration
AR	(1) *Alabama Review* (2) Appeal against Removal (3) AR (Anno Regni), the year of the reign of (4) Alien Registration
AR/Ark	Arkansas
ARA/ ARAB	Arabia
arb	arbitrator, arbitrate, arbitration
arc	arcade
ARC	American (National) Red Cross
ARC	Automated Resource Center, Family History Library, 35 North West Temple Street, Salt Lake City, UT 84150
arch	(1) archaeological (2) architect (3) architecture (4) architectural (5) archives
Arch.	Archbishop
Archd	Archdeaconry
archit	architectural
Archiv	*Achiv für das Studium der Neueren Sprachen und Literaturen*
archt	architect
ArcM	Master of Architecture
Arfr	Artificer
arg	(1) argent, silver (heraldry) (2) argentum blue (a silver color)
Arg	Argyllshire, Scotland
ARG/ ARGE/Argt	Argentina

ARGUS	ARGUS, Marysville, Union Co. newspaper	arsl	arsenal
ARGY/ ARL	Argyllshire, Great Britain	art	article
Argyll	Argyll, Scotland	art/artill/ arty/artl	artillery
ArHQ	*Arkansas Historical Quarterly*	Arth/Art^r/ Arth^r	Arthur
ARI	Automated Research Inc., 1160 South State St., Suite 220, Orem, UT 84097	arti/artif	artificer
Ariz/AZ	Arizona	Artl	Artillery
ARIZO	abbreviation for Arizona LDS Temple	AS	(1) Adopted Son (2) Alsase, France (3) Anglo-Saxon (4) *anno salutis* (in the year of salvation) (5) at Sea (6) Azores
Ark	Arkansas		
Ark & Dove	Society of the Ark and the Dove	AS/ASM	American Samoa
ARL	Ancestry Reference Library (CD-ROM)	ASA	Advertising Standards Authority (of England)
ARL	Ancestry Reference Library, Ancestry, Inc., P.O. Box 990, Orem, UT 84059	A–Sbg	Aabenraa, Sonderborg
ARL	Association of Research Libraries, 21 Dupont Circle, Washington, DC 20036	ASC	(1) Army Service Corps (2) Army Survivor's Certificate (3) Isle of Ascension (4) *The Anglo-Saxon Chronicle*
Arm/ Armagh	Armagh, Ireland	ASCAP	American Society of Composers, Authors, and Writers
ARME	Armenia	ASCII	American Standard Code for Information Interchange (a common communications format for personal computers). Text not formatted with HTML.
Armr	Armorer		
Armst	Armstadt		
Arnold	James N. Arnold, *Vital Record of Rhode Island, 1636B1850*	AscM	assistant schoolmaster/mistress
arprt	airport	ASEA	At Sea
arr	(1) arranged (2) arrangement (3) arrival (4) arrived	Aser	agricultural servant
		ASF	Archivio di Stato, Florence
ARR	Anno Regina Register	ASG	American Society of Genealogists, P.O. Box 1515, Derry, NH 03038-1515
ARS	Automated Records System (General Land Office), GLO Records Access Staff, Bureau of Land Management, Eastern States, 7450 Boston Boulevard, Springfield, Virginia 22153-3121	ASGR	Association of Germans from Russia
		ASGRA	Association of Scottish Genealogists and Record Agents, P.O. Box 174, Edinburgh EH35QZ Scotland
arrv	arrived		

ASGS	Arizona State Genealogical Society, P.O. Box 42075, Tucson, AZ 85733-2075
ASI	(1) Adopted Sister (2) Asia
ASIA	Asia
ASJA	*American Society of Journalists and Authors*
Asmb	(1) assemblies (2) assembly
asmblr	assembler
ASN	Archivio di Stato, Naples
A-Sndr	Aaberaa, Denmark
asoc	associate
ASon	adopted son
asr	assessor
assd	assigned
assgn	(1) assign (2) assignee
assist/asst	assistant
assn/assoc/ assocn	association
asso./assoc.	(1) associate (2) association
AssocSc	Associate in Science
Asso.Pres. Ch	Associated Presbyterian Church
asst/Asst	assistant
Ass't Q.M. General	Assistant to Quarter Master General
assy	assembly
ASTED	Association des sciences et des techniques de la documentation, 3414, avenue du parc, Suite 202, Montréal, Québec, Canada H2X 2H5
Astl	Australia
ast mrshll	assistant marshal
ast srvyor	assistant surveyor
A Sus	Anna Susanna
ASV	Archivio di Stato, Venice
at	(1) archives, testamentary record (2) attendant
At	Attendant
AT	Atlanta Georgia LDS Temple
atba	able to bear arms
Atch	assistant teacher
ATG	Applied Technology Gallery
Atl	Atlantic Ocean
ATLAN	Atlanta Georgia LDS Temple
at lge	at large
atndt	attendant
a&tr	administration and testamentary record
ATS	at Sea
att	(1) attached; attached to (2) attest
att/atty	attorney
attn	attention
attt/ attachmt/ attachm	attachment, as in law
attrib	attributed to
atty	attorney
ATut	assistant tutor
au	(1) aunt (2) gold
AU	Austria
auc	*ab urbe condita* (from the founding of the city, i.e., Rome, in 753 B.C.)
AUC	Atlantic Union College
aud	auditor

Aug/Augs/ August
Augst/Ag

AUH   Austria Hungary

AunL   aunt-in-law

AUS   Arm of the United States

AUS/Aust/ Austria
Austr/OES

AUS/   Australia
AUSL/
Austl/AUT

auto   autobiography

aux   auxiliary

Aux Sons   Auxiliary to Sons of Union Veterans of the
of Union   Civil War Veterans Site for Sons of Union
     Veterans of the Civil War

av   *annos vixit* (he lived [so many] years)

av/aver   average

a/v   ad valorem

Av/Ave   avenue

AV   Appeal against vagrancy

ava/us   grandmother/father

avail   available

ave   avenue

AVGS   Antelope Valley Genealogical Society, P.O. Box
     1049, Lancaster, CA 93584-1049

AW   *Arizona and the West*

awc   admon (letters of administration) with will and
     codicil annexed

AWC   Army Widow's Certificate

AWmn   almswoman

AWOL   absent without official leave

Ayr/AYR   Ayrshire, Scotland

Az/az   azure (a blue color) (heraldry)

AZ/Ariz   Arizona; Arizona LDS Temple

AzGAB   Arizona Genealogical Advisory Board, P.O. Box
     5641, Mesa, AZ 85211-5641

AzHS/AHS Arizona Pioneers Historical Society, 949 East
     Second Street, Tucson, AZ 85719

AzMBL   Arizona Mesa Branch Genealogical Library,
     Mesa, AZ (Family History Center)

AZOR   Azores

Aztec Club Aztec Club of 1847

B

b   (1) bachelor (2) baptism; *baptême* (French) (3) birth (4) book (5) born (6) brother (7) on maps and chartsSBay or Bayou

b.   before

B   (1) Baptist (2) Black (3) British (language) (4) Brother (5) Burials

ba/bach   bachelor

ba/bap/bapt   baptized

BA   (1) Bachelor of Arts (2) Bahamas (3) Bastard (4) Bastardy Allegation (5) Bavaria (6) Boston Athenaeum (7) Buenos Aires Argentina Temple

BAAF   British Agencies for Adoption and Fostering (11 Southwark Street, London, England SE1 1RQ)

baby   baby

bach/bachr   bachelor

BACSA   British Association for Cemeteries in South Asia

Bad/BAD/BADE   Baden

BAE   Bureau of American Ethnology

bag   baggage

BAg/BAgr   Bachelor of Agriculture

BAH/BAHA   Bahama Islands

Bai   Baierne/Bairn/Baier

BaiD   bailiff's daughter

Baier   Baiern

Bail   bailiff

Bair   (see Bai)

BAIRE   Buenos Aires Argentina LDS Temple

BaiS   bailiff's son

BaiW   bailiff's wife

bakr   baker

bal   balance

bal/ball   an account balance

Balth   Balthasar

Ban   Banel

BAN   Banffshire

B and S   Bargain and Sale

BANF   Banff, Great Britain

bank cashr   cashier of the Alton Bank

bank intrp   interpreter in bank

bank tellr   teller in bank

bap(t)/bp   baptize/d

Bapt   Baptist

bar   (1) baron (2) baroness (3) bartender (4) boar

Bar   (1) Barisha (2) Bartender

BAr/BArch   Bachelor of Architecture

BAR/BARB   Barbados

BarA   bar assistant

Barb[a]   Barbara

bark	bar keeper	bbl(s)	barrel(s)
BarM	barmaid, barman	B Boy	bound boy
Baronial Ord	Baronial Order of Magna Charter	BBS	Blairs' Book Service, 1661 Strine Drive, McLean, VA 22101
bart/bt	baronet	BBS	Bulletin Board System; Bulletin Board Service (users exchange files and leave messages)
Bart^{me}	Bartomone		
BarW	barwoman	BC/B.C.	(1) bachelor (2) Bachelor of Chemistry (3) Bail Court (4) Bas-Canada (i.e., Lower Canada or Québec) and British Columbia, Canada in 1881, 1891, and 1901 (5) Becker College (6) before Christ (7) Bible Church (8) Borough Council
Bas	bastard		
BASc	Bachelor of Applied Science		
Bat.	Battery (military regiment)	BCC	(1) Bellevue Community College, 3000 Landerholm Circle, Bellevue, WA 98007 (2) British Council of Churches (see CCBI)
batch	bachelor		
batln/bat/ batt	battalion	BCC/UCF	Brevard Community College, University of Central Florida, 1519 Clearlake Rd., Cocoa, FL 32922-6597
BatM	bath man		
batt	battery	BCD	(1) binary code decimal (2) Bristol County, Massachusetts, Deeds
BAUS	Bingham Association in the United States		
Baut^a, B^t	Bautista	BCE	(1) Bachelor of Chemical Engineering (2) Bachelor of Civil Engineering (3) before the Christian Era (4) before the common era
Bautzn	Bautzen, Sax.		
Bav/Ger/ Bava	Bavaria, Germany	b/cer	birth certificate
BAV/BAVA	Bavaria (Bayern)	BCG	Board for Certification of Genealogists, P.O. Box 14291, Washington, DC 20044
Bay	Bayden	BCGS	British Columbia Genealogical Society, P.O. Box 88054, Lansdowne Mall, Richmond, BC, Canada V6X3T6
BB	(1) Bail Bond (2) Barbados (3) Bastardy Bond		
BBA	Bachelor of Business Administration	bch	beach
BBC	British Broadcasting Corporation	Bch	Bachelor of Surgery
BBCS	Bulletin of the Board of Celtic Studies	BCHS	Bucks County Historical Society, 84 South Pine Street, Doylestown, PA 18901-4999
Bbd	Bombardier	BCL	Bachelor of Civil Law
bbl	barrel(s)	BCMS	Bible Churchmen's Missionary Society
Bbl	Bible	bd	(1) birth date (2) board (3) boarder (4) bound (5) buried

Bd	(1) Baden, Germany (2) Bedfordshire, England
BD	Bachelor of Divinity
Bda. Arch.	Bermuda Archives, Hamilton, Bermuda
Bdau	boarder's daughter
bde	brigade
BDF	Bedfordshire, England
bdl	bundle
Bdle	beadle
BDN	Baden
bds	(1) beds (2) boards
BDS	Bachelor of Dental Surgery
bdt	birth date
Bdy	Broadway
BE	(1) Bastardy Examination (2) Belgium
BE/BEd	(1) Bachelor of Education (2) Bachelor of Engineering
BEA	Bureau of Economic Analysis
bec	became
BEDF/ Beds	(1) Bedford, England (2) Bedfordshire, England
BEE	Bachelor of Electrical Engineering
bef	before
BEF	British Expeditionary Force(s)
beh	beheaded
BeHLUM	Bentley Historical Library, University of Michigan, 1150 Beal Ave., Ann Arbor, MI 48109-2113
Bei	Beirn/Biern/Beiyens
BEK	Berkshire, England

Bel/BEL/ Belg	Belgium
BelI	Belfast, Ireland
Bened	Benedikt, Benedict
BENG	Bengal
Benj^a/ Benjn/ Benj	Benjamin
BEO	Board of Economic Operation
beq	(1) bequeathed (2) bequest
Ber	(1) Berlin/Bernstadt (2) Bermuda (3) Berne (4) Berwickshire, Scotland
BerG	Berlin, Germany
Bergen	Bergen, Norway
BERK/ Berks	Berkshire (England)
Berli	Berlin
BERM	Bermuda
Bern^{do}	Bernardo
Berw	Berwick, Scotland
BER	Bermuda
BERW	Berwick, Great Britain
bet/betw	between
BEW	Berwickshire
Bey	Beyens
bf	(1) before, such as before 1850 (2) black female (3) boldface type
BF	(1) Bachelor of Finance (2) Bachelor of Forestry
BFA	Bachelor of Fine Arts
B&FUA	British and Foreign Unitarian Association

bg	big	BI	British Isles
BG	(1) Bugler (2) burial grounds (3) Burg	Bia	Bian
Bgd	Brigadier	BIA	Bureau of Indian Affairs
BgdMaj	Brigade Major	Bib	(1) Bible (2) Biblical
BGen	Brigadier General	bibl	*bibliotheca*; library
bgemn	baggageman	bibl/bibliog	bibliography
Bgg/Mstr	Baggage Master	Bic	Bickerburg
B Girl	bound girl	BIC	born in the covenant (an LDS Church term). Indicates that a child's parents were married and sealed in an LDS temple prior to the child's birth.
BGL	Branch Genealogical Library of The Church of Jesus Christ of Latter-day Saints (now known as Family History Centers)		
		Bicent	Bicentennial
bglr	bugler	BIDC	Business/Industry Data Center
BGMI	*Biography and Genealogy Master Index* (Detroit: Gale Research Co., 1975-)	bien	biennial
		Biera	Bieran
BGS	Buckinghamshire Genealogical Society, Mrs. Eve McLaughlin, Varneys, Rudds Lane, Haddenham, Bucks, England HP17 8JP	Biern	Bierne/Bierren
		BIFHS-US	British Isles Family History Society-USA
BGS	Bachelor in General Studies	BIGHR	British Institute of Genealogy and Historical Research
BGSU	Center for Archival Collections; Bowling Green State University, Bowling Green, OH	BIGR	*British Isles Genealogical Register* (project of the Federation of Family History Societies)
BH	(1) Bohemia (2) Board of Health		
BHC	British High Commission	BIGRA	British Isles Genealogical Research Association
BHC	Burton Historical Collection, Detroit Public Library, 5201 Woodward Ave., Detroit, MI 48202	BIGWILL	British Interest Group of Wisconsin and Illinois
		BIHR	*Bulletin of the Institute of Historical Research* (British)
Bhlm	Bornholm, Denmark	Bil	Bilafelt
BHM	*Bangor Historical Magazine*	b-i-l	brother-in-law
BHR	*Business History Review*	Bills/Colic	Billious Colic
BHS	Bahamas	Bills/Fev.	Billious Fever
BHS	Beverly Historical Society, 117 Cabot Street, Beverly, MA 01201	bi-m	every 2 months
BHU	Bhutan	bio/biog/ biogr	(1) biographical (2) biography

biol	(1) biological (2) biologist (3) biology
Bir	(1) Birmingham (2) Biron
BIRDIE	British Isles Regional Display of IGI Extracts
bish	bishop
bi-w	biweekly
BJ	Bachelor of Journalism
BJS	Bureau of Justice Statistics
bk/bks	(1) bank (2) barracks (3) block (4) book(s) (5) brook
Bk	Buckinghamshire, England
BK	Brother's Keeper (genealogy software program)
bkbndr	bookbinder
bkpr	bookkeeper
bksm	blacksmith
bk statnry	book & stationary mercha
BKW	Brother's Keeper for Windows (genealogy software program)
Bl	(1) British Library (2) brother-in-law
BL	(1) Bachelor of Law (2) Belgium (3) British Library, London England (4) Brother-in-law
Blaw	by law
bldg(s)/blg	building(s)
bldr	builder
Blek	Blekinge, Sweden
blf	bluff
BLG	Belgium
BLit(t)	(1) Bachelor of Letters (2) Bachelor of Literature
blk	(1) black (2) block

blksmith/ Blk/Smth	Black Smith
BLM	Bureau of Land Management, U.S. Department of the Interior, Eastern States Office, 7450 Boston Blvd., Springfield, VA 22153 *See also* GLO
BLN	Bounty Land Number
bl reg	bounty land rejected
blrmkr	boilermaker
BLS	(1) Bachelor of Library Sciences (2) Bureau of Labor Statistics
bltd	billeted
Blu	Blumberg
Blvd	Boulevard
BLW/ BLWT	Bounty Land Warrant (a right to free land in the Public Domain)
bm	(1) *beatae memoriae* (of blessed memory) (2) bi-monthly (3) black males (4) bondsman
BM	(1) Bachelor of Medicine (2) Bench Mark used in surveying land (3) Bermuda (4) Brigade Major (5) British Museum
BMA	Bureau of Missing Ancestors (Everton Publishers, Logan, UT)
BMAA	Baptist Missionary Association of America
BMan	(1) bar manager (2) bondsman
BMD	births, marriages, deaths
bmdr	bombardier
bmo	business machine operator
Bmot	boarder's mother
BMP	Bit-mapped graphics format (Windows Bitmap)
BMS	Boston Marine Society, 1st and 6th Avenue #32, Charlestown, MA
bmt	basement

BMus	Bachelor of Music	BorB	boarder's brother
Bn	(1) Battalion (2) births	BorC	boarder's child
BN	Baden, Germany	Bord	boarder/boardress
BNA	British North America	BorD	boarder's daughter
bnd	(1) bend (2) bond (marriage)	BorG	boarder's grandson
bndsmn	bondsman	BorN	boarder's niece
Bnf	Banffshire, Scotland	BORO	Borough
Bnq	Bibliotheque nationale du Québec	BorS	boarder's son
bns	banns (marriage)	BorW	boarder's wife
bo	(1) Boarder (2) born (3) bottom (4) bought (5) bound	Bos/Carp	Boss Carpenter
		Bosn	Boatswain
b/o	brother of	BOSN	Bosnia
Bo	Boarder	bot	bought
BO	(1) as found inland records of colonial period probably means British Oak or Bur Oak, inferred from WO meaning White Oak (2) Bohemia (3) Boise Idaho LDS Temple	BotB	boat boy
		BotM	boatman
boat ngner	engineer on boat	botp	both of this parish
Bodl. Libr.	Bodleian Library, Oxford England, Bodieian Library, Broad Street, Oxford OXI 3BG	BoU	Boston University, Boston, MA
		boul	boulevard
Boe	Boehm/Boern	BOUNT	Bountiful, Utah LDS Temple
BOGOT	Bogotá Colombia LDS Temple	boy	boy
Boh/Bohe	Bohemia	Boyds	Boyd's Marriage Index
Bohme	Bohmen/Bahmen	bp	(1) baptized (2) before the present (3) birthplace (4) bishop
BOISE	Boise, Idaho LDS Temple		
BOL	Bolivia	BP	Black Polls
bona	goods, chattels, moveable property	BPd/BPe	Bachelor of Pedagogy
boot	boots	BPE	Bachelor of Physical Education
bor	borough	BPh/BPhil	Bachelor of Philosophy
BOR	(1) Borough (2) Island of Borneo	bpl	birthplace

BPL	Boston Public Library, 700 Boulston Street Copley Square, Boston MA 02117	Bre/BREC	(1) Brecknock, Wales (2) Brecon, Great Britain
BPOE	Benevolent and Protective Order of Elks	BRE	(1) Bachelor of Religious Education (2) Breconshire
bps	bits per second (computer term)	Brec	Bible record
bpt	baptized	Breme/ BREM	Bremen
Bpt/Mins	Baptist Minister		
bq	*bene quiescat* (may he rest well)	Brev	Brevet
br	brought	brew	brewer
br/bro	brother	brg	(1) bridge (2) burg
Br	(1) Britain (2) British	BRG	British Guiana
BR	(1) Book of Remembrance (2) Branch (3) Brazil (4) Bremen, Germany (5) British (6) British Rail (7) Bromskirschen	BrHCDPL	Burton Historical Collection, Detroit Public Library, Detroit, MI
Bra	Bradenburg/Braunsweig	bri	bridge
BRA/Braz	Brazil	BRI	British East Indies
Brain/Fev	Brain Fever	brick brnr	brick burner
Brain/Inf	Brain Infirmation or Inflamation	Brid[a]	Brigida
BraL	Braslaw	BriE	Bristol, England
BRAN	Brandenburg	Brig	(1) Brigade (2) Brigadier
Brand	Brandenburg	Brig Gen	Brigadier General
brassfnshr	brass finisher	Brig Insp	Brigadier Inspector
BRAZ	(1) Brazil (2) Brazilian	Brig Q.M.	Brigadier Quarter Master
BRBL	Beinecke Rare Book and Manuscript Library, Yale University, New Haven, CT 06520	br-in-l	brother-in-law
		Brio	Brion/Briosson
brd	buried	Bris	Brisen
BRD	Germany (1991)	Brit.	(1) Britain (2) British (3) Briton (4) Great Britain
Brdbg	Brandenburg, Prussia		
brdng hs	boarding house	Brit. Mus.	British Museum, London, England
		Brit Ref	British Reference
Bre	(1) Brecknockshire, Wales (2) Breman	BriYU	Brigham Young University, Provo, UT 84602

brk	brook
Brk	Berkshire, England
brklyr	bricklayer
brkmn	brakeman
BrLD	brother-in-law's daughter
BrLS	brother-in-law's son
BrLW	brother-in-law's wife
Brm	Bermby
BRM	Business Reply Mail
BRN	born
bro	brother
br/o	brother of
Bro	Bromane
BroD	brother's daughter
BroL/ bro-i-l/ bro-il	brother-in-law
bro/o	brother of
BroR	brother in religion
bros/bro(s)	brothers
BroS	brother's son
BroW	brother's wife
BRS	Belarus (Belorussia)
BRS	*British Record Society*
BrSi	boarder's sister
Bru/Brun/ Bruns/Brunsw	Brunswick (Braunschweig), Germany
BRU	Brunei

Bryn	Bryan Public Library, 107 East High Street, Bryan, Ohio 43506
bs/B/S	bill of sale
Bs/Stllr	Boss Stiller
BS	(1) Bachelor of Science (2) Bahamas (3) British Standard
BSA	Boy Scouts of America
BSAg	Bachelor of Science in Agriculture
BSBA	Bachelor of Science in Business Administration
BSc	Bachelor of Science
BSch	boarding scholar
BSE	Bachelor of Science in Engineering
BSEd	Bachelor of Science in Education
Bser	bakery servant
bshp	bishop
bshp tr	bishop's transcript(s)
Bskd	Buskerud, Norway
BSL	Bachelor of Science in Law
BSN	Bachelor of Science in Nursing
BSnL	boarder's sister-in-law
Bt	(1) Baronet (2) Beat (3) Brevet
BT	(1) Bishop's Transcript(s) (England) (2) Board of Trade, Public Record Office, Kew, England
BT/BTh/ B Theology	Bachelor of Theology
BTA	British Tourist Authority (formerly British Travel Association)
btch	butcher
Bte	Buteshire, Scotland
btlr	butler

BtlS	butler's son	BUR/ BURM	Burma
BtlW	butler's wife	Bur Gr	burying ground
btm	bottom	Burkh	Burkhard, Burkhart
Btm	Boatman	Bur Plot	burial plot
Btry/Bttry/ Bty	Battery (army unit)	Bürg	Bürger, citizen
BTs	Bishops Transcripts	burs	bursar
Btss	Baronetess	bus/busn	business
bttn	battalion	BUS	Business Services
BTU	British thermal unit(s)	BUT	Bute
btw	(1) a bulletin board (computer) abbreviation (2) between (3) by the way	Bute/ BUTE	Bute, Scotland
btwn	between	bv	beide von (both from)
bu	(1) burial (2) buried (3) bushel	BV	Bavaria
Bu	butler	BVI	British Virgin Islands
BU	Baptist Union of Great Britain and Ireland	BVM	Blessed Virgin Mary
BUCH	Buchau	BVR	Bureau of Vital Records
Buck/ Bucks/BUK	Buckinghamshire, England	BVRHS	Bureau of Vital Records and Health Statistics
BUD	Budapest	Bvt	Brevet
BUGB	Baptist Union of Great Britain	bw	bi-weekly
bul/bull	bulletin	b/w	black and white
BUL/ BULG	Bulgaria	BW	Brunswick
		BWI	British West Indies
Bulletin	Genealogical Forum of Oregon quarterly, 2130 SW 5th Avenue, Suite 200, Portland, OR 97201-4934	Bwid	brother's widow
		bx	box (archival)
BUP	British United Press	Bye	Byern
BUPNS	Bulletin of the Ulster Place-Name Society	byp	bypass
bur	(1) bureau (2) burial (3) buried	Byr	Byrne/Byren/Byern/Bayern

byu   bayou

BYU   Brigham Young University, Provo, UT 84602

BYU   *Brigham Young University Studies*, Brigham
Studies   Young University, Provo, UT 84602

C

c/ca.   *circa* (about; frequently used before an uncertain or approximate date; around). For example, c. 1790 or ca. 1790.

C/c   (1) Baptisms (2) Cambridgeshire, England (3) case number (4) Celtic (5) cemetery record (6) centigrade (7) century (8) Chancery (9) chapter (in law citations) (10) child (11) christened (12) Christening Register (13) *circa* (about) (14) Colored (15) controlled extraction (LDS term) (16) copyright (17) Corporal (18) cousin (19) indicates christenings (or births) extracted in Controlled Extraction Program of LDS church (20) name cleared for LDS temple (21) 1890 Union pension census (22) cousin

C1   First Corporal

C2   Second Corporal

C3   Third Corporal

C4   Fourth Corporal

C5   Fifth Corporal

C6   Sixth Corporal

C7   Seventh Corporal

C8   Eighth Corporal

ca.   circa (approximately)

Ca/Can   Canada

CA   (1) Central America (2) Chartered Accountant (3) Coast Artillery (4) Common Wealth Award (Virginia Genealogical Society) (5) Court of Appeals

CA   Church Archives, Historical Department of The Church of Jesus Christ of Latter-day Saints, 50 East North Temple, Salt Lake City, UT 84150

CA/Calif   California

C of A   Coat of Arms

CaAR   California State Archives, 1020 "O" Street, Sacramento, CA 95814

cabtmkr   cabinetmaker

CAC   Center for Archival Collections, Bowling Green State University, Jerome Library, Bowling Green, OH 43403-0175

CACC   Council for the Accreditation of Correspondence Colleges (British)

Cache   Cache Genealogical Library, Logan, Utah

CAD   Certificate of Arrival Division, Ellis Island

cadet   cadet

CAE   Caenarvonshire

CAEDM   Computer Aided Engineering Design and Manufacturing

CAER/Caerns   Caernarvon, Wales

CAGG   Computer-Assisted Genealogy Group

Cai/CAIT/Caith   Caithness, Scotland

CAI   Caithnesshire

CAILS   Certified American Indian Lineage Specialist (Board for Certification of Genealogists, P.O. Box 14291, Washington, DC 20044). See CLS.

Cal   (1) California (2) calendar

calc   calculated

CALG   Certified American Lineage Genealogist

Calif Pioneers	Society of California Pioneers, The Alice Phelan Sullivan Library and Archives, 300 4th Street, San Francisco, CA 94107-1272
CALS	Certified American Lineage Specialist (Board for Certification of Genealogists, P.O. Box 14291, Washington, DC 20044). Now known as Certified Lineage Specialist SM (CLS).
CALUPL	Council of Administrators of Large Urban Public Libraries (Canada)
CAM/ Camb/Cambs	Cambridgeshire (England)
Camb/ Cambs	(1) Cambridge, England (2) Cambridgeshire
CAME	Central America
CAMLS	Cleveland Area Metropolitan Library System (Cleveland, Ohio) 20600 Chagrin Blvd, Ste 500, Shaker Heights, OH 44122-5334
campn	campaign
CAN/ CANA	(1) Canada (2) Canadian
Cana	Canada
CanaW	Canada West
cand	candidate
Can$	Canadian dollar
CanP	Canadian Press
Cantab	*Cantabrigiensis* (of Cambridge)
CAO	Conference of Administrative Officers
cap	(1) capital (2) capitalized
cap/capt/ captn	Captain (military)
Cap	(1) Cape Britton (2) Captain
CAP/ CAPE	Cape of Good Hope

CAPG	Colorado Chapter, Association of Professional Genealogists, P.O. Box 40817, Denver, CO 80204-0817
capt	(1) captive (2) captured
CaptLt	Captain Lieutenant
Car	Carlow, Republic of Ireland
CAR	Caribbean
CAR	Children of the American Revolution
CarC	care child
card	carder
Card	Cardiganshire
CARD/ Cards	Cardigan, Wales
CARI	Caribbean Islands
CARL	Canadian Association of Research Libraries
Carls	Carlsruhe
Carm	Carmarthenshire
CARM/ Carms	Carmarthen, Wales
Carn	Carnarvonshire
CARN	County Archives Research Network (British)
Carol	Carolina
carp/carpt	carpenter
carpt jonr	carpenter & joiner
carr	carriage
carr drvr	carriage driver
carr mkr	carriage maker
carr trmr	carriage trimmer
cart	carter

Carvan	Carvan, Ireland	Cbern	pr. Canton Berne, Sw.
Cas	Cassel	CBI	China, Burma, India
cash	cashier	Cbnt/Mkr	Cabinet Maker
casl	casual	Cboy	cart boy
CaSL/CSL	California State Library, Sacramento, CA Library and Courts Building 914 Capitol Mall, Sacramento, CA 95814	CBT	Computer-based training
		cc	(1) carbon copy (2) cubic centimeters (3) LDS Church census
CASLIS	Canadian Association of Special Libraries and Information Services	CC	(1) chain carrier (2) Clerk of Court (3) Company Commander (4) Country Club (5) County Clerk (6) County Commissioner (7) County Court
CaSlSu	California State Library, Sutra, CA		
Casp	Kaspar, Caspar		
CAST	Center for Applied Special Technology	C of C	Chamber of Commerce
cat	(1) catalog (2) catalogue	CCAPG	Colorado Chapter, Association of Professional Genealogists (APG) Ruth Herlacher Christian, 19341 Knotty Pine Way, Monument, CO 80132-9438
cath	cathedral		
Cath	(1) Catharina (2) Catherine (3) Catholic (4) Katharina		
		CCBI	Council of Churches for Britain and Ireland Inter-Church House, 35-41 Lower Marsh, London SE1 7RL
cath bshp	Catholic Bishop		
cathclergy	Catholic clergyman		
cathpriest	Catholic Priest	CCC	(1) Civilian Conservation Corps (2) Clerk of the County Court (3) Copyright Clearance Center (4) Chapman County Codes (British)
CATNYP	Catalog of the New York Public Library, New York, NY		
		CCCGS	Contra Costa County Genealogical Society, P.O. Box 910, Concord, CA 94522
cav.	Cavalry (military regiment)		
Cav	Cavan, Republic of Ireland	CCD	(1) census county divisions (2) Computer Council of Dallas, Texas
Cawel	Cawell		
cb	(1) chain bearer (2) county borough	CCF	Collections Control Facility (Library of Congress)
Cb	Cuba		
CB	(1) Bachelor of Surgery (2) Christenings & Burials (3) Color Bearer (4) Companion of the Order of the Bath (5) Court Baron (England)	CCG	Connecticut Coordinated Genesearch, P.O. Box 757, Watertown, CT 06795
		CCGS	Chautauqua County Genealogical Society, P.O. Box 404, Fredonia, NY 14063
		CCGS	Clark County Genealogical Society, P.O. Box 2728, Vancouver, WA 98668-2728
CBA	Council for British Archaeology		
		CCGS	Coctaw County Genealogical Society, P.O. Box 1056, Hugo, OK 74743
CBE	Commander of the Order of the British Empire		

CCGS	Colorado Council of Genealogical Societies, P.O. Box 24379, Denver, CO 80224-0379
CchD	coachman's daughter
CChem	Chartered Chemist
Cchm	coachman
CchS	coachman's son
CchW	coachman's wife
CCN	*Century Cyclopedia of Names*
CCNGS	Clark County Nevada Genealogical Society, P.O. Box 1929, Las Vegas, NV 89125-1929
CCP	Court of Common Pleas
CCPL	Cuyahoga County Public Library, 2111 Snow Road, Parma, OH 44134-2792
CCRA	Certified Clinical Research Assistant
cd	(1) civil docket (2) contrary to the Discipline (Quaker)
CD	(1) Canada (2) compact disc, i.e., CD-ROM
CDA	Colonial Dames of America
CDIB	Certified Degree of Indian Blood
Cdr	Commander
Cdre	Commodore
CD-ROM	Compact Disk, Read Only Memory
CD XVII	Colonial Dames of the Seventeenth Century
CE	(1) Canada East (i.e., Canada-East or Québec) (2) Caveat Emptor (3) Central America (4) Chief of Engineers (5) Christian Era (6) church extension (7) Church Elder (8) Church of England (9) Civil Engineer (10) common era
C of E	Church of England
CEF	Canadian Expeditionary Force
cem/Cem	cemetery

CEM	Central America
cen/cens	census
CEng	Chartered Engineer
cent	(1) centennial (2) centigrade (3) centimeter (4) central (5) century
CEO	Chief Executive Officer
cer/cert	(1) certain (2) certificate(s) (3) certified (4) certify
Cest	Cheshire
CEY/ CEYL	Ceylon
cf	(1) cardboard file box (2) *confer* (compare)
CF	(1) Connecticut Firelands (2) Chaplain to the Forces
CFA	Canadian Field Artillery
CFAR	Church Unit Checking Account (LDS Family History Center term)
CFGFHS	Canadian Federation of Genealogical and Family History Societies
CFI	Computer File Index (now known as International Genealogical Index® and the Ordinance Index™)
CFL	Council of Federal Libraries (Canada)
cft	croft
cftr	confectioner
CG	Certified Genealogist[SM] (Board for Certification of Genealogists, P.O. Box 14291, Washington, DC 20044). One who has passed the rigorous tests administered in this specialty by BCG.
CG	(1) Coast Guard (2) Color Guard
CG	*The Computer Genealogist*, New England Historic Genealogical Society, 101 Newbury Street, Boston, MA 02116-3007
CGA	Color Graphs Adapter

CGC	Council of Genealogy Columnists
CG(C)	Certified Genealogist (Canada)
CGE	Centennia Genealogy Edition Clockwork Software, Inc. P.O. Box 148036, Chicago, IL 60614
CGI	Certified Genealogical Instructor[SM] (Board for Certification of Genealogists, P.O. Box 14291, Washington, DC 20044). One who has passed the rigorous tests administered in this teaching specialty by BCG.
CGI	Common Gateway Interface (Internet web page scripts)
CG-Intern	Certified Genealogist-Intern (a term formerly used by the Board for Certification of Genealogists)
CGL	Certified Genealogical Lecturer[SM] (Board for Certification of Genealogists, P.O. Box 14291, Washington, DC 20044). One who has passed the rigorous tests administered in this teaching specialty by BCG.
CGL	Computerized Genealogical Library
CGN	Cardiganshire
CGNDB	Canadian Geographical Names Database
CGPR	Canadian Genealogical Projects Registry
Cgr/Mkr	Cigar Maker
CGRS	Certified Genealogical Records Specialist[SM] (Board for Certification of Genealogists, P.O. Box 14291, Washington, DC 20044). One who has passed the rigorous tests administered in this specialty by BCG. (Formerly known as Certified Genealogical Records Searcher).
CGS	California Genealogical Society, P.O. Box 77105, San Francisco, CA 94107-0105
CGS	Cape Cod Genealogical Society, P.O. Box 906, Brewster, MA 02631
CGS	Chicago Genealogical Society, P.O. Box 1160, Chicago, IL 60690

CGS	(1) Chief of the General Staff (2) *The Companion to Gaelic Scotland*
CGS	Colorado Genealogical Society, P.O. Box 9218, Denver, CO 80209-0218
CGSSD	Computer Genealogy Society of San Diego, P.O. Box 370357, San Diego, CA 92137-0357
CGSI	Czechoslovak Genealogical Society International
Ch	Cheshire, England
Ch/ch	(1) Chancery record, Common Pleas Court (2) chaplain (3) chapter (4) chief (5) child/children, issue, offspring (6) church (7) courthouse (8) custom house
CH	(1) Chancery record, Common Pleas Court (2) Chaplain (3) Chicago Illinois LDS Temple (4) China (5) Chinese (6) county court houses (7) Couer Hessen (8) Switzerland
Cha	chamber maid
Cha[s]/ Char[s]/Chas	Charles
CHAI	Channel Islands
chan	(1) chancel (2) chancery
Chanc.	Chancellor; Chancery
Chan. Proc.	Chancery Proceedings
chap	(1) chaperon (2) chaplain (3) chapter
char	charwoman
CHAR	Charleston
chauf	chauffeur
ChB	Bachelor of Surgery
CHC	*A Comprehensive History of the Church*, by B. H. Roberts
Ch Ch	Christ Church
chd	child
ChD	Doctor of Chemistry

CHD	County Health District		chmn	chairman
ChE	Chemical Engineer		Chmntz	Chemnitz, Sax.
Ch E	Chemical Engineer		chn	children
Chelsea P	Chelsea pensioner (sometimes Chelsea out pensioner) (Scotland)		CHN	China
			Chnd	chandler
chem	(1) chemical (2) chemist (3) chemistry		chng	change
Ches/ CHES	Cheshire, England		ch/o; c/o	child of
CHess	Corhessen		ChoB	choirboy
chf	chief		Chol/Inf	Cholera Infantum
chg	chargeable		chp	chaplain
chh	church		Chp/Chpn	chaplain
CHH	Carmarthenshire		chpt	chapter
CHH	Cincinnati Historical Society, Museum Center, 1301 Western Avenue, Cincinnati, OH 45203-1129		CHQ	Church Headquarters (refers to The Church of Jesus Christ of Latter-day Saints, 50 East North Temple, Salt Lake City, UT 84150)
ChHS	Chicago Historical Society, Clark Street at North Avenue, Chicago, IL 60614		chr	charter
			chr/chrs	church(s)
CHI	(1) Channel Islands (2) China		Chr	(1) Christian (2) Chronic
CHICA	Chicago Illinois LDS Temple		CHR/chr/ chris	(1) christened (2) christening (a child is baptized and named)
child	children			
Children, Amer	National Society Children of the American Colonist		chrg	charge
			chrm	chairman
CHIN/ CHN	China		chron	chronologically
chkr	checker		Chron	Chronicles
CHL/CHIL	Chile		CHS	Cheshire
chld	child		CHS	Chicago Historical Society, Clark Street at North Avenue, Chicago, IL 60614-6099
chldn/chn	(1) children (2) condemned his/her misconduct			
chm	chairman		CHS	Connecticut Historical Society, 1 Elizabeth Street at Asylum Avenue, Hartford, CT 06105
ChMd	chambermaid			

CHS	Cincinnati Historical Society, Museum Center, 1301 Western Avenue, Cincinnati, OH 45203-1129	Cinci/CinO	Cincinnati, Ohio
CHSA	Chinese Historical Society of America, 650 Commercial Street, San Francisco, CA 94111	CIO	Congress of Industrial Organizations
ChsM	cheese man	CIP	(1) Cataloging in Publication (Library of Congress) (2) Cataloguing in Publication (National Library of Canada)
CHSRS	Canadian History and Society Research Service, National Library of Canada, 395 Wellington Street) Ottawa, Ontario, Canada K1A 0N4	cir	circle
		cir/circ	(1) circa (about, around) (2) circulation
ChsW	cheese woman	circ	circus
CHSW	Collections of the State Historical Society of Wisconsin, 816 State St. Madison, WI 53706	C Is	Cannel Islands
ch w	church warden	CIS	Congressional Information Service
Chwm	Chairwoman	CIS	Central Index System
chyd	churchyard	CISE	Computer and Information Science and Engineering
CI	Channel Islands	CISL	Canary Islands
Cia	Compañia (company)	CISTI	Canada Institute for Scientific and Technical Information
CIBS	Canadian Information by Subject	cit	(1) citato (work cited) (2) citizen
C.I.C.	Clerk of the Inferior Court	City Clk	City Clerk
Cie	Compagnie (company)	cityhospkp	keeper of city hospital
CIE	Companion of the Order of the Indian Empire	city recdr	city recorder
CIG	Computer Interest Group. For example, National Genealogical Society Computer Interest Group.	civ/civl	civil
		cj	(1) chief justice (2) county jail (3) county judge
CIHM	Canadian Institute for Historical Micro-reproductions, 395 Wellington, Room 468, Ottawa, Ontario, Canada KIA ON4	CJHS	Columbus Jewish Historical Society, 1175 College Ave., Columbus, OH 43209-2890
cil/Cil	cousin-in-law	ck	(1) check (2) cook (3) creek
CILLA	Coordinated Inter Library Loan Administration (Canada)	cl	(1) carload (2) child (3) class (4) colonel
C-in C	Commander-in-Chief	Cl	child
CIMS	Centre for Immigration and Multicultural Studies	CL	(1) Continental Line (2) Courier of Liberty, West Union, Adams Co. (2) William L. Clements Library, University of Michigan, Ann Arbor (3) Continental

Cla — Clare, Republic of Ireland

CLA — California Library Association, 717 K Street Ste 300, Sacramento, CA 95814-3477

CLA — Canadian Library Association, 200 Elgin Street, Suite 602, Ottawa, Ontario, Canada K2P 1L5

CLA — Cemetery Listing Association

CLAC/ Clack — Clackmannan, Scotland

ClaI — Clare County, Ireland

clb — club

CLB — Columbia

cl cts — clerk of courts

clerk — clerk

cler serv — clerical survey

Cleve — Cleveland, Ohio

CLF — Clayton Library Friends, P.O. Box 271078 Houston, TX 77277-1078

clfs — cliffs

clg — (1) clergyman (2) college

clk — clerk

Clk/CLK — Clackmannanshire, Scotland

Clk/Clke/ Cl/Cl Ct/ Clrk/Clr — Clerk (of a court or county)

Clk Chan Ct — Clerk of Chancery Court

Clk Cir Ct — Clerk of Circuit Court

Clk Cts — Clerk of Courts

Clk Dis Ct — Clerk of District Court

Clk/Mkr; Clk M — clockmaker

Clk of Peace — Clerk of the Peace

Clk Sup Ct — Clerk of Superior Court

Cllr — Councillor

Clmt/Ccpl — Clermont County Public Library, Batavia 180 South 3rd Street, Batavia, OH 45103

cln — cleaning; cleaner

clo — (1) close (2) clothing

clos — closing

cloth drsr — clothe dresser

clothngmct — clothing merchant

clr — clear

Clrg — clergyman

clrgymn ME — clergyman Methodist

clrgymn RC — clergyman Roman Catholic

CLRO — Corporation of London Record Office

CLS — Certified Lineage Specialist[SM] (Board for Certification of Genealogists, P.O. Box 14291, Washington, DC 20044). One who has passed the rigorous tests administered in this specialty by BCG.

CLS — Charleston Library Society, 164 King Street, Charleston, SC 29401

clth — clothier

cm — (1) catholic missionary (2) centimeter (3) christenings & marriages (4) Commissary

c/m — Chinese male

CMA — Clan McAlister of America

Cman — cellarman

c marshall — city marshall

CMB — (1) all types of parish registers (2) christenings, marriages, and burials

cmd	command
CMD	Collections Management Division (Library of Congress)
cmd'd	commanded
cmdg	commanding
cmdr	commander
Cmdt	Commandant
CME	*Cambridge Medieval History*
CMG	Companion of the Order of St. Michael and St. George
CMGS	Central Massachusetts Genealogical Society, P.O. Box 811, Westminster, MA 01473-0811
CMH	Center of Military History
Cmkr	cheesemaker
Cmman	Court Martial man
CMOf	Court Martial Officer
cmpy	company
CMS	Collection Management Services
CMSR	Compiled Military Service Records (National Archives)
Cmsry	Commissary
cmst	chemist
CMW	Complete Maps of the World (Hammond, Inc.)
cn	(1) census (2) concubine
CN	(1) Capital News (2) *Church News*: A weekly supplement to the *Deseret News* Salt Lake City, Utah: also called *Church Section* during certain years (3) Cherokee Nation (4) Continental Navy
CN/CND	Canada
CnHS	Connecticut Historical Society, 1 Elizabeth Street at Asylum Avenue, Hartford, CT 06105
CNRI	Corporation for National Research Initiatives
CNS	(1) Catholic News Service (2) Copley News Service
CnSL	Connecticut State Library, 231 Capitol Ave., Hartford, CT 06106
cn soapmn	candle & soap man
Cnt	Cornet
cntb	constable
Cntrctr	Contractor
CntS	canteen steward
cnty	county
cnty clerk	county clerk
CNY	Canary Islands
c/o	(1) in care of (2) child of
Co	(1) Cornish (2) Cornwall, England
Co/co	(1) chosen overseer (used in Quaker records) (2) company (3) county (4) cousin
CO	(1) Chief of Ordnance (2) Colonial Office, Public Record Office, Kew (3) Commanding Officer (4) conscientious objector (5) county
CO/Colo	Colorado
coa/Coa	coachman
COA	Coat of Arms
coal drvr	driver in coal tank
Co Asr	County Assessor
Co Aud	County Auditor
CobG	Coburg Gata
Cobug	Cobugh
Co Clk	County Clerk
cod	codicil

COD	(1) cash on delivery (2) collect on delivery	collect	collection
COED	Census of Overland Emigrant Documents	colloq	(1)colloquial (2) colloquialism (3) colloquially
co/f	colored female	Col Lords of Manors	Order of Colonial Lords of Manors in America
Coff	chief officer		
coffehskpr	coffee house keeper	collr	collector
cog	consent of guardian	colls	collaterals
coh	co-heir, co-heiress	coll/stu	college student
Co Health	County Health Department	ColM	college matron
CoHu	cook's husband	Colo	Colorado
COI	Central Office of Information (British)	Col Ord of the Crown	Colonial Order of the Crown
Co Judge	County Judge	ColP	college porter
col	(1) collection (2) colonel (military) (3) colony/-ial (4) colored (5) column	Cols/Colum	Columbus, the state capital of Ohio
col/cold	abbreviation for Negro or African American person, often found in legal documents and censuses	ColS	college student
		Col Soc of Pa	Colonial Society of Pennsylvania
COL/ Clmb/COLO	Columbia	com	(1) comitatus; county as used in English visitation pedigrees (2) command; commander (3) commentary (4) commerce (5) commission; commissioner (6) committee (7) commodore (8) common; commoner (9) communicate (10) companion (11) complain; complained of (12) complete
ColC	(1) college cook (2) Columbia, Connecticut		
col^d	colored		
Col Dames of Amer	Colonial Dames of America	co/m	colored male
Col Dames XVII Cent	National Society Colonial Dames of the Seventeenth Century	Com	companion
		COM	Comoro Islands
Col Dau, XVII Cent	National Society Colonial Daughters of the Seventeenth Century	COM	Component Object Model
Colg	colleague	comd	command
Colket	Meredith B. Colket, *Founders of Early American Families* (Cleveland: Founders' Project, 1985)	comdg	commanding
		comdr	commander
coll	(1) college (2) collegiate	comdt	commandant
coll/colln Col	(1) collection(s) (2) collector	coml	commercial

comm	(1) commander (2) commissary (3) commis-sioner(s) (4) committee (5) community
commiss	(1) commission (2) commissioner
commn	commission
commn'd	commissioned
Commo	Commodore
commr	commissioner
Commun	community
comn	commission
comnr	commissioner
comp/ comps	(1) accompt (account) (2) company (3) companion (4) comparative degree (5) compater, sponsor(s) (6) compiler(s); compiled by (7) complained; complained of (8) compositor
Com Pleas Ct	Common Pleas Court
complt	(1) complainant (2) complaint
compt	account
compt	comptroller
comr	commissioner
comssn mct	commission merchant
Com^te	Committee
con	(1) condemned (2) conjunx (3) consent (4) contra; against (5) country
CON	(1) Consular (British) (2) Cornwall
Conc	concubine
Concep^on	Concepcion
cond	conditional
condr	conductor
conf	(1) confederate (2) conference (3) confirmed

Conf/Chills	Confective Chills
confect	confectionary
confectnr	confectioner
Confed	Confederate
confedn	confederation
confest	confessed, as in confession of a judgement
confr	confectioner
cong	(1) congregational (2) congress (3) congressional
Cong	Congressman; Congress; Congressional
Cong/Brain	Congestion of the Brain
Cong/Lungs	Congestion of the Lungs
congl	congressional
conj	(1) conjunction (2) conjugation
Conn.	Connecticut
Conn/CT	Connecticut
ConnHS/ CHS	Connecticut Historical Society, 1 Elizabeth Street at Asylum Avenue, Hartford, CT 06105
ConnSL/ CSL CSL	Connecticut State Library, History and Genealogy Unit, 231 Capitol Avenue, Hartford, CT 06106
con/o	consent
Conr	Konrad, Conrad
cons	(1) consonant (2) consultant (3) consultative (4) consulting
consang	consanguinity
cons/o	consort of
consol	consolidated
const	(1) consistory (2) constitute (3) constitution(al)
constl	constitutional

constn	construction	COR	Corfu Island
constr	(1) construction (2) constructor	COR/ Co. R	Costa Rica
Consumpt	Consumption	Corbin	Corbin Collection (New England Historic Genealogical Society, Boston, MA). Microfilmed.
consv	conservation		
cont	(1) continued (2) contract (of marriage) (3) contesting	CORC	Cooperative Online Resource Catalog
		Co Rcdr	County Recorder
Cont/Contl	Continental	Corn/ CORN/ Cornw	Cornwall, England
contd/ cont'd	continued		
contl	continental	corp/corpl	corporal
contr	(1) contract (2) contractor (3) contraction (4) contrast (5) controlled	CORP	(1) Corporal (2) Corporation
		corpn	corporation
conv	(1) convention (2) convict	corr	(1) correction (2) correspondence (3) correspondent
CooD	cook's daughter		
cook	cook	corres	(1) correspondence (2) correspondent (3) corresponding
Cook	Cook Islands		
coop	cooperative	Corresp. Mem.	Corresponding Member
co-op	co-operative		
Co Ord	County Ordinary	Cor(s)	corner(s)
coord	(1) coordination (2) coordinator	cort/crte	court
cop	consent of parents	cos	(1) cousin(s) (2) counties
cop	copy service	COS	(1) Chief of Staff (2) Commercial Online Service (3) Costa Rica
Coph	Copenhagen, Denmark		
Coph	Roskilde, Denmark	CosM	costume maker
Copp^r	Cooper	CoSn	cousin's son
copr	copyright	COT	Chronicle of the Times, Batavia, Clermont Co.
cor/cors	corner(s)	cotts	cottages
cor/corr/ corresp	(1) correspondence (2) correspondencing	CoU	Colorado University, University of Colorado at Boulder, Boulder, CO 80309
		Couc	cousin's child
		CouD	cousin's daughter

CouH	cousin's husband
CouL	cousin-in-law
coun/counc	council
cou/o	cousin of
couns	(1) counsellor (2) councillor
Court of P's and Q's	Court of Common Pleas and Quarter Sessions
Court Rec	Legislative Records of the Governor's Council (Massachusetts Archives)
cous/coz/ csn	cousin
cous-i-l	cousin-in-law
CouW	cousin's wife
cov	entered into covenant without coming to communion (church)
CowB	cowboy
CowL	cow lad
CowM	cowman
CowS	cowman's son
CowW	cowman's wife
cp	(1) camp (2) civil parish (British) (3) compare
CP	(1) Cape of Good HopeCCape Province (2) Catholic Priest (3) Common Pleas (Court) (4) G. E. Cokayne, *Complete Peerage*
CPA	Certified Public Accountant
cpad	Common Pleas Court Appearance Docket
CPART	Center for the Preservation of Ancient Religious Texts, Brigham Young University, Provo, UT 84602
CPC	Canterbury Prerogative Court, London
CPC	Cumberland Presbyterian Church

CPCGN	Canadian Permanent Committee on Geographical Names
cpe	cape
cpl	Corporal (military)
CPL	Cleveland Public Library, 325 Superior Avenue, NE, Cleveland, OH 44114-1271
cpmb	Common Pleas Court Minute Book
CPNS	Soldier's Children Were Pensioned
CPO	Chief Petty Officer
cpob	Common Pleas Court Order Book
CPR	Civilian Personnel Records
cprb	Common Pleas Court Record Book
Cprv	Provost of college
cptn	captain
CPU	central processing unit (computer hardware)
CQ	(1) Congressional Quarterly (2) Congressional Quarterly Service
cr/CR	(1) church record(s) (2) court record (3) created (4) credit, creditor (5) creek
CR	(1) Carolina (2) carriage return on your computer, or press ENTER (3) Costa Rica (4) County Recorder
CR	*Conference Reports* (LDS)
CRA	Church Records Archives of the LDS Church, Family History Library, Salt Lake City, Utah
Crd	Cardiganshire, Wales
CRE	Crete
cred	creditor
crem	cremated
cres	crescent
crft	crofter

CRIC	Costa Rica
crim	criminal
crk	creek
Crk	Cork, Republic of Ireland
CRL	Center for Research Libraries (a cooperative library)
Crm	Carmarthenshire, Wales
Crn	Caernarvonshire, Wales
CrnS	crown servant
CRO/ C.R.O.	County Record Office (England)
CRO/ CROA	Croatia
crpl	corporal
Crpntr	Carpenter
Crrg/Mkr	Carriage Maker
Crrg/Smth	Carriage Smith
crs/crspd	correspond; correspondence
CRT	Canadian Refugee Tract
Crte	Curate
CRW	Custom Report Writer (The Master Genealogist)
cs	census
CS	(1) Civil Service (2) Church of Scotland (3) Color Sergeant (4) County census
CS/CZ/ Cze/CZH	Czechoslovakia
C of S	(1) Chief of Staff (2) Church of Scotland
CSA	(1) Confederate States Army (2) Confederate States of America; the southern states that succeeded from the U.S. before the Civil War
CSB	Bachelor of Christian Science

CSC	Carl Sandburg College, Galesburg, Illinois 2232 South Lake Storey Road, Galesburg, IL 61401
CSC	Clerk of Superior Court
CSCC	Chapter Support Committee Chairman
CSer	college servant
CSG	Connecticut Society of Genealogists, P.O. Box 435, Glastonbury, CT 06033-0435
CSGA	California State Genealogical Alliance, P.O. Box 311, Danville, CA 94526-0311
CSi	CompuServe Interactive (online service)
CSL	California State Library
CSL	Connecticut State Library, History and Genealogy Unit, 231 Capitol Avenue, Hartford, CT 06106
CSM	*Christian Science Monitor*
csn	cousin
CSN	Confederate States Navy
CSNEH	Center for the Study of New England History
CSP	Christian Science Practitioner
CSPI	Canadian Studies Publisher, 519 Mill St., P.O. Box 336, Lockport, NY 14095
CST	(1) Central Standard Time (2) *Chicago Sun Times*
C/S/Tch	C. S. Teacher
cstm h of	Custom House Office
CT/Conn	Connecticut
Ct	court
ct(s)	(1) Captain (2) cent(s) (3) certificate/certificate to (4) county (5) court(s)
cta	*cum testamento annexo* (with will attached)
CTAHS	Commerce Township Area Historical Society, 207 Liberty Street, P.O. Box 264, Walled Lake, MI

CTC	Certified Travel Consultant
Ctchg	Cutchogue
Ctgr	cottager
CTGS	Cumberland Trail Genealogical Society, P.O. Box 576, St. Clairsville, OH 43950-0576
Ctkr	caretaker
ctl	central
ctl/ctrl	control key (on computers)
CTBNYT	*Chicago Tribune—New York Times*
ctr	(1) center (2) cutter
ct.r.	court record
ctre	centre
CtRec	court record
CtrM	counterman
CTSSAR	Connecticut Society of the Sons of the American Revolution, P.O. Box 270275, West Hartford, CT 06127-0275
cttee	committee
cty	county
cty crtclk	city court clerk
CtyLt	County Lieutenant
cu	cubic
Cu	(1) Cumberland, England (2) Cumbric (language)
CU	(1) Cambridge University (England) (2) Clark University, 950 Main Street, Worcester, MA 01610
CU/CUB/ CUBA	Cuba
CUL	Columbia University Library, New York, NY 612 West 115th St. NYC, NT 10025

Cumb/ CUMB/ Cumbld	Cumberland, Great Britain
CUP	(1) Cambridge University Press, 40 West 20th St. NYC, NY 10011-4211 (2) Canadian United Press
CUPP	Canada-Ukraine Partners Program
cur	curate
Curon	curation
curr/cur	current, now
custdn	custodian
Cutr	cutter
Cuyu	Cuyahoga County, Ohio
cv/c.v.	(1) cove (2) curriculum vitae
CVGA	Central Virginia Genealogical Association, Inc., P.O. Box 5583, Charlottesville, VA 22905-5583
CVO	Commander of the Royal Victorian Order
CVR	Connecticut Vital Records
cw	case will
CW	(1) Canada West (i.e., Ontario) (2) carriage wheels (3) Church Warden (4) Choctaw Nation (5) Civil War (6) Civil War Families, Ohio Genealogical Society, 713 S. Main St. Mansfield, OH 44907-1644 (7) Colonial Williamsburg, Williamsburg, VA
Cwdr	chief warder
CWFO	Society of Civil War Families of Ohio, Ohio Genealogical Society, 713 South Main Street, Mansfield, OH 44907-1644
cwo	cash with order
CWom	chairwoman
CWR	Connecticut Western Reserve (northeastern Ohio)
CwrD	chief warden's daughter

CWrd   chief warden

CWrS   chief warden's son

CWrW   chief warden's wife

CWSAC   Civil War Sites Advisory Commission

CWSS   Civil War Soldiers and Sailors System (Civil War military database)

cwsy   causeway

cwt   a hundredweight; one hundred and twelve pounds, e.g., "The inventory revealed three cwt of bronze."

cy   (1) city (2) county

cyn   canyon

CYP/CYR   Cyprus

CZ   Territory of Canal Zone

CZ/CZH/   Czechoslovakia
Czec/Czech

CZR   Czech Republic

D

d   (1) daily (2) date (3) daughter (4) day (5) death or mortality censuses (6) décès (death) (7) *decessit* (died) (8) died (9) ditto (10) *dorso* (back) (11) Old penny; denarius

-d   ("-" is a number) penny, pence (Penny is used to show the size of nails.)

D   (1) Daughter (2) Democrat; Democratic (3) deputy (4) Devon, England (5) divorced (6) docket (7) Doctorate (in) (8) *Dominus* (the Lord) (9) Duke (10) Dutch

D197101   110 year file (Family History Department)

da   (1) daughter (2) day(s)

DA   (1) Dakota (2) Dallas Texas LDS Temple (3) *Journal of the Devonshire Association of Art, Sciences, and Literature*

D.A.   District Attorney

D^a   Doña [title]

DAAG   Deputy Assistant Adjutant General

DAB   Dictionary of American Biography

DAC   Dominion (Public) Archives of Canada, Ottawa

DAC   National Society Daughters of the American Colonists, Alabama Society, 433 West Vista Court, Mobile, AL 36609

DAG   Deputy Adjutant General

dagureoian   daguerreoian

DakT   Dakota Territory

Da/Labor   Day Laborer

DalC   daughter-in-law's daughter

DalF   daughter-in-law's father

DalH   daughter-in-law's husband

DALLA   Dallas Texas LDS Temple

DalM   daughter-in-law's mother

DALM   Dalmatia

DalS   daughter-in-law's son

DalU   daugher-in-law's uncle

Dames, Court of Honor   National Society of the Dames of the Court of Honor

Dames of Loyal Legion   Dames of the Loyal Legion of the United States

DAMRUS   *Directory of Archives and Manuscript Repositories in the United States*

Danl/Dan¹   Daniel

Dar   (1) Darmstadt (2) Darnsted

DAR   National Society, Daughters of the American Revolution, 1776 D Street NW, Washington, DC 20006-5392

DAR   Official Rosters, Revolutionary Soldiers in Ohio

DARL   Daughters of the American Revolution Library, 1776 D Street NW, Washington, DC 20006-5303

Darm   Darmstadt

DAR Misc Rec   Daughters of the American Revolution, Miscellaneous Records

DaSS   daughter's stepson

dat   (1) date (2) dated (3) dative case

dau/daur(s)/ dau^r/daus   (1) daughter(s) (2) daughter(s) of

Dau Barons of Runnemede — National Society Daughters of the Barons of Runnemede

DauC — daughter's child

Dau of Col Wars — National Society Daughters of Colonial Wars

DauD — daughter's daughter

Dau of 1812 — National Society United States Daughters of 1812

Dau Founders — The National Society of the Daughters of Founders & Patriots of Patriots of America, 706 Woodlawn Avenue West, North Augusta, SC 29841-3372

DauH — daughter's husband

dau-i-l — daughter-in-law

DauL — daughter-in-law

Dau Rep of Tex — Daughters of the Republic of Texas, DRT Library P.O. DRTL Box 1401, San Antonio, TX 78295-1401

daus/daut — daughters

DauS — daughter's son

Dau Union Veterans — Daughters of Union Veterans of the Civil War 1861-1865, 503 S Walnut St., Springfield, IL 62704-1932

Dau of Utah Pioneers — National Society of the Daughters of Utah Pioneers, 300 North Main, Salt Lake City, UT 84103-1699

Dav^d — David

DAV — Disabled American Veterans

db — (1) deed book (Recorder's Office) (2) domesday

Db — Derbyshire, England

DB — (1) database (2) Deed Book (3) *Divinitatis Baccalaureus* (Bachelor of Divinity) (4) Domesday Book

dba — doing business as

DBA — Doctor of Business Administration

DBE — Dame Commander of the Order of the British Empire

DBG — Denbighshire

dbn — *de bonis non* (concerning goods not settled by preceding administrator)

dbncta — *de bonis non cum testo annexo*

DBY — Derbyshire

dc — docket

DC — (1) District of Columbia (Washington) (2) Doctor of Chiropractic

D & C — Dean and Chapter

d & coh — daughter & coheiress

DCB — *Dictionary of Canadian Biography*

DCC — Society of Descendants of Colonial Clergy

dce — *Writ of diem clausit extremum* (he has closed his last day)

DCG — Descendants of Colonial Governors

DCGS — Dutchess County [NY] Genealogical Society, P.O. Box 708, Poughkeesie, NY 12602

DCH — (1) Dames of the Court of Honor (2) Diploma in Children's Health

DCHS — Dutchess County Historical Society, P.O. Box 88, Poughkeepsie, NY 12602

DCJ — District Court Judge

DCL — (1) Dartmouth College Library, Hanover, New Hampshire (2) Doctor of Canon Law (3) Doctor of Civil Law

DCM — Distinguished Conduct Medal

DcoPL — Denver Public Library, 10 West Fourteenth Ave. Pkwy., Denver, CO 80204

DCW — National Society Daughters of Colonial Wars

dd	(1) dated (2) *de dato* (on this date) (3) death date (4) deed (5) died
DD	(1) deaths (2) dishonorable discharge (3) *Divinitatis Doctor* (Doctor of Divinity)
DDC	Dewey Decimal Classification
DDR	(1) Death Duty Register(s) (British) (2) German Democratic Republic (formerly East Germany)
DDS	(1) Dewey Decimal System (2) Doctor of Dental Surgery
de	(1) day (2) dead (3) docket of estates (4) God (5) of (6) to die
DE/Del	Delaware
de & De	from
Dea/Deac/ Deacn	Deacon
dean	dean
Debrett's	*Debrett's Genealogical Peerage of Great Britain and Ireland*
debt	debtor
dec	(1) deacon (2) deceased (3) decimal (4) declare
dec/decla/ declae	declaration
decd/dec^d/ deced/dcd/ dec'd/d'd	deceased
Decmb/ Dec/ Dcmbr/D	December
D. Ed	Doctor of Education
def	(1) defense (2) definite (3) definition
def/deft	defunt (deceased - masculine); defunte (deceased - feminine)
def sen	definitive sentence

deft/ defendt/ defend/ defdt	defendant
del	(1) delegate (2) delivery
Del/Delaw/ DL/De	(1) Delaware (2) Delaware, Ohio
DEL	Del-Gen-Data-Bank
deld	delivered
deleg	delegate, delegation
DelHS/ DHS	Delaware Historical Society, 505 Market Street, Wilmington, DE 19801
Deln	Delegations
DelPAr/ DPA	Delaware Public Archives, Dover, DE, Roll of Records, 121 Duke of York St., Dover, DE 19907
Dem	Democratic
demi/dem/ di/d	one half or smaller than
Den	Denbighshire, Wales
DEN/ DENM	Denmark
Denb/ DENB	Denbigh, Wales
DEng	Devonshire, England
DENVE	Denver, Colorado LDS Temple
dep	(1) deposed (2) depot
dep/depty	deputy
depo/ depot/depos	deposition
dept	(1) department (2) deputy
DEQ	National Society Descendants of Early Quakers

DERB/ / Derby/ / Derbys — Derbyshire, England

deriv — derivative

Derry — Londonderry, Ireland

des — designate

desc/desct — (1) descend (2) descendant(s) (3) descended (4) descends

DESCEND — Descendant Chart (genealogy software program)

Desc of Col Clergy — Society of the Descendants of the Colonial Clergy

Desc of Col Governors — Hereditary Order of the Descendants of Colonial Governors

Desc, Founders of Hartford — Society of the Descendants of the Founders of Hartford

Desc, Sons & Dau of Kings of Britain — Descendants of the Illegitimate Sons and Illegitimate Daughters of the Kings of Britain

Desc Knight of Most Noble Ord of the Garter — Society of Descendants of Knights of the Most Noble Order of the Garter

Desc of Lords of Md Manors — National Society of Descendants of Lords of the Maryland Manors

Desc, Loyalists Amer Rev — Hereditary Order of Descendants of the Loyalists and Patriots of the American Revolution

Desc, NJ Settlers — Descendants of the New Jersey Settlers

Desc of Signers of Decl of Indep — Descendants of the Signers of the Declaration of Independence

descr — describe, description

descs — descendants

DesL — Doctor of Letters (French)

desr — desire

DesS — Doctor of Science (French)

DESSAR — Delaware Society of the Sons of the American Revolution

Det/Detch — Detachment

DETC — Distance Education and Training Council

DetM — Detroit, Michigan

Deu — Deutschland (Germany)

dev — (1) developing (2) development

DEV/ DevE/DEVO/ Devon — Devonshire, England

DEW — distant early warning

DFA — Descents from Antiquity

DFAW — Descendants of the Founders of Ancient Windsor

DFC — Distinguished Flying Cross Society, 8430 Production Ave. San Diego, CA 92121

DFHS — Dutch Family Heritage Society, 2463 Ledgewood Drive, West Jordan, UT 84084

Dfnc — Defiance Public Library, Defiance, 320 Fort Street, Defiance, OH 43521

DFPA — National Society, Daughters of Founders and Patriots of America, National Headquarters, Park Lane Building, Suites 300-05, 2025 Eye Street, NW, Washington, DC 20006

dft — defendant

dg — degree of gift

dg/d.of.g — deed of gift

DGS — Dallas Genealogical Society, P.O. Box 12446, Dallas, TX 75225-0446

DGS — Delaware Genealogical Society, 505 North Market Street, Wilmington, DE 19801-3091

DGSJ	*Delaware Genealogical Society Journal*	Dis Ct	District Court
dh	namely	disp	(1) dispensation (for marriage) (2) dispenser
DH	(1) *Delaware History* (2) Doctor of Humanities	dispr	dispatcher
DHC	*Documentary History of the Church*, B. H. Roberts, ed.	diss	dismissed (church)
DHD	Daughters of Holland Dames	diss	(1) dissertation (2) dissolved
DHHS	New Hampshire Department of Health and Human Services	dist	(1) distinguished (2) distributor (3) district
		distrib	(1) distribute (2) distribution
di	(1) das ist (that is) (2) demi (one-half)	Ditto, Do	a repeat of what was previously written domicile
dia^d	diamond	div/DIV	(1) divide (2) divided (3) divinity (4) division (5) divorce (6) divorced
dial	(1) dialect (2)dialectical		
Dialogue	*Dialogue: A Journal of Mormon Thought*	divnl	divisional
diam^d	diamond	divs	divisions
dict	dictionary	DJ	Dow Jones
dietn	dietitian	DJAG	Deputy Judge Advocate General
dil	daughter-in-law	Djur	*Doctor Juris* (Doctor of Law)
dim	diminutive	DK	(1) Dakota Territory (2) Denmark
dio/dioc	diocese	dl	dale
dip FHS	Diploma in Family Historical Studies (Australia). Awarded by the Society of Australian Genealogists to those who take its course of study and subsequently pass its rigorous exams.	Dl/DL	(1) daughter-in-law (2) daughter lawful
		DL	(1) Deputy Lieutenant (2) Doctor of Laws
		DL	Old Dartmouth Historical Society, New Bedford, MA 02740
dir	director	Dla	day laborer
direct	directory	DLC	Donation Land Claim (e.g., Oregon Donation Land Claim)
dis	disowned, disowned for		
dis/disc	discharge(d)	dld	delivered
disb	disbursement	DLit/DLitt	(1) Doctor of Letters (2) Doctor of Literature
disc	disciples	DLP	Descendants of Loyalists and Patriots
disch/ dischd/discd	discharged		

DLP	Hereditary Order of the Descendants of the Loyalists and Patriots of the American Revolution, 608 South Overlook Drive, Coffeyville, KS 67337-2531
dlr	dealer
DLS	Doctor of Library Science
dm	(1) dam (2) domestic
DM	Denmark
DM/ DrmMaj	Drum Major
Dmag	dairy manager
DMD	Doctor of Dental Medicine
DMF	Death Master File (Social Security Administration)
Dmf	Dumfriesshire, Scotland
Dmi	*Domini*
Dmkr	dressmaker
DMn	Doctor of Ministry
dmnstr	demonstrator
DMR/ Dm. R	Dominican Republic
Dmstc	Domestic
DMus	Doctor of Music
DMV	Research Center-Delmarva History and Culture
d-m-y	day, month, year
DMZ	demilitarized zone
DN	(1) Denmark (2) *Deseret News*, Salt Lake City, Utah (3) *Dominica*, Sunday (4) *Dominus Noster* (Latin) Our Lord
D^n	*Don* [title]
DNA	deoxyribonucleic acid

Dnb	Dunbartonshire, Scotland
DNB	*Dictionary of National Biography*
Dnca	*Dominica*, Sunday
DNK	Denmark
DNM	deceased non-member
DNS	Domain Name Server (connected to the Internet)
do/do°	(1) ditto (the same), used in many older records (2) same as above
d/o, da/o, dau/o	daughter of
Do	Dorset, England
DO	Doctor of Osteopathy
DOA	dead on arrival
dob/DOB	date of birth
doc (docs)	document(s)
doc est	docket of estates
doct	doctor
dod	date of death
DOD	Department of Defense
d of g	degree of gift
d.of.t/dt	deed of trust
dol	dollar
dol/$	U.S. dollar, Spanish milled dollar, and occasionally an early Peso
dom	date of marriage
dom	domicile
dom/ domc/Dom	domestic

Dom	(1) *Dominica*, Sunday (2) *dominus master* (used as a title)	dpl	(1) death place (2) diploma
Dom/Dut	Domestic Duties	DPL	Dallas Public Library, 1515 Young Street, Dallas, TX 75201
DOMS	Diploma in Ophthalmic Medicine and Surgery	DPL	Denver Public Library, Genealogy Division, Western History Collection, 1357 Broadway, Denver, CO 80203-2165
dom serv	domestic servant		
Don	Donegal, Republic of Ireland	DPL	Dover Public Library, 525 North Walnut Street, Dover, OH 44622
Donca	*Dominica*, Sunday		
Doneg	Donegal, Ireland	dpo	depot
DOR/ Dors/	Dorsetshire, England	dpob	date, place of birth
		DPS	Dead People's Society
Doroth	Dorothea	dpt	department
DORS	Dorset	Dr./dr	(1) as now, a debtor, debt, debit, or indebted to, especially in account ledgers (2) daughter (3) dram (4) drive (5) when found in Quaker records this term stands for drinking spiritous liquor to excess
DOS	Disk Operating System		
dow	dowager		
DOW	died of wounds		
doz	dozen	Dr./D^r	doctor, physician, or surgeon
dp	(1) death place (2) dropped plain dress and/or speech	DR	(1) Darmstadt, Germany (2) death record (3) The National Society Daughters of the Revolution of 1776
DP	(1) data processing (2) Delaware Patron (3) displaced person (4) National Archives and Records Administration descriptive pamphlet/publication		
		DR/Drm	Drummer
		DRAM	Dynamic Random-Access Memory
DPA	(1) Delaware Public Archives (2) Doctor of Public Administration, Hall of Records, 121 Duke of York Street, Dover, DE 19901	drap	draper
		drct	director
		Dresdn	Dresden, Saxony
DPCN	Decentralized Program for Canadian Newspapers	drest	dressed (as in meat)
Dpen	dependent	drftsmn	draftsman
DpGv	deputy governor	Drgns	Dragoons
DPh/DPhil	Doctor of Philosophy	dr-in-l	daughter-in-law
DPH	Diploma of Doctor of Public Health	driv	driver
DPI	dots per inch	Dr. Jur	Doctor of Laws or Jurisprudence

DRL	Dutch Reformed Church
drm	drummer
DrmMaj	Drum Major
DrnM	drawing master
DRO	Diocesan Record Office (England)
Dro/Brain	Dropsy of the Brain
Dro/Heart	Dropsy of the Heart
drov	drover
drpd	dropped
drsmkr	dressmaker
Drsr	dresser
DRSW	Documentary Relations of the Southwest
DRT	Daughters of the Republic of Texas, Caddel-Smith Chapter, 909 South Park, Uvalde, TX 78801
drum	drummer
DryB	dairy boy
drygds&gro	dry goods & groceries
drygoodmct	dry good merchant
DryM	dairymaid, dairyman
DryS	dairy servant
ds	(1) deserted (2) died single (3) document signed
d(s)s	document(s) signed
DS	Democratic Standard
DS/DSc	Doctor of Science
DSC	Distinguished Service Cross
Dser	domestic servant

DSGR/ DSGRM	*The Detroit Society for Genealogical Research Magazine*, Detroit Society for Genealogical Research, Inc., Detroit Public Library, Burton Historical Collection, 5201 Woodward Avenue, Detroit, MI 48202
DSL	State Library of Delaware, 43 South Dupont Highway, Dover, DE 19901
DSM	Distinguished Service Medal
DSO	Companion of the Distinguished Service Order
dsp/DSP	*decessit sine prole* (died without issue)
dspl/dspleg/ dsp legit	*decessit sine prole legitima* (died without legitimate issue)
dspm	*decessit sine prole mascula* (died without male issue)
dspms	*decessit sine prole mascula superstite* (died without surviving male issue)
dsps	*decessit sine prole supersite* (died without surviving issue)
DSSSL	Document Style Semantics and Specification Language (computer term)
DST	(1) Daylight Saving Time (2) District
dt	(1) date (2) daughter(s), daughter of (used in Quaker records) (3) delirium tremens
DT	(1) Dakota Territory (2) Darmstadt (3) deed of trust (4) Donation Tract
dtd	dated
DTD	Document Type Definition
DTER	Dakota Territory
dth	death
DTh/ DTheol	Doctor of Theology
dto	ditto
DTP	desktop publishing
dtr	(1) daughter (2) doctor

Du	Durham, England
Dub/DubI	Dublin, Ireland
DUF	Dumfriesshire
DUL	Duke University Library, Durham, NC
dum/d.unm	died unmarried
Dumb	Dumbarton, Scotland
Dumf/ DUMF	Dumfries, Scotland
DUN	Dunbartonshire
Dunb/ DUNB	Dunbarton, Scotland
dunm	died unmarried
DUP	duplicate
dur	during
DUR/ Durh/ DURH	Durham, Great Britain
Dutch Col Soc of Del	Dutch Colonial Society of Delaware
DuU	Duke University, Durham, North Carolina
DUV	Daughters of Union Veterans of the Civil War
DUVCW	Daughters of Union Veterans of the Civil War, National Headquarters, D.U.V. Registrar's Office, 503 South Walnut Street, Springfield, IL 62704
DV	(1) Denver, Colorado LDS Temple (2) Deo Volente; God willing (found in cemeteries)
DVD	Digital Versatile Disk
dvm	*decessit vita matris* (died in the lifetime of the mother)
DVM	(1) Doctor of Veterinary Medicine (2) Verbi Dei minister, which means Minister of the Word of God
dvp	*decessit vita patris* (died in the lifetime of the father)
DVR	Society of the Descendents of Washington's Army at Valley Forge
dvu	*decessit vitae uxoris* (died in the lifetime of the husband/wife)
dw/Dw	dishwasher
DWB	*Dictionary of Welsh Biography*
dwi	died without issue
DWL	Dr. Williams' Library, 14 Gordon Square, London, England WC1H OAG
dwli	died without legitimate issue–also dsp (leg)
dwmi	died without male issue
Dwn	Down, Northern Ireland
dwsi	died without surviving male issue – also dwsmi
dwt	pennyweight(s)
DX	Dixie
dy	died young
DY	(1) Dakota Territory (2) Dorothy
dyet	food, meals, as in a prisoner's dyet
dyg	died young

E

E/e   (1) Earl (2) East (3) ein-, a(n) (4) eldest (5) endowed previously (LDS) (6) endowment (LDS) (7) Estate (8) evening (newspaper) (9) Exchequer, Public Record Office, Kew, England

ea   each

ead   *eadem* (in the same way)

EAD   Encoded Archival Description

EAN   (1) European Academic Network (2) European Article Number

EAP   Electronic Access Project (National Archives and Records Administration)

EaTU   East Tennessee State University, Johnson City, TN 37614-0717

EB   *Encyclopedia Britannica*

EBB   Electronic Bulletin Board

Eben^r   Ebenezer

EC   (1) East Central (2) European Community (3) Executive Committee

ECAT   Everybody's Catalog

eccl/eccles   ecclesiastical

Eccles   Ecclesiastical Society

Ecc^lia   church

ECGS   Eaton County Genealogical Society, P.O. Box 337, Charlotte, MI 48813-0337

ECHO   Exporting Cultural Heritage Overseas, 1500 Broadway, Suite 1010, New York, NY 10036

ECIF   Early Church Information File (alphabetical card index to LDS Church and other records; microfilmed)

econ   (1) economics (2) economy

ECPA   Electronic Communications Privacy Act

ECU/ECUA   Ecuador

ecux   a female executor (of probate)

ed/Ed/ED   (1) edited by; edited; editor (2) edition (3) *eodem die* (old date; to the same place or same point; the same day) (4) estate docket

ED   (1) Efficiency Decoration (2) Enumeration District, a term used with U.S. census population schedules

EdB   Bachelor of Education

ed cit   *editio citata* (edition cited)

edcn   education

edcnalist   educationalist

EdD   Doctor of Education

Edin   Edinburgh, Scotland

edit   editorial

EdM   Master of Education

edn   edition

EDN   Edinburgh/Midlothian

Edon   Edon Public Library, Edon

eds   editors

educ	(1) educated (2) educated at (3) education (4) educational
Edw	Edward
EE	(1) Early English (2) Electrical Engineer
EEI	Essential Elements of Instruction
EEO	Equal Employment Opportunity
e et OR	*errore et omissione reservata* (error and omission reserved)
EFA	Evangelical Friends International
EFC	Evangelical Friends Church, Eastern Region (Ohio Y.M.)
EFIC	Early Families in Cleveland (Ohio), Genealogical Committee of the Western Reserve Historical Society, 10825 East Blvd., Cleveland, OH 44106-1777
EFOIA	Electronic Freedom of Information Act
EFTA	European Free Trade Association
e.g.	*exempli gratia* (for example)
EG/Eg	(1) Egypt (2) Egyptian
EGA	Enhanced Graphics Adapter
EgnW	engineer's wife
EGS	Elgin Genealogical Society, P.O. Box 1418, Elgin, IL 60121-1418
EGY/ EGYP	Egypt
EH	Endowment House (used for LDS temple ordinances and located in Salt Lake City, Utah)
Ehefr	Ehefrau, wife
ehel/ehl	ehelich (legitimate)
Ehl	Eheleute, a married couple
E. Hmptn	East Hampton
EHR	*Economic History Review*

Ei/E.I./EIn	East Indies
EI	Essex Institute, Salem, Massachusetts
EIA	Energy Information Administration
EIC	East India Company
1812 vet	War of 1812 veteran
EIN/EIND	East Indies
ej	*ejus* (his; hers; of him)
ejusd	*ejusdem* (in the same month or year); of the same (month)
El	Elisabeth/Elizabeth
EL	Election
ELCA	Evangelical Lutheran Church of America
eld	(1) elder (2) eldest
elec/elect	electrical or electric
electn	electrician
electro	electrotyper
elev	elevator
ELG	Elgin/Morayshire
Eliz/Eliz^th	Elizabeth
ELN/E. Loth	East Lothian (see Haddington)
Elnr	Eleanor
ELo/ELOT	East Lothian, Scotland
Els/ElsP	Elsace, Prussia
ELS	El Salvador
Elsac	Elsac/Elsase
Elsb	Elsbeth
Elsba	Elsbetha, Elisabetha

ElSG	Elsah, Germany	Eng	(1) England (2) English
ElsL	Elsace, Lorraine	EngD	(1) Doctor of Engineering (2) engineer/engine driver
e-mail	electronic mail		
em	emigrated	engg/engrg	engineering
em/emp/ empl	employed, employee, employing	Eng. Hist. Rev.	*English Historical Review*
EM	Efficiency Medal	Engn/ engr(s)	engineer(s)
E-mail	electronic mail (communication using the Internet)	E. Nian	East Niantic dialect
embk	embankment	enl	(1) enlarged (2) enlisted-drafted-volunteered-etc.
EMC	Episcopal Methodist Church	Enlg/Bowels	Enlargement of the Bowels
emig	emigrant	eno	enough
emigr	emigrate from	Enriq^e	Enrique
Emp	Employee	Ens	Ensign
empd	employed	Ensign	*The Ensign.* A periodical published by The Church of Jesus Christ of Latter-day Saints, Salt Lake City, Utah.
empl	employees		
EMS	Expanded Memory Specification	entd	entered
emyr	employer	entg	entering
en/En	(1) and (2) engineer (3) English	EO	Executive Officer
En/Ens	Ensign	Eod/eod	*eodem* (on the same date)
EN/ENG/ Eng/ENGL	England	*eodem die*	in court records, same place, same day
ency/encyc	encyclopedia	eoe	errors and omissions excepted
end	endorsed	EOTR	End of the Trail Researchers, 145 24th Avenue, SE, Salem, OR 97301
end/END	(1) endowed (2) endowment (an LDS temple ordinance)	ep	ecclesiastical parish (British)
ENE	East Northeast	Ep	Epiphania, Epiphany
enfeoff	to invest with a fee	EPC	Episcopal Protestant Church
eng/engr	engineer	Epi	bishop's
		Epis/Episc	Episcopal

Epit.	Epitaph
EPNS	English Place-Name Society
EPPP	Electronic Publications Pilot Project
EPRU	East Prussia (Ostpreussen)
EPS	Encapsulated Post Script
eq	(1) equation (pl. eqq. or eqs.) (2) for example
equip	equipment
e.r.	*errore reservata* (error reserved)
ER	(1) East Riding (2) Examination of Removal Order (*see also* E II R)
E&R	Evangelical and Reformed Church
Era	*The Improvement Era.* A periodical previously published by The Church of Jesus Christ of Latter-day Saints, Salt Lake City, Utah.
ERA	earned run average
Eres	Electronic Reserves
ERIC	Educational Resources Information Center
Erlle	Erllebrun
Ernd	errand boy, errand girl
Erptn/Vssl	Eruption of Vessel
ERR	Editorial Research Reports
ERS	Economic Research Service
ERY	East Riding of Yorkshire, England
es	east side
ES	Bureau of Land Management, Eastern States Office, Springfield, VA (*see* BLM)
ESA	Economics and Statistics Administration
Escot	Edinburgh, Scotland
ESE	East Southeast

E II R	Elizabeth II Regina (Queen Elizabeth)
ESF	extra surveillance, folio, large
esp	(1) especially (2) esplanade (3) extrasensory perception
ESP	Espagne / España (Spain)
esq/esqr/ Esqr	esquire
ESQ	extra surveillance, large
ESRC	Economic and Social Research Council (Scotland)
ESS	Experimental Search System (Library of Congress)
Ess/ESS/ ESSX	Essex, Great Britain
est	(1) established (2) estate (3) estimate
EST	(1) Eastern Standard Time (2) Estonia
estd	estimated
est div	estate division
et	(1) also (2) and (3) yet
et al.	(1) *et alii* (and others); in a deed, the names of at least two others besides the grantor and grantee. An *et al.* deed is often, but not always, a deed of settlement of an estate and contains the names of heirs.
etc.	*et cetera* (and so forth; and the rest)
ETH	Ethiopia/Abyssinia
ETO	European Theater of Operations
et passim	(and) here and there
et seq	*et sequentes* (and the following)
Et ux	(1) and wife (2) one other; this type of deed contains the name of one other person besides the grantor or grantee
et uxor	and wife

EU/EUR/ (1) Europe (2) European
Euro/
EURO/Europ

Eucl — Euclid, Ohio

Eug — Eugene

Eur — European

EV — entries have been evaluated by the Family History Department, Salt Lake City, Utah

EV/Evan/ Evangelical
Evang

E Va/EVA — East Virginia

EVA — extravehicular activity

evang — evangelisch

eve — evening

Everton — Everton Publishers, P.O. Box 368, Logan, UT 84321

EWGS — Eastern Washington Genealogical Society, P.O. Box 1826, Spokane, WA 99210-1826

ex/exec/ executor
exc'r/exec^r/
ex^r/ex^{or}

Ex — (1) example (pl. exx.) (2) excommunication (3) from

exam — examination, examiner

exec — (1) executed (2) executives

exec^x/ex^x/ executrix
ex^{ix}/exc'x/
extx

exc — (1) except (2) excepted (3) exclusive (4) exchange

Exc/Excelly Excellancy

exch — (1) exchange (2) Exchequer, Court of

exec — executive(s)

EXEC — Executive Services

exh — exhibit

exit — it goes forth, the issuance of a process, writ, etc., by a court

exit. atta — attachment was signed and issued by the court

exon/excn/ execution, as in law suits
exec/execn

Exon — Exeter

exor — executor (probate)

exp — (1) expanded (2) express

expd — expired

expdn — expedition

expdny — expeditionary

Expy — Expressway

exr — executor

ex rul — *ex relatione* (at the instance of)

ext — (1) extended (2) extension (3) extra (4) extraordinary

extr — executor

extraord — extraordinary

extrix/ executrix (probate)
exrx/exx

EYC — Clay, Charles Travis, *Early Yorkshire Charters*

Ez/Ezr — Ezra

Ezek — Ezekiel

F

f	(1) father (2) flourished
f/ff	following page or pages
F	(1) and following (pl. ff.) (2) Fahrenheit (3) farm and ranch censuses (4) Father (5) fellow (6) female (7) female form (8) Female Sealing List (LDS) (9) feminine (10) file/docket (11) *filius* (son) (12) film (microfilm) (13) folder (14) folio
F/fa/fr	father
F/Feb/ FebR/Febr	February
F/Fri	Friday
fa	filled alphabetically
FA	(1) Field of Artillery (2) French America
FAA	Fleet Air Arm
Faamer AcadOpt	Fellow of the American Academy of Opticians
FAAP	Family Album Archive Project
fac	factory
facs (facsim)	facsimile
FACS	Fellow American College of Surgeons
Faer	Faeroerne, Denmark
FAGS	Fellow, American Geographical Society
FaH	farm hand
fai	faithful
FaL	farm laborer
FAL	Falkland Islands

FalD	father-in-law's daughter
FaLS	father-in-law's son
FaLW	father-in-law's wife
fam	family
F & A M	Free and Accepted Masons
fam bible/ fb	family Bible
fam. hist.	family histories
FaMo	farmer's mother
fam rec	family records
fam rep	family representative
FAO	Food and Agriculture Organization
FAQ	Frequently Asked Question(s)
Far	Farleben
FARC	Federal Archives and Records Centers (branches of the National Archives in Washington, DC)
FarD	farmer's daughter
FarF	farmer's father
farm	farmer
Farmer	John Farmer, *A Genealogical Register of the First Settlers of New England*
farmer rtr	farmer renter
FARMS	Foundation for Ancient Research and Mormon Studies, Brigham Young University, P.O. Box 7113, Provo, UT 84602
farr	farrier

FarS	farmer's son	FBro	foster brother
FarW	farmer's wife	Fc/Fchd	foster child
FAS	Free African Society	FC	Free Church (Presbyterian)
fasc	fascicle	FC&AGR	*French Canadian and Acadian Genealogical Review*
FASG	Fellow of the American Society of Genealogists (P.O.Box 1515, Derry, NH 03038-1515). Fellowship in ASG, an honor society established in 1940, is limited to fifty living inductees elected on the basis of their genealogical scholarship, as evidenced by the quality and extent of their scholarly publications. A person is voted on without prior knowledge of his or her consideration as a candidate for the honor.	FCC	Federal Communications Commission
		FCHQ	*Filson Club Historical Quarterly*
		FCP	Free Person of Color
		fctry labr	laborer in factory
		fcty	factory
		fcy	faculty
		fd	(1) fiduciary docket (2) file drawer(s)
FatB	father's brother	FDau	foster daughter
fath	father	FDD	floppy disk drive
father-i -l/F-in-l	father-in-law	fdr	founder
FatL	father-in-law	FDRL	Franklin D. Roosevelt Library, Hyde Park, New York, NY
FatS	father's sister		
FatW	father's wife	fdry	foundry
FaW	farm worker	fe	for example
FAZA	Friends of Arizona Archives	Feb	February
fb	(1) family Bible (2) file (3) file box	Fed	Federal, Federated
FB	(1) foreign born (2) foster brother	Fed/Fedn	Federation
FBA	Fellow of the British Academy	FEDIX	Federal Information Exchange, Inc.
Fbai	farm bailiff	Fedl	Federal
FBG	Friends burial grounds (Society of Friends, Quaker)	Fedn	Federation
FBH	Friends of the Blue Hills Trust, 1894 Canton Avenue, Milton, MA 02186	FEEFHS	Federation of Eastern European Family History Societies, P.O. Box 510898, Salt Lake City, UT 84151-0898
FBI	Federal Bureau of Investigation	fell	fellow
Fboy	farm boy	felw	fellow

fem	feminine
fem/feml	female
Fem. Dis	Female Disease
FERA	Federal Emergency Relief Administration
Ferdº	Fernando
Ferman	Fermanagh, Ireland
FERPA	Family Educational Rights and Privacy Act
FesB	Feshbag
feu	late (deceased)
Fev	Fever
ff	(1) and the following; and following pages (2) Fifer (3) more than one microfilm or microfiche number in a series
FF	First Families of Ohio, Ohio Genealogical Society, 713 South Main Street, Mansfield, OH 44907-1644
FF	(1) foster father (2) frates: brothers
FFA	Fellow, Faculty of Actuaries (in Scotland)
FFHS	Federation of Family History Societies, c/o Benson Room, Birmingham and Midland Institute, Margaret Street, Birmingham, England B3 3BS
FFI	Family Finder Index, Broderbund, P.O. Box 6125, Novato, CA 94948-6125
FFO	First Families of Ohio, Ohio Genealogical Society, 713 South Main Street, Mansfield, OH 44907-1644
FF's	First Families
FFTT	First Families of the Twin Territories (Oklahoma Genealogical Society), P.O. Box 12986, Oklahoma, OK 73157-2986
FFV	Order of First Families of Virginia, 1607-1624/25
FG	French Grants

FGBS	Fellow, the New York Genealogical and Biographical Society
FGCU	Florida Gulf Coast University
FGR/fgr	family group record
FGRA	Family Group Records Archives at the Family History Library, Salt Lake City, Utah (microfilmed)
FGRC	Family Group Records Collection at the Family History Library, Salt Lake City, Utah (microfilmed)
fgs	family group sheet
FGS	Federation of Genealogical Societies, P.O. Box 200940, Austin, TX 78720-0940
FGS/OGS	Federation of Genealogical Societies/Ohio Genealogical Society
FGSP	Fellow of the Genealogical Society of Pennsylvania
FH	(1) family histories (2) family history
FHC	Family History Center™ of The Church of Jesus Christ of Latter-day Saints (local branch genealogical library)
FHCs	Family History Centers™
FHD	Family History Department, 50 East North Temple, Salt Lake City, UT 84150 (the Family History Library is part of the Family History Department)
FHG	Fellow of the Institute of Heraldic and Genealogical Studies
FHH	Family History Hero (Treasure Maps How-to Genealogy Internet Web Site)
FHiTL	Family History Technology Laboratory, Brigham Young University, Provo, Utah
FHL	Family History Library™, 35 North West Temple Street, Salt Lake City, UT 84150
FHLC	Family History Library Catalog™, Family History Library, Salt Lake City, Utah

FHND	*Family History News and Digest*
FHQ	*Florida Historical Quarterly*
FHS	family history society
FHS	Fellow, Heraldry Society
FHSA	Family History Society of Arizona, P.O. Box 63094, Phoenix, AZ 8082-3094
Fi/fi	(1) fireman (2) for instance
FI/FIN	Finland
FIAG	Fellow of the Institute of American Genealogy (defunct)
F&IW	French and Indian War
fiche	microfiche (e.g., frequently used as a Family History Library microfiche number)
fid	(1) fidelity (2) fiduciary: held in trust
FID	International Federation for Information and Documentation
FIELD	*Field News Service* (formerly Chicago Daily News-Sun Times)
Fif/FIF	Fife, Fifer, Scotland
fi fa	a writ of fieri facias
FifMaj/FM	Fife Major
fig	(1) figuratively (2) figure
FIGRS	Fellow of the Irish Genealogical Research Society (Ireland), an honor awarded in recognition of outstanding service to the society and/or outstanding contributions to Irish genealogy.
FIGS	Family Search® Internet Genealogy Service
FIIC	Fellow, International Institute for Conservation of Historic and Artistic Works
FIJ	Fiji Islands
FIL/Fil/ f-i-l	father-in-law

Filby	Frequently refers to P. William Filby's *Passenger and Immigration Lists Index* (Detroit: Gale Research)
FilCK	Filson Club, Louisville, KY
FilDr	Doctor of Philosophy
filia	daughter
filius	son
fille	daughter
film	film number, microfilm number (e.g., Family History Library microfilm number)
fils	son
fin	finance, financial
FIN/Finn/ FINL	Finland
Finla	Finland
FIOP	Foreign and International Official Publications
first C/ First C	first cousin
First Fam of Miss	Order of The First Families of Mississippi
First Fam of Ohio	First Families of Ohio (Ohio Genealogical Society, 713 South Main Street, Mansfield, OH 44907-1644)
FI SG	Fellow of the Institute of American Genealogy
fk	fork, as in the Salt Fork of the river
FKC	Fellow, King's College London
fl/FL	(1) fall (2) father-in-law (3) floor (4) floruit (5) he/she flourished, lived
FL	Family Line Publications, Rear 63 E Main Street, Westminster, MD 21157
FL/Fla	Florida
FLA	Fellow, Library Association

Flab	farm laborer
Flagon & Trencher	Flagon and Trencher (Descendants of Colonial Tavern Keepers)
FLAI	Fellow, Library Association of Ireland
fld/flds	field(s)
Flem	Flemish
FLHS	Fellow, London Historical Society
FLIN	Flint, Great Britain
Flint/FLN	Flintshire
FLOW	Franconia, Lower (Unterfranken)
flr pkr	flower packer
fls	falls
FlSU	Florida State University, Tallahassee, FL
flt	(1) flats (2) flight
Flt	Flintshire, Wales
F/Lt	Flight Lieutenant
FLT	an inscription of the cemetery stone of an I00F member, meaning Friendship, Love, and Truth
FM/fm	(1) Field-Marshal (2) foster mother (3) free mulatto (4) funeral marker
FMA	Fellow, Museums Association
Fmag	farm manager
FMID	Franconia, Middle (Mittelfranken)
Fmn	Fermanagh, Northern Ireland
Fmot	foster mother
fn	(1) footnote (2) free negro
FN	(1) field-name(s) (2) Finland (3) First Name (4) free Negro(es) (5) Register of births, deaths, and marriages in foreign countries
fndl	foundling

fndry clk	foundery clerk
fndry fnsh	finisher in foundery
fndry frmn	foundery foreman
fndry mldr	moulder in foundery
fndry tnshr	tinesher in foundery
FNGS	Fellow of the National Genealogical Society (4527 17th Street North, Arlington, VA 22207-2399). An honor accorded in recognition of outstanding service to NGS and/or worthy contributions to American genealogy.
FNS	Family Name System (Family History Department, Salt Lake City, UT)
fnshr	finisher
fnshr mshp	finisher in machine shop
fo	folio
f/o, fa/o	father of
f/o	formerly of
FO	Family Origins (genealogy software program)
FO	(1) Fidelity Oath (2) Field Officer (3) Foreign Office (4) Foreign Officer
F/O	Flying Officer
fob	free on board
FoB	(1) foreign birth (2) foster brother
FOE	Fraternal Order of Eagles
Fof F	Feet of Fines
FOIA	Freedom of Information Act
fol	following
fol.	folder
FOLDOC	Free On-Line Dictionary of Computing
Folle	Follenze

for	(1) foreign (2) foreigner
FOR	Forfar/Angus
form	formerly
formn	foreman
fortn	fortnightly
FORUM	*Federation of Genealogical Societies Forum,* P.O. Box 200940, Austin, TX 78720-0940
forwn	forewoman
FoS	foster son
FoSi	foster sister
FOTW	Flags of the World
found	foundation
Founders of Norwich, Conn	Society of the Founders of Norwich, Connecticut
Founders & Patriots of Amer	Order of the Founders and Patriots of America
Four-H (4-H)	Four-H (head, hands, heart, and health)
FOW	Family Origins genealogy software
fower	four
FP/f.p.	(1) foreign parts (2) Free Polls
F & PA	The Order of the Founders and Patriots of America
FPC	Free Persons of Color
FPhS	Fellow, Philosophical Society of England
FPO	Fleet Post Office
FPR	Fairview Park Regional, Cuyaboga County Public Library, 21255 Lorain Road, Fairview Park, OH 44126-2120
Fpup	farm pupil

fr	(1) family records (2) father (3) final record (4) friend (5) from
Fr/FR	(1) France; French (2) Frau, wife
FR	(1) Family Records program within PAF (2) Family Registry (3) Family Representative (4) Father (Roman Catholic Priest) (5) France (6) Frankfurt Germany Temple (6) see FRA
FR	Frame reference of an entry on a microfilm copy (especially Scottich parish registers)
FrA	French Army
FRA	Fellow, Royal Academy (British)
FRA/Fran	France
frac	fractional
FraF	Frankfurt, Germany
FRAHS	Fellow, Royal Austalian Historical Society
FraM	Frankfort on the Maine
Franc/ FRAN	France
Fran^{ca}/ Fran^{co}	Francisca/Francisco
FRANK	Frankfort Germany LDS Temple
Frankl^{n}/ Frank/Frank^{n}	Franklin
frat	fraternity
Frbg	Frederiksborg, Denmark
FRC	Family Records Centre, 1 Myddelton Street, London, England EC1R 1UW
frd	(1) ford (2) friend
Frds	Friends (Society of Friends, Quakers)
Fre	Freiburg
FRE	family record extraction (LDS Church term)

Fredk   Frederick
Fred^ck/Fredr^k

freem/frm   oath of freeman

Frei   Freisland

FREIB   Freiberg Germany LDS Temple

Freibg   Freiburg, Baden

freq   (1) frequent (2) frequently

frg   forge

FRG   Federal Republic of Germany

F.R.Hist.S.   Fellow of the Royal Historical Society

Fri   (1) Friday (2) Frieberberg (3) Frieburg

Fried   Friedrich

frir   friar

frk/frks   fork(s)

Frk   Frankfort

frk(s)   fork(s)

frm   Freeman, a voter in a colony. The date following is usually the date he was admitted.

Frm/Hnd   Farm Hand

frmn   foreman, forewoman

frms   farms

Frm/Wife   Farmer's Wife

FrN   French Navy

FRN   France

FRNC   Franconia

frnd   friend

FRNH   Frankenhausen

FRNK   Frankfurt

fro   from

frs   francs (French or Swiss money)

FRS   Fellow of the Royal Society (British)

FRSA   Fellow of the Royal Society of Arts

FRSAI   Fellow of the Royal Society of Antiquaries of Ireland

FRSC   Fellow of the Royal Society of Canada

FRSE   Fellow of the Royal Society of Edinburgh

FRSL   Fellow of the Royal Society, London

FRSNZ   Fellow of the Royal Society of New Zealand

frst   forest

frt   freight

FRU   Family Records Utilities (a genealogy software utility for use with Personal Ancestral File 2.31)

fry   ferry

fs   (1) facsimile (2) footstone

FS   Female servant

FSA   (1) Farm Security Administration (2) Fellow of the Society of Antiquaries

FSAG   Fellow of the Society of Australian Genealogists

FSAI   Fellow of the Society of Antiquaries of Ireland

FSAL   Fellow of the Society of Antiquaries of London

FSAS/FSA Scot   Fellow of the Society of Antiquaries of Scotland

FSC   Family Studies Center (Brigham Young University, Provo, UT 84602-5516)

FSC   Fitchburg State College

FSCK   filesystem check (computer)

Fser   farm servant

FSG   Fellow of the Society of Genealogists (London). Society of Genealogists, 14 Charterhouse Buildings, Goswell Road, London, England EC1M 7BA. An honor accorded in recognition of outstanding service to the society and/or worthy contributions to British genealogy.

FSGs   foster step grandson

FSGS   Florida State Genealogical Society, P.O. Box 10249, Tallahassee, FL 32302-2249

FSHSW   Friends of the State Historical Society of Wisconsin

Fsi   Foster sister

Fsis   foster sister

FSon   foster son

Fsta   Kaubisch Memorial Public Library, Fostoria

Fstw   farm steward

ft   (1) feet, foot (2) fort

ft.   linear feet. Used for large quantities of loose papers.

FTB   Franchise Tax Board

FTC   Federal Trade Commission

fteen   fifteen

FTG   Form Tool Gold (computer software program)

FTJP   Family Tree of the Jewish People

FTM   Family Tree Maker™ (Brøderbund Software, Banner Blue Division, P.O. Box 6125, Norato, CA 94948-6125)

FTML   Fort Ticonderoga Museum Library, Ticonderoga, NY

Ftmn   footman

ftn   fountain

FTP   Family Tree Print (a genealogy software utility)

FTP   File Transfer Protocol (transferring files from one computer to another via the Internet)

ftr   fitter

FTSGS   Fellow, Texas State Genealogical Society

FUGA   Fellow of the Utah Genealogical Association (P.O. Box 1144, Salt Lake City, UT 84110). An honor accorded in recognition of outstanding service to the society and/or worthy contributions to genealogy at large.

funrl/mort   funeral and mortuary records

FUPP   Franconia, Upper (Oberfranken)

furn   (1) furnace (2) furniture

furngs   furnishings

furntr dlr   furniture dealer

furntr mct   furniture merchant

furntr str   furniture store

Fus   Fusiliers

fut   future

fv   folio verso; on the back of the page

F-v   Catherine Fedorchak's Monroe County Records

FVGS   Fellow of the Virginia Genealogical Society

FVGS   Flathead Valley Genealogical Society, P.O. Box 584, Kalispell, MT 59903-0584

FW   Allen County Public Library, 900 Webster Street, Fort Wayne, IN 46802

fwd   (1) forward (2) forwarded

FWif   friend's wife

FWIW   for what it's worth

FWK   framework knitter (may be found in British
             census)

Fwy   Freeway

FYI   for your information

FxGS   Fairfax Genealogical Society, P.O. Box 2290,
             Merrifield, VA 22116-2290

G

g/gr   (1) grand (2) great

G   (1) corresponding record is in computer file (LDS) (2) Gaelic (3) German (4) guardianship record (5) gulf

G/GER   German, Germany

GA   Great aunt

GA/Ga   Georgia

GAB   Gene/Logical Aids Bulletin, Miami Valley Genealogical Society quarterly

Gab^l   Gabriel

GACP   Great American Census Program

Gael   Gaelic

GAESRE   Genealogical Association of English Speaking Researchers in Europe

GAHA   German American Heritage Association of Oklahoma, Modern Language Department, Oklahoma City University, 2501 North Blackwelder, Oklahoma City, OK 73106

gal/gall   gallon

Gal   Galway, Republic of Ireland

GALI   Galicia

galr   gaoler

GAM   (1) Gambia (2) Guam

GamK   game keeper

Gang/Dipth   Gangrenous Diphtheria

GAR   Grand Army of the Republic (veteran's group of Union soldiers)

gardnr& frm   gardener & farmer

GasAR   Georgia State Department of Archives and History, Atlanta, GA

GAT   Guatemala

GATE   *Gateway to the West: Ohio*, genealogical periodical (defunct)

gatertendr   gater tender

GaU   Georgia University, Athens, GA

Gaun   (1) grandaunt (2) great-aunt

Gavlbg   Gavleborg, Sweden

Gaz   Gazetteer

gb   Guardian bond

GB   (1) gigabytes (2) Great Britain

G&B   *The New York Genealogical and Biographical Record. See* NYGBR.

GBBS   Genealogy Bulletin Board System(s)

GBE   Knight (or Dame) Grand Cross of the Order of the British Empire

Gboy   garden boy

GBR/ GBRI   Great Britain

GbSC   Glassboro State College, New Jersey

GC   (1) *Genealogical Computing* (2) General Code (3) George Cross (4) grandchild (5) Greece

GCAH	General Commission on Archives and History, United Methodist Church
G/Capt	Group Captain
GCB	Knight Grand Cross of the Order of the Bath
GCC	Genealogical Coordination Committee (a coordinating committee organized 1980-1995)
g. ch/gch/ g chn	grandchildren
GChd/Gcl	grandchild
GCMG	Knight or Dame Grand Cross, Order of St. Michael and St. George
GCO	Genealogical Council of Oregon, P.O. Box 628, Ashland, OR 95420-0021
gct	granted a certificate to
GCVO	Knight (or Dame) Grand Cross of the Royal Victorian Order
gd	(1) grand (2) granddaughter (3) guard (4) guardian
GD	(1) Genealogical Department (now Family History Department, Salt Lake City) (2) German Documents (3) gifts and deposits (manuscripts; British term) (4) Granddaughter
GDaH	granddaughter's husband
GDaL	granddaughter-in-law
GDau	granddaughter
GdGS	God-grandson
GDL	Granddaughter-in-law
GDM	Genealogical Data Model
GDMNH	Noyes, Libby, and Davis, *Genealogical Dictionary of Maine and New Hampshire*
gdn(s)	(1) garden(s) (2) guardian

GdnC	gardener's child
GdnD	gardener's daughter
gdn/o	guardian of
gdnr	gardener
gdnship	guardianship
GdnW	gardener's wife
Gd/o	granddaughter of
gdp	grandparent
GDPBM	*Gale Directory of Publications and Broadcast Media*, 2 vols. (Detroit: Gale Research, 1997)
GDR	German Democratic Republic (Soviet Germany; East Germany)
gds	(1) goods (2) guards
GE	Greece
GE/ge	(1) German (2) Germany
geb	*geboren* (born, maiden name)
GED	(1) Genealogical Event Database (2) General Education Development
GeDC	Georgetown, D.C.
GEDCOM	GEnealogical Data COMmunications. A format for genealogical data developed by the Family History Department, Salt Lake City, Utah, for transferring data from one type of genealogical software to another. As an example, data may be downloaded (copied) from the Ancestral File™ into the Personal Ancestral File®.
GEDISS	Genealogical Data Interchange and Storage Standard
GEG	Genealogical Educators Group of Greater Monroe County, New York
Gem/GeM	Gemeindsmann

gen   (1) genealogy/genealogical (2) general (3) generation (4) genitive case; genus

Gen   Geneva

GEN   Generations genealogy software

Gen/Genl/   General (military rank)
Gen'l

GENCAP   Genealogical Computing Association of Pennsylvania

Gen. Dept.   Genealogical Department; now the Family History Department, Salt Lake City, UT 84150

Gen/Dipth   General Debility

GENDIS   Genealogical Death Indexing System (Michigan Division of Vital Records and Health Statistics)

GENE   (1) genealogy (2) genealogical

geneal   (1) genealogical (2) genealogist (3) genealogy

GeneaNet   Genealogical Database Network

GENEVA   Genealogical Events and Activities

GenH   general help

GENLOC   Genealogy and Local History Discussion Group

Gen. Mag.   *The Genealogists' Magazine* (Society of Genealogists, London, England)

GENO   Genoa

genr   generation

GENRT   Genealogy Roundtable

Gen Soc   Genealogical Society of Utah (see Family History Library), 35 North West Temple, Salt Lake City, UT 84150

GEN SOURCE   GENealogy Source (Advanced Resources, Inc.)

GENSUP   Genealogical Support Forum

gent/gentl[n]/   (1) gentleman/gentlewoman (2) gentlemen/
gent   gentle-women

Gent   (1) Gentleman (a title, not an adjective) (2) Gentlemen

GENTECH   Genealogy Technology. An independent, non-profit organization chartered in Texas to educate genealogists in the use of technology.

GENUKI   UK and Ireland Genealogical Information Service

Geo/G[o]   George

Geof   Geoffrey

geog   (1) geographer (2) geographic (3) geographical (4) geography

geol   (1) geological (2) geologist (3) geology

geom   (1) geometrical (2) geometry

Geor   Georgian

ger   gerund

GER/Ger/   (1) German (2) German Old Empire
Germ   (3) Germanic (4) Germany

Gert   Gertrude

gest   (1) *gestorben* (died) (2) guest

get   *getauft* (baptized, christened)

getr   *getraut* (married)

Gev/Gevat   Gevatter(n), sponsor(s)

gf/gfa/   grandfather
GFat/grf/
g fr/gff/GF

GF   Genealogical Forum of Oregon

G & F   Georgia & Florida Railroad

GFaL   grandfather-in-law

GFO   Genealogical Forum of Oregon, P.O. Box 42567, Portland, OR 97242-0567

GFOA   Government Finance Officers Association

GFR   German Federal Republic (West Germany)

GFWC	General Federation of Women's Clubs
gg/gtgr	great grand
Gg	Georg
GGCd	great-grandchild
ggch	great-grandchild
ggd/ggda	great-granddaughter
GGD	*Genealogical Research Directory* (surname queries listing)
GGD	*German Genealogical Digest*
ggf/ggfa/ GGF	great-grandfather
ggg	great, great grand
gggch	great-great-grandchild
g-g-gfr/ gggf/GGGF	great-great-grandfather
g-g-gmor/ gggm/GGGM	great-great-grandmother
g-g-gp	great-great-grandparent
ggm/GGM	great-grandmother
GGMo	great-grandmother
GGNe	great-grandnephew
GGNi	great-grandniece
GGS/GGSn	great-grandson
GGSA	German Genealogical Society of America, P.O. Box 291818, Los Angeles, CA 90029
GH	*Genealogical Helper*
GHMA	*Genealogical and Historical Magazine of the Arizona Temple District*
GHQ	General Headquarters
GI	General (or Government) Issue; a private soldier

GIA	Genealogical Indexing Associates
GIB/GIBR	Gibraltar
GICS	Geographic Information Coding Scheme (US Census)
GIE	Genealogical Information Exchange (a program in Personal Ancestral File® 2.31 and older versions). This program is not available in PAF 3.0 or PAF 4.0.
GIF	Graphic Interchange Format (computer format)
GIG	German Interest Group, P.O. Box 2185, Janesville, WI 53547-2185
GIGO	garbage in garbage out
Gil/Gilb^t/ Gil^{rt}	Gilbert
GIL	General Information Leaflet (National Archives and Records Administration, Washington, D.C.)
GIL(s)	General Information Leaflet(s) (National Archives and Records Administration, Washington, DC)
GILS	Government Information Locator Service (Canada)
GIM	Genealogical Institute of the Maritimes
GIM/ GIMA	Genealogical Institute of Mid-America, Continuing Education, University of Illinois at Springfield, Springfield, IL 62794-9243
GIPSI	Genealogical Index Processing System and Interpreter (genealogy software utility)
GIS	Geographic Information Systems
GIT	Genealogical Institute of Texas (now Institute of Genealogical Studies), P.O. Box 25556, Dallas, TX 75225-5556
giv	(1) given (2) giving
GIX	Government Information Exchange
GJ	*Genealogical Journal*, Utah Genealogical Association, P.O. Box 1144, Salt Lake City, UT 84110

Gk	Greek	GLO	General Land Office (*see also* BLM, Bureau of Land Management)
GKpr	gatekeeper		
gl	granted letter	Glocs/Glos/ GLOU/Glouc	Gloucestershire (England)
Gl	Gloucestershire, England	Gloucs	Gloucester, England
GL	(1) Grand Lodge (2) Greater London, England (3) Guildhall Library, Aldermanbury, London, England EC2	GLRO	Greater London Record Office, 40 Northampton Road, Clerkenwell, London, England EC1R OAB
GL	Graduate in Law	GLS	Gloucestershire
GLA/Glam	Glamorganshire, Wales	Gls/Blo	Glass Blower
GLaB	General laborer	glt	granted letter to
GLAM/ Glams	Glamorgan, Wales	gm	gram(s)
Glas	Glasgow, Scotland	gm/gma/ grm/g mr/ GM	grandmother
GlaS	Glaris, Switzerland		
GLC	Greater London Council	GM	*The Gentleman's Magazine*
gld	guild	Gmc.	Germanic
GLH	Genealogy and Local History Collection on microfiche (published by University Microfilms). Includes compiled genealogies, local histories, genealogical serials, printed vital records, biographies, and other sources.	GMD	Georgia Military District
		GML/Gml	Grandmother-in-law
		GMN	*Great Migration Newsletter,* Great Migration Study Project, 101 Newbury St., Boston, MA 02116
G&LHBIP	*Genealogical and Local History Books in Print* (Baltimore: Genealogical Publishing Company)	GMNJ	*The Genealogical Magazine of New Jersey*
GLHD	Genealogy & Local History Department, Mid-Continent Public Library, Independence, MO	gmo	grandmother
GLIN	Global Legal Information Network (Library of Congress)	GmoL	grandmother-in-law
		GMot	grandmother
GLLDS	Genealogical Library, The Church of Jesus Christ of Latter-day Saints. See FHL	GMT	Greenwich Meal Time
Glm	Glamorgan, Wales	GMW	Genealogy's Most Wanted
GLMC	Genealogical Library Master Catalog (bibliographical references)	Gn/GN	(1) General (2) great or grand nephew
		GNE	Grandnephew
gln	glen	GneL	grandnephew-in-law

GNep	grandnephew, Great-nephew
GNI/GNie	grandniece, Great-niece
G94	deceased member file (LDS term)
GNiL	grandniece-in-law
GNIS	Geographic Names Information System (USGS)
Gnr	Gunner
GNS	Gannett News Service
Gn/s	Guineas-21 shillings
Go	governess
GO	(1) General Office (2) general order(s)
GOA	Goa, East Indies
GOC	General Officer Commanding
GOC-in-C	General Officer Commanding-in-Chief
GodC/ God C1	Godchild
GodD	Goddaughter
godf	Godfather
godm/ GodM	Godmother
God'r	Godmanchester
GodS	Godson
GOP	Grand Old Party
Got & B	Goteborg & Bohus
Gotld	Gotland, Sweden
Gottf	Gottfried
Gottl	Gottlieb
gov	governing
gov/govt	government

Gov/Govr	(1) governor (2) Royal Governor
Gov-Gen/ Gov.Gen	Governor General
gov^n	governor
govt	government
govtl	governmental
gp	grandparent(s)
GP	General Practitioner
GPAI	*Genealogical Periodical Annual Index*. Heritage Books, 1540-E Pointer Ridge Place, Bowie, MD 20716
GPC	Genealogical Publishing Company, 1001 North Calvert Street, Baltimore, MD 21202-3897
GPO	general post office
GPO	Government Printing Office
GPR	Genealogical Projects Registry
GPrt	gate porter
GPS	Genealogical Proof Standard (a genealogical term to replace preponderance of the evidence)
gr	(1) grain (2) grand (3) grant or granted, grantor or grantee (4) grave (5) great (6) gross (7) grove
gr	grandfather
gr-gr	great-grandfather
GR	(1) Germany (2) gravestone record (3) Greece (4) Greek
gra	grange
GRA	Genealogy Research Associates, Inc., 2600 Garden Rd., Suite 224, Monterey, CA 93940-5322; and Salt Lake City, UT
GRA	German Research Association, P.O. Box 711600, San Diego, CA 92171-1600
GRA	Grand Army of the Republic

grad	(1) graduate (2) graduated
GRHS	Germans from Russia Heritage Society
gram	grammar
grand jr/ grand jur	grand jury
grat	great
GRBN	*Genealogical Reference Builders Newsletter*
Gr Br/ Gr Brit	Great Britain
GRC	*Gravestone Records Committee*
GRC	Greece
GR(C)	Certified Record Searcher (Canada)
grch/grchn/ grchildmn	grandchildren
grchild	grandchild
grd	(1) ground (2) guard
grd/grdn	guardian
GRD	*Genealogical Research Directory* (research queries). Available in printed form and on compact disc from Lois Burlo, 737 Calle Pensamiento, Thousand Oaks, CA 91360-4839.
gr/dau/ grdau	granddaughter
grd/o or gr/d/o	granddaughter of
grd(s)	guard(s)
grdshp/est	guardianship and estate records
grdsn	grandson
GREE	Greece
Greg	Gregory
Gren	Grenadier

GREN	Grenada
grf	grandfather
gr-father	grandfather
grgrch	great-grandchild
GrHM	Greensboro Historical Museum, North Carolina
GRHS	Germans from Russia Heritage Society, 1008 East Central Avenue, Bismarck, ND 58501
GRINZ	Genealogical Research Institute of New Zealand
Grl	Guerilla
grm	grammar (school)
grn	green
grnd	grand
Grnpt	Greenport
gro	(1) gross (2) grove
GRO	General Register Office England (*see also* ONS, Office for National Statistics)
GRO	General Register Office of Scotland
groc	grocer/grocery
gro clk	clerk in grocer store
gro kpr	grocery keeper
grom	groom
GROS/ GRO(S)	General Register Office for Scotland, New Register House, Edinburgh, Scotland EH1 34T
GRS	Graves Registration Service
grs/o or gr/s/o	grandson of
gr/son/grs grson/gson	grandson
grtd.	granted
grv	grove
Gr Yd	graveyard

gs/GS	(1) grandson (2) gravestone	g son	grandson
Gs	grandson	GSP	Genealogical Society of Pennsylvania, 1305 Locust Street, Philadelphia, PA 19107-5405
GS	genealogical serials		
GS	(1) Genealogical Society (Family History Library, Salt Lake City, UT) (2) General Staff	GSP	Genealogical Standard of Proof
		GSS	Grand-stepson
GSA	(1) General Services Administration (2) Girl Scouts of America	GSS	Genealogical Search Services
GSC	General Staff Corps	GS ser no.	Genealogical Society serial number (Family History Library, Salt Lake City, UT)
GS call no.	Genealogical Society call number (Family History Library, Salt Lake City, UT)	GSSI	Genealogy Society of Southern Illinois
GSCW	General Society of Colonial Wars	GSU	Genealogical Society of Utah, 35 North West Temple Street, Salt Lake City, UT 84150. *See* FHL, Family History Library™
GSDa	grandstepdaughter		
GSDS	Genealogical Software Distribution System		
Gser	general servant	g.s.w.	gunshot wound (military)
GSF	Genealogical Society (Family History Library) film number	GSW 1812	General Society of the War of 1812
		GSY	Guernsey
GSG	Genealogical Speakers Guild, 2818 Pennsylvania Avenue, Suite 159, Washington, DC 20007	gt	great
		GT	GENTECH
GSHA-SC	Genealogical Society of Hispanic American-Southern California	GT	(1) Germany (2) Grant
GsL/Gsl	grand son-in-law	GTA	*Germans to America* (Genealogical Publishing Co., Baltimore, MD)
GSL	Great Salt Lake (Salt Lake City, Utah)	GTA	Greater Toronto Area (Canada)
GSMD	General Society of Mayflower Descendants	Gt Br	Great Britain
GSnD	grandson's daughter	GTI	GENTECH, Inc. *see* GENTECH.
GSNJ	Genealogical Society of New Jersey, P.O. Box 1291, New Brunswick, NJ 08903	Gtlm	gentleman
		GTT	Gone to Texas
GSnL	grandson-in-law	GTTW	*Gateway to the West*
GSnS	grandson's son	gtwy	gateway
GSnU	grandson's uncle	Gu/gu	gules, red (heraldry)
GSnW	grandson's wife	GU	(1) Great Uncle (2) Guatemala City LDS Temple (3) Guinea, Africa
Gs/o	grandson of		
GSO	General Staff Officer		

gua/guard/Gua	(1) guardian (2) guardianship
GUA/GU/GUAM	Guam
GUAD	Guadaloupe
guar	(1) guarantee (2) guardianship
Guat/GUE	Guatemala
GUATE	Guatemala City Guatemala LDS Temple
GUAYA	Guayaquil Ecuador LDS Temple
Gue	Isd of Guenesey
Guern	Guernsey, C. Is.
Guest	Guest
GUI	Graphical User Interface
Gunc	(1) granduncle (2) great-uncle
gunr	gunner
gurd	guard
Gus	(1) Augustus (2) Gustave
GUTT	Guttenburg
GUY	Guiana
GUYA	Guyana
GvnD	governess's daughter
gvnr	governor
gvns/go	governess
GvrD	governor's daughter
GvrS	governor's son
GW	(1) *Gateway to the West* (2) George Washington
GWPDA	Great War Primary Document Archive
GWR	Great Western Railway
GWU	George Washington University
GWSC	Genealogical Websites of Societies and CIG's
GY	Guayaquil Ecuador LDS Temple
gz	gazetteer

H

h   (1) heir/heiress (2) hot (3) hour (4) house (5) householder (6) husband (of)

H   (1) Herr, a title of respect, often stylized (2) Historical Dept. (PBO deaths)

1/h, 2/y   First husband, second husband, etc.

Ha   Hampshire, England

HA   (1) Historical Association (2) Hawaii LDS Temple

HAC   Honourable Artillery Company (British) Armoury House, City Road, London, ECIY23Q

HAD   Haddington/East Lothian

Hag   Haggai

HAGA   Houston Area Genealogical Association, 2507 Tannehill, Houston, TX 77008-3052

HAI/HAIT   Haiti

hairdrsr   hairdresser

Halafax   see Nova Scotia

HalB   hall boy

HalF/HalX   Halifax

half bro   half brother

half sis   half sister

Hall   Halland, Sweden

Ham/ Hambg/ Hambu/HAMB   Hamburg, Germany

HAM   Hampshire/Hants/Southampton

Hamil   Hamilton

Hammon   Hammonassett dialect

HAMP/ Hamps   Hampshire (England)

Han/Hanah   Hannah

Han/ HANO   Hanover

handks/hk/ hhk   handkerchief or handkerchiefs

Hann   Hannover, Prussia

Hants   Hampshire, England

HAPI   Hispanic American Periodical Index (available on Local Area Networks)

Harl mss   Harleian Manuscripts (British Library, London)

Harl. Soc. Pub.   Harleian Society Publications

Harv.   Harvard

HAT   Haiti

HAWAI   Hawaii LDS Temple

hawk   hawker

Hb   half brother

HB   Hamburg, Germany

HB   Heritage Books, 1540-E Pointer Ridge Place, Bowie, MD 20716

HBC   The Hudson's Bay Company Archives, Provincial Archives of Manitoba, 200 Vaughan St., Winnipeg, Manitoba Canada, R3C 1T5

Hbl   half brother-in-law

HBLL	Harold B. Lee Library, Brigham Young University, Provo, UT 84602
HBM	His or Her Britannic Majesty
Hb/o	half brother of
Hboy	house boy
hbr	harbor
Hbro	half brother
hc	*honoris causa* (honorary)
HC	(1) Havana, Cuba (2) Harvard College (3) Haut-Canada (i.e., Upper Canada or Ontario) (4) heads of cattle (5) Holy Cross (6) Joseph Smith, *History of the Church of Jesus Christ of Latter-day Saints,* Century 1, B. H. Roberts, ed., 7 vols. (Salt Lake City: Deseret Book Co., 1952-1962)
HCA	High Court of Admiralty
HCAS	Hesse Cassel (Kurheessen)
HCC	Historical Chattahoockee Commission, P.O. Box 33, Eufawla, AL 36072-0033
HCGI	Historical Collections of the Great Lakes, Bowling Green State University, Jerome Library, Bowling Green, OH 43403
HCL	Haverford College Library, 370 Lancaster Ave., Haverford, PA 19041-1392
HCL	Hebrew College Library, 43 Haves St., Brookline, MA 02446
HCou	half cousin
Hd	Hundred
Hd/HDAR	*Hesse Darmstadt* (German)
HD	(1) hard disk/ hard drive (2) high density
HD	Holland
Hdau	half daughter

HDC	Historical Department of The Church of Jesus Christ of Latter-day Saints, Salt Lake City, UT 84150
HDD	hard disk drive (computer term)
HDFA	Higher Diploma in Fine Art
HDipEd	Higher Diploma in Education
Hdlbg	Heidelberg, Baden
HDoc	house doctor
H'don	Huntingdon
Hdqrs	Headquarters (*see also* HQ)
hds	hands
Hdsl	Haderslev, Denmark
hdw	(1) handwritten (2) hardware
he/He	herder
He	Herefordshire, England
HE	His (or Her) Excellency; His Eminence
head	head
HeaM	headmaster, headmistress
Heart/ Comp	Heart Complaint
Hedm	Hedmark, Norway
HEF/ HERE/ Heref	Herefordshire, England
HEH	Henry E. Huntington Library, 1151 Oxford Rd., San Marino, CA 91108
HEH	His (or Her) Exalted Highness
HEIC	Honourable East India Company
HEICS	Honourable East India Company Service
Heini	Heinrich

heir-app	heir-apparent
Hel	Helle/Hellen
help/Help	help, helper
HELPER	*Everton's Genealogical Helper*, P.O. Box 368, Logan, UT 84323-0368
Hen	Henry
her	heraldry
Her	Hersotom
HERE	Herefordshire
Herefs	Hereford, England
Her & Gen	*The Herald and Genealogist*
Hernand^z	Hernandez
hers	herself
HERT/ Herts	(1) Hertford, England (2) Hertfordshire, England
Hes/HESS	Hesse/Hessen/Hessian/Hissin
HES	Hesse-Darmstadt
HesC	Hesse Castle
HesD	Hesse Darmstadt/Hessendame
HesM	Hessendame
HesN	Hesse Nausau
HESS	Hess Darne/Darm
Hess/HessD	Hesse-Darmstadt
HessC	Hesse Cassel
Hesse	Hessen/Hesse
HesseH	Hesse Holstein
Hessna	Hessen-Nassau, Purssia
HFRA	Honorary Foreign Member of the Royal Academy

HG	(1) Hagley Museum and Library, P.O. Box 3630, Wilmington, DE 19807-0630 (2) High German (3) Home Guard (4) Hungary
HGF	Houston Genealogical Forum, P.O. Box 271466, Houston, TX 77277-1466
hgi/H.Gi	hired girl
hglds	highlands
HGR	Hungary
HGS	Heartland Genealogy Society
hgts	heights
hh/Hh	hired hand
HH	Hempstead House, New London, Connecticut
HH	His or Her Highness (Holiness)
hhd/hd	hogshead
HHD	Doctor of Humanities (US)
HHEC	Hohenzollern Hechingen
HHOM	Hesse Homberg
HHS	Hearst Headline Service, 1701 Pennsylvania Ave. N.W., Washington, DC 20006
hi	high
HI	(1) Hawaii (2) Hawaiian Islands
HI and RH	His or Her Imperial and Royal Highness
HIAS	Hebrew Immigration Aid Society, 333 Seventh Avenue, New York, NY 10001
hic jacet	here lies
hic sit	here is buried
Highrs	Highlanders
HIH	His or Her Imperial Highness
HIM	His or Her Imperial Majesty
hims	himself

hind	hind	hls	hills
hird	hired	Hls	Holistine
hist	(1) historical (2) historian (3) history	HLS	*Hoc Loco Situs* (laid in this place)
Hist Coll	Charles A. Hanna, *Historical Collections of Harrison County, Ohio*	HLSMCa	Henry Huntington Library, San Marino, CA
HISTGEN	New England Historic Genealogical Society, 101 Newbury Street, Boston, MA 02116-3007	HLW	hand loom weaver
		hm	*hoc mense* (in this month)
histl	historical	Hm	Hired man
Hist MSS Comm	Royal Commission on Historical Manuscripts	HM	(1) His Majesty or Her Majesty (2) Honorable Mention (3) horses and mules
histn	historian	HMaid	housemaid
hist soc	historical society	HMan	headman
Hist. Soc.	Historical Society	HMC/. H.M.C	Historical Manuscripts Commission, London
HJ	(1) Here lies (2) *Historical Journal* (British)	HMCS	His or Her Majesty's Canadian Ship
Hjor	Hjorring, Denmark	Hmgr	hotel manager
HJS	Hic Jacet Sepultus; here lies buried	Hmls	homeless
hk/Hk	housekeeper	HMS	His or Her Majesty's Service or Ship
HKONG	Hong Kong LDS Temple	HMSO	Her Majesty's Stationery Office, Publications Centre, P.O. Box 276, London, England SW8 5DT
hk(s)	hank(s)		
hl/hls	hill(s)		
HL	Hayes Library, Edenton, North Carolina	Hmst	housemaster
HL/HLD	Holland	HMth	housemother
HLD	Doctor of Humane Letters	HN	(1) Hanover (2) Holstein, Germany (3) HotNotes! (Silicon Roots! Associates, P.O. Box 20541, San Jose, CA 95160-0541)
hldr	householder		
hlg/Hlg	hireling	hnd	hundred
HLI	Highland Light Infantry	HND	Honduras
HlpM	helpmate	hndlr	handler
hlpr	helper	HNG/ Hngr/ HUN/HU	Hungary
HLQ	*Huntington Library Quarterly*		

HNie	half niece	Hoop/Cgh	Hooping Cough
HNK	Hong Kong	HorS	horseler
Hntng	Huntting	horse dr	horse doctor
Hnur	house nurse	horse farr	horse farrier
ho	house	hort	horticulture
h/o	husband of	hortcltist	horticulturist
HO	(1) Historian's Office, The Church of Jesus Christ of Latter-day Saints, Salt Lake City, Utah (2) Holland (3) Home Office, Public Record Office, Kew, Richmond, Survey, England TW9 4DU	hosp	hospital
		Host	hostler
		hou/hous	house/houses
Hoanz	Hoanzoller	housecarpt	house carpenter
H of C	House of Commons	house devel	house development
H of L	House of Lords	house kpr	house keeper
HOHE	Hohenzollern	HP/hp	(1) Hewlett-Packard (2) horsepower
Hohenz	Hohenzollern, Purssia	HPNS	Heirs Pensioned
Hol	Holiday	Hprt	house porter
Hol/HOL/ Holl	Holland	Hprus	Hesse Prusia
Holb	Holbaek, Denmark	HPSO	Historical and Philosophical Society of Ohio
HOLD	Hesse Olddorf	HPSO	*Historical & Philosophical Society of Ohio Bulletin*
Holland Soc	Holland Society of New York, 122 East 58th Street, New York, NY	hq	headquarters
Hols/Holst	Holstein	HQ	*Heritage Quest Magazine*, P.O. Box 329, Bountiful, UT 84011-0329
holw	hollow	HQRL	Heritage Quest Research Library
hon	(1) honor (2) honorable (3) honorary	hr	(1) heir (2) hour(s)
hon/ honble/hon^ble	honorable	HR	(1) House of Representatives (2) Human Resources
Hon	(The) Honourable	Hrdl	Hordaland, Norway
Hond	Honduras	HrdM	herdsman
hons/Hons.	honors	hrdwa mct	hardware merchant

H.R.H.	His or Her Royal Highness
HRIP	*Hic Requiescit Pace* (here rests in peace)
HrnM	harnessmaker
hrnss mkr	harness maker
hrs	hours
HRS	Historical Records Survey
HRSA	Honorary Member, Royal Scottish Academy
HrsD	horse dealer
Hrt/HRT	Hertfordshire, England
hs	(1) half sister (2) *hic sepultus* (here is buried) (3) house
Hs	Hans
HS	(1) Hesse-Darmstadt, Germany (2) High School (3) Holland Society
HS	Hocking Sentinel, Logan, Hocking Co.
HSA	Huguenot Society of America, 122 East, 58th Street, New York, NY 10022
HsBr	husband's brother
HsConr	Hans Konrad, Hans Conrad
HSD	Historical Society of Delaware, 505 Market Street, Wilmington, DE 19801
hse	house
HSH	His or Her Serene Highness
HSi/HSis	half sister
HSIG	Hohenzollern Sigmaringen
Hsil	half sister-in-law
Hs Jb	Hans Jakob, Hans Jacob
HskC	housekeeper's child
HskD	housekeeper's daughter

HskF	housekeeper's father
HskH	housekeeper's husband
HskN	housekeeper's nephew or niece
Hskp/ HsKpr	housekeeper
HskS	housekeeper's son
HsMd	housemaid
Hs/o	half sister of
HSon	half son
HSP	Historical Society of Pennsylvania, 1300 Locust Street, Philadelphia, PA 19107-5699
Hs/Pntr	House Painter
Hsrg	house surgeon
Hs Rud	Hans Rudolf
HSrv	house servant
Hss/Ger	Hesse, Germany
Hst	Holstein
Hstw	house steward
Hs Uli	Hans Ulrich
Hs Wilh	Hans Wilhelm
ht	(1) height (2) *hoc tempore* (at this time)
HT	(1) Haiti (2) Hearth Tax
htg	heating
HtlG	hotel guest
HTML	Hyper Text Mark-up Language (Internet web pages are written in HTML language)
Hts	heights
HTTP	Hyper Text Transfer (Transport) Protocol
Htz	Holtenzen

Hu	Huntingdonshire, England		hw	his wife
HU	(1) Harvard University Library, Cambridge, Massachusetts (2) Hungary (3) Husband		hw/Hw	houseworker
HubD	husband's daughter		Hwy	Highway
HUD	Hudson Tombstone Collection		hy	heavy
HuGM	husband's grandmother		Hy	Henry
Huguenot Soc, Founders of	Huguenot Society of the Founders of Manakin in the Colony of Virginia		Hz	hertz
Huguenot Soc of SC	Huguenot Society of South Carolina, 138 Logan Street, Charleston, SC 29401			
HUL	Henry E. Huntington Library, San Marino, CA			
hun/hds/ hund	hundred(s)			
HUN	(1) Hungary (2) Huntingdonshire			
HUNG	Hungary			
HUNT/ Hunts	Huntingdonshire, England			
hus/husb/ husbn	husband			
Hus	Hussars			
husbm	husbandman			
HusF	husband's father			
HusM	husband's mother			
HusN	husband's nephew or niece			
HusS	husband's sister			
HusU	husband's uncle			
HV	Hannover, Germany			
hvn	haven			
HVR	Hocking Valley Republican, Logan, Hocking Co.			
Hvy Art	Heavy Artillery (military regiment)			

I

i	(1) instant (2) inventory (3) island (4) isle (5) issue	ICA	International Council of Archives
I	(1) independent (newspaper) (2) inmate (3) Instance Books (4) inventory (5) Ireland (6) Irish	ICC	Interstate Commerce Commission
		ICCS	International Council for Canadian Studies
I–	institution	ICE	Iceland
i.a.	*in absentia*	ICEL	Iceland, Icelandic
Ia	(1) Iowa (2) old abbreviation for Indiana	Ichg	in charge
IA	(1) Indian Army (2) Invalid's Application (3) Iowa (4) used for Indiana in 1850	ICOMOS	International Council on Monuments and Sites
		ICPSR	Inter-university Consortium for Political and Social Research, Ann Arbor, MI
IACI	The Irish American Cultural Institute, University of Saint Thomas, 2115 Summit Avenue, Mail #5026, Saint Paul, MN 55105-1096	id	*idem* (the same)
IAF	Internet Address Finder	ID	(1) identification (2) *Independent Democratic* (newspaper)
IAJGS	International Association of Jewish Genealogical Societies, 104 Franklin Avenue, Yorkers, NY 10705-2808	ID/Ida	Idaho
		IDA/IDI	India
IaHS	Iowa Historical Society, Iowa City, IA	IDN	*In Dei Nomie*
IASS	International Association for Scandinavian Studies	IDRC	International Development Research Centre
IaU	Iowa University, Iowa City	IdSHS	Idaho State Historical Society, Genealogical Library, 450 North Fourth Street, Boise, ID 83702
ib	inventory book		
ib/ibid/ Ibid/ibm	*ibidem* (in the same place; the same)	i.e.	*id est* (that is)
IBA	International Bar Association	IE	(1) *Improvement Era* (2) Indo-European (3) Internet Explorer (Microsoft's web browser)
IBSSG	International Blacksheep Society of Genealogists (homepages.rootsweb.com)	ien	Indian masculine (feminist)
		if	*ipse fecit* (he did it himself)
i/c	in charge of	IF	(1) Idaho Falls LDS Temple (2) Invalid's File
IC	(1) Iceland (2) Invalid's Certificate	IFALL	Idaho Falls LDS Temple

IFF	Internet Family Finder (Family Tree Maker)	IHRC	Immigration History Research Center, University of Minnesota, 826 Berry Street, St. Paul, MN 55114
IFGSX	Irish Family Group Sheet Exchange, P.O. Box 535, Farmington, MI 48332	IHS	first 3 letters of Greek name for Jesus Christ; a symbol of the Holy Name
IFLA	International Federation of Library Associations and Institutions	IHS	Indiana Historical Society, 315 West Ohio Street, Indianapolis, IN 46202-3299
IG	Inspector General		
IGCh	illegitimate grandchild	II	India
Ig^{co}	Ignacio	IIGS	International Internet Genealogical Society
IGDa	illegitimate granddaughter	IJGS	Illiana Jewish Genealogical Society, P.O. Box 384, Flossmoor, IL 60422-0384
IGG	Italian Genealogical Group		
IGHL	Institute of Genealogy and History for Latin America	IJH	*Iowa Journal of History*
		IJHP	*Iowa Journal of History and Politics*
IGHR	Institute of Genealogy and Historical Research, Samford University, Harwell G. Davis Library, 800 Lakeshore Drive, Birmingham, AL 35229-7008	Ikep	innkeeper
		il/i-l	in-law
IGI	International Genealogical Index® (database in Family Search®)	Il	Illegitimate
		IL	Kaskaskia Campaign (Illinois)
ign	ignorant; ignotus	IL/Ill	Illinois
IGS	Indiana Genealogical Society, P.O. Box 10507, Fort Wayne, IN 46852-0507	ILA	International Law Association
IGS	Institute of Genealogical Studies, P.O. Box 25556, Dallas, TX 75225-5556 (formerly Genealogical Institute of Texas)	IlHS	Illinois State Historical Society, Old State Capitol, Springfield, IL 62701
		ill	illuminated (document)
IGS	Iowa Genealogical Society, P.O. Box 7735, Des Moines, IA 50322-7735	ILL	Interlibrary loan
IGSI	Irish Genealogical Society, Intl., P.O. Box 13585, St. Paul, MN 55116-0585	IllC	illegitimate child
		IllD	illegitimate daughter
IGSn	illegitimate grandson	illeg	(1) illegible (2) illegitimate
IGV	Indische Genealogische Vereniging (Dutch Indische Genealogical Association)	illg/illeg/ illegit/ille`gitime	illegitimate
ih	*iacet hic* (here lies)		
		IllN	illegitimate niece or nephew
IHGS	Institute of Heraldic and Genealogical Studies, Northgate, Canterbury, Kent, England CT1 1BA	ills/illus/ill	illustrated
IHR	*Iowa Historical Record*	IllS	illegitimate son

ILO	International Labor Organization
IlSAr	Illinois State Archives, Springfield, IL
i/m	Indian male
IMAP	Internet Message Access Protocol
IM, I/M	Isle of Man
I. Man	Isle of Man, Great Britain
IMH	*Indiana Magazine of History*
IMHO	In my Humble Opinion
IMLS	Institute of Museum and Library Services
imm	(1) immigrant(s) (2) emigrated (3) migrated (4) immigrated
immig/pass	immigration and passenger lists
immigr	immigrate to
imp/Imp^s	*imprimis* (in the first place)
Imp	Imperial
imper	imperative
impl	implement
implts	implements
importacon	importation
impr	impression
imprimis	in the first place, first
improvem^t/ improv^t	improvement
imps	imprimis
impts	improvements
impv	improver
IMSI	International Microcomputer Software, Inc., San Rafael, CA

In	(1) inch(es) (2) Inmate
IN/Ind/ IND	Indiana (at Vincennes)
inc	(1) inclosure (2) incomplete (3) incorporated
Inc	Incumbent
incl	(1) include(d) (2) includes (3)including (4) inclusive
inconm	surname not known
incorp	incorporated
ind	(1) independent (2) Indian(s) (3) indictment (4) industrial
Ind.	(1) a person of independent means (2) Indian (3) Indiana
IND	Indonesia
I.N.D.	*In Nomine Die* (in God's name)
indef	indefinite
Indents	small page, often found before an original will
IndHS	Indiana Historical Society, 315 West Ohio Street, P.O. Box 88255, Indianapolis, IN 46202
INDI	India
indic	indicative
indien	Indian (masculine)
indiene	Indian (feminine)
indl	industrial
indpt	independent
indr	indenture
Inds	Indians
IND. S.C.	Indian Survivors' Certificates
IndSL	Indiana State Library, Indianapolis, IN

Ind. S.O.	used in pension files—Indian Wars Survivor's Original certificate	InmF	inmate's father
indt	indictment	InmM	inmate's mother
IndT/ Ind T/ Ind Ter/ Indty	Indian territory	InmR	inmate of refuge
		InmS	inmate's son
Ind. W.C.	Indian Wars Widow's Certificate	Inmt	inmate
indy	industry	InmW	inmate's wife
ined	*ineditus* (not made known; unpublished)	INO	Indonesia
in esse	in being, usually refers to an unborn child	INPCRP	Indiana Pioneer Cemeteries Restoration Project
inf	(1) infancy (2) infant (3) infinitive (4) informant (5) information (6) informed (7) infra, below	in poss of	in possession of
		in pr	in principio (in the beginning)
Inf.	Infantry (military regiment)	inq	Inquisition Post Mortem
Inf/Bowels	Infirmation or Inflamation of Bowels	inq/inqr	inquiry
Inf/Brain	Infirmation or Inflamation of Brain	inqst	inquest, as in coroner's inquest
infin	infinitive	INRI	*Jesus Nazarene Rex Judaeorum* (Jesus of Nazareth, King of the Jews)
Inf/Lungs	Infirmation or Inflamation of Lungs		
info	information	ins	(1) insert (2) insurance
infra	below	INS	Immigration and Naturalization Service, 425 I Street NW, Washington, DC 20536
infra dig	Infra dignitatem; undignified		
inft	infant	INS	International News Service
inh	inherited	ins agt	insurance agent
inhab	inhabitant	Inscr	inscriptions
INHS	Indiana State Historical Society, Indianapolis, IN	InsL	intended son-in-law
		INSL	Indiana State Library, Indianapolis, IN
in loco	in place of	insp	(1) inspection (2) inspector
in loco citata	in the place cited	inst	(1) instant, this month, or within the same month (2) institute (3) institution (4) instructor
inlt	inlet	instn	institution
InLw	in-law	instr	(1) instructor (2) instrumental
InmD	inmate's daughter		

int	(1) intention(s) (marriage) (2) interest (3) interred (4) intestate
int dec	interior decorator
interj	interjection
internat	international
InterNIC	Internet Network Information Center
intest	intestate
Int/Fever	Intermittent Fever
Intl	International
intrans	intransitive
intrd	introduced
int rev	Internal Revenue
introd/intro	introduction
inv	(1) investment (2) inventory
inv/invd	invalid
inv/invt/ invent^y	(1) inventory (of possessions) (2) inventoried (estate)
Inv/INV/ INVE	Inverness-shire, Scotland
Invern	Inverness, Scotland
IOAA	Independent Offices Appropriation Act
IOFC	Isle of Corsica
IOFG	Isle of Guernsey
IOFM/ IOM	Isle of Man
IOFW	Isle of Wight
IOLR	India Office Library and Records
IOM	Isle of Man (British Isles)
IOMFS	Isle of Man Family History Society, 6 Selbourne Drive, Douglas, Isle of Man

ION	Ionian Islands
IOOF	Independent Order of Odd Fellows
IOS	Isles of Sicilly
IOU	I owe you
IOW	Isle of Wight
IowC	Iowa City, Iowa
IP	Internet Protocol address (computer term)
IPA	International Phonetic Alphabet
IPGS	Imperial Polk Genealogical Society, Box 10, Kathleen, FL 33849
IPL	Internet Public Library
i.p.m./ inq pm	*inquisition post mortem* (an inquest held to determine a deceased person's land holdings, usually dated by "regnal year", for example: 3 Hen. 4; 3 Hen IV= third year of the reign of Henry IV)
ipso facto	by the act itself
iq	*idem quod* (the same as)
IQ	intelligence quotient
ir/irreg	irregular
IR	(1) *Independent Republican* (newspaper) (2) Irish
IR/IRE/ IRL	Ireland
IRA	(1) Iraq (2) Persia
IRAD	Illinois Regional Archives Depositories
IRC	Internet Relay Chat
IRE	Ireland
IREL	Ireland
IRIS	Illinois Research Information Systems (Service), University of Illinois at Urbana-Champaign, 901 South Mathews Avenue, Urbana, IL 61801

irnr	ironer	IsTr	Isle of Trinidad
IRO	International Refugee Organization	it.	item
is	(1) island(s) (2) isle	IT	(1) Indian Territory (2) Indian Territory, Oklahoma (3) information technology
Is	Isaiah		
IS	In Slavery	IT/ITA/ ITL/ITAL	(1) Italian (2) Italy
ISBGFH	International Society for British Genealogy and Family History, P.O. Box 3115, Salt Lake City, UT 84110-3115	ital	italic type
		ite	item
ISBN	International Standard Book Number	ITER	Indian Territory
ISDN	Integrated Services Digital Network	ITO	International Trade Organization
ISFHWE	International Society of Family History Writers and Editors	ITV	in this village
ISGS	Illinois State Genealogical Society, Illinois State Archives Building, P.O. Box 10195, Springfield, IL 62791-0195	IU	Indiana University Library, Bloomington, IN
		IVC	Ivory Coast
IsJ	Island of Jersey	IWW	International Workers of the World
isl/isld	island	IY	(1) *Idaho Yesterday* (2) Italy
ISL	Indiana State Library, Indianapolis, IN		
IsMan	Isle of Man		
ISO	International Standards Organization		
ISOA	*In Search of Ancestors*		
ISP	Internet Service Provider		
ISPC	International Statistical Programs Center		
ISR	Israel		
ISRR	International Soundex Reunion Registry, P.O. Box 2312, Carson City, NV 89702-2312		
ISSA	International Society Security Association		
ISSN	International Standard Serial Number		
IsT	Isle of Teneriff		
ISTG	Immigrant Ship Transcribers Guild		

J

j — (1) joined (2) journal

J — (1) Jahr(e), year(s) (2) Johann or Johannes (3) journeyman

Ja/JA/ JAM/JAMA — Jamaica

JAMA — *The Journal of the American Medical Association*

Ja/Jan/Janry JanRy — January

JA — (1) Japan (2) Judge Advocate

JAD — Joint Application Development

JAG — Judge Advocate General

JAH — *Journal of American History*

Jamtld — Jamtland, Sweden

jan — janitor

JAP/JAPA — (1) Japan (2) Japanese

jas — joined another society

Jas/Ja^s — James

jASF — joined Anti-Slavery Friends

JAV — Batavia (Java)

Jb — (1) Jacob (2) Jakob

jC — found in Quaker records this indicates that a member joined a group of Conservative Friends

JC — (1) June Court (2) Justiciary Court (British)

JCAL — Jewish Calendar (genealogy software utility)

JCBL — John Carter Brown Library, Providence, Rhode Island

jccp — judge court of common pleas

JCD — (1) Doctor of Canon Law (2) Doctor of Civil Law

jcky — jockey

J Conr — Johann Konrad, Johann Conrad

Jct. — Junction

JD — (1) Doctor of Jurisprudence (2) Journal of Discourses, George D. Watt, et. al., eds., 26 vols. (London: Latter-day Saints Book Depot, 1854–1886) (3) Judicial (probate) districts (Connecticut and Vermont) (4) Juris Doctor (Doctor of Law)

JEH — *Journal of Economic History*

JEPN — *Journal of the English Place-Name Society*

Jer — Jeremy

Jer/Jer^a/ Jerem^a — Jeremiah

Jersey Blues — The Ancient and Honorable Order of the Jersey Blues

JERU — Jerusalem

JFH — *Journal of Family History*

Jfr. — Jungfrau (maiden, virgin)

JG — Junior Grade

Jgfr/Jngfr — Jungfrau, a girl never married

JGS — Jefferson Genealogical Society, P.O. Box 961, Metairie, LA 70004-0961

JGS — Jewish Genealogical Society, Inc., P.O. Box 6398, New York, NY 10128

JGSBCNJ	Jewish Genealogical Society of Bergen County, New Jersey, 155 N. Washington Ave., Bergenfield, NJ
JGSG	Jewish Genealogical Society of Georgia, Inc., 2700 Claridge Court, Atlanta, GA 30360
JGSGB	Jewish Genealogical Society of Great Britain, P.O. Box 13288, London, England N3 3WD
JGSGB	Jewish Genealogical Society of Greater Boston, P.O. Box 610366, Newton, MA 02461-0366
JGSGO	Jewish Genealogical Society of Greater Orlando, P.O. Box 941332, Maitland, FL 32794-1332
JGSGW	Jewish Genealogical Society of Greater Washington, D.C., P.O. Box 31122, Bethesada, MD 20824-1122
JGSLA	Jewish Genealogical Society of Los Angeles, P.O. Box 55443, Sherman Oaks, CA 91413
JGSP	Jewish Genealogical Society of Philadelphia
JGSR	Jewish Genealogical Society of Rochester, New York
JGSS	Jewish Genealogical Society of Sacramento, 2351 Wyda Way, Sacramento, CA 95825
jH	found in Quaker records which meant that member joined the Hicksite Friends
JHUL	Johns Hopkins University Library, Baltimore
JHSCJ	Jewish Historical Society of Central Jersey, 228 Livingston Ave., New Brunswick, NJ 08901
JIAS	*Journal of International and Area Studies,* Brigham Young University, 280 HRCB, Provo, UT 84602
JISHS	*Journal of the Illinois State Historical Society*
J./Jour	journeyman
J Jb	(1) Johann Jacob (2) Johann Jakob
jl(s)	Journal(s)
J Lud	Johann Ludwig
Jmc	Jamaica

jMeth	a Quaker abbreviation indicating that a member joined the Methodist Church
JMH	*Journal of Mississippi History*
JMH	*Journal of Modern History*
JMSIUS	Journal of the Military service institution of the United States
jn	(1) journeyman (2) journeymen
Jn	John
JNH	*Journal of Negro History*
jnl	journal
Jno	(1) John (2) Jonathan
jnr	junior
Jntn	Johnstown Public Library, Johnstown
Jo	(1) Johann (2) Johannes
JO	Johannesburg, South Africa LDS Temple
Jocu	joint occupant
Joes	Johannes
Joh	Johann or Johannes
Joh/Jo/ Ioh/Jno	John
JOHAN	Johannesburg, South Africa LDS Temple
Johes	Johannes
join	joiner
Jois	Johannis (of Johannes)
Jon/Jon^a/ Jon^n/Jonath^n	Jonathan
Jonkpg	Jonkoping, Sweden
Jos	Joseph
Jos^h	Josiah

Josh	Joshua	jtly	jointly
jour	journal	j.u.	*Jure uxoris* (right of wife)
JP	Justice of the Peace	Ju/Je	June
J-PCT	Justice Precinct	jud	(1) judge (county common court) (2) judicial
JPEG	graphics file	JUD	Juris Utriusque Doctor; Doctor of Laws
JPG	Compressed version of GIF	judg	judges
JPG	Joint Photographic Experts Group	Judge Ad.	Judge Advocate
JPN	Japan	judgmt/ judgmnt	judgement, as at law
JPS	Jewish Publication Society		
Jr/Jr./Junr/ Junr/J^r	Junior	judic	judicious
		Jul/Jl	July
JR	Jordan River LDS Temple	J Uli	Johann Ulrich
Jr blksmth	junior blacksmith	Jun	(1) June (2) junior
Jr hrnssmk	junior harness maker	junc	junction
JRI	Jewish Records Indexing	jur	(1) *juratum* (it has been sworn) (2) jurisprudence (3) jury or juror
JRIVE	Jordan River LDS Temple		
JRN	Jordan	Jur D	*Juris Doctorate* (Doctor of Law)
jrnl	journal	JUSCA	*Journal of the United States Calvary Association*
jrnm	journeyman	JUTL	Jutland
J Rud	Johann Rudolf	juv	*juvenis* (young)
jr wagnmkr	junior wagon maker	jwlr	jeweler
JSB	Joseph Smith Building, Brigham Young University, Provo, UT 84602		
JSH	*Journal of Southern History*		
JSMB	Joseph Smith Memorial Building, Salt Lake City, UT 84150		
Jst/Pce	Justice of the Peace		
JSY	Jersey		
jt	joint		

K

k	(1) killed (2) king
K	(1) Kent, England (2) Kinder (children)
ka	killed in action
Kan	Kanada/Canada
Kan/KS	Kansas
KANA	Kashubian Association of North America
Karls/Karlsr	Karlsruhe, Baden
KaSHS	Kansas State Historical Society, Reference Services, 120 West Tenth Street, Topeka, KS 66612
Kat	Katham
Kath	Katherine
KB	(1) kilobyte(s) (2) Kirchenbuch, parish register (3) Knight of the Bath
KBE	Knight Commander of the Order of the British Empire
kc	kilocycle(s)
KC	Kansas City (Missouri or Kansas)
K.C.	(1) King's Counsel (2) Knights of Columbus
Kcb	Kirkcudbrightshire, Scotland
KCB	Knight Commander of the Order of the Bath
KCGS	Kansas Council of Genealogical Societies, P.O. Box 3858, Topeka, KS 66604-6858
KCL	King's College London, England
KCPL-	Kansas City Public Library S. Missouri Valley Special

KVSC	Collections
KCVO	Knight Commander of the Royal Victorian Order
keep	keeper
KeHS	Kentucky Historical Society, P.O. Box H, Frankfort, KY 40602-2108
Kel	Keller
KEN/ KENT	Kent
KepC	keeper in charge
kept	(1) keep (2) kept
Ker	Kerry, Republic of Ireland
KeSCF	Kentucky State College, Frankfort, KY
kg	(1) keg(s) (2) kilogram(s)
KG	Knight of the Order of the Garter
KGS	Kansas Genealogical Society, P.O. Box 103, Dodge City, KS 67801
kh	Keeping house/housekeeper
KHess	Kurhessen
KHQ	*Kansas Historical Quarterly*
KHS	Kansas State Historical Society, Reference Services, 120 West Tenth Street, Topeka, KS 66612
KIA	killed in action
Kild	Kildare, Ireland
Kilk	Kilkenny, Ireland
kilo	(1) kilogram (2) kilometer

Kinc/KINC Kincardine, Scotland

kind   kindred

Kinr/KINR Kinross, Scotland

kinsm   kinsman

kinsw   kinswoman

Kirk/KIRK Kirkcudbright, Scotland

KitM   kitchen maid

KitP   kitchen porter

KitS   kitchen superintendent

KKK   Klu Klux Klan

Kld   Kildare, Republic of Ireland

Klk   Kilkenny, Republic of Ireland

kln   kilderkin

kn   known

Knc/KNC Kincardineshire, Scotland

knls   knolls

Knr/KNR Kinrosshire, Scotland

knt/kt   knight

KO   knockout

KO/KOA/ Korea
KOR

K. of C.   Knights of Columbus

K of P   Knights of Pythias

Kol   Kollans

Konstz   Konstanz, Baden

Koppg   Kopparberg, Sweden

KOR   Korea

KP   Knights of Pythias

kpr   keeper

Krist   Kristianstad, Sweden

KRK   Kircudbrightshire

Kronbg   Kronoberg, Sweden

KS/Kans   Kansas

KSHS   Kansas State Historical Society, Reference Services, 120 West Tenth Street, Topeka KS 66612

KST   Kansas Territory

KSU   Kent State University Network Center, Kent

kt   knight

KT   (1) Knight of the Thistle (Scotland) (2) Knight Templar

ktd   knighted

KurH   KurHessen/Kurkessen

KVGS   Kalamazoo Valley Genealogical Society, P.O. Box 405, Comstock, MI 49041

ky   key

KY/Ky   Kentucky

L

l	(1) law (2) leaf (leaves) (3) liber/libre: book or freespoken (4) license (5) line (6) lived (7) lodger
-l	(word ending in l.) = root word + lichB or -lein; there is a similar scriptural notation that means simply that the end of the word is missing
L	(1) American Indian (2) Latin (3) Lawful (4) left (in stage directions) (5) Liber (6) Libra. Pound (7) Licentiate (8) living (less than 110 years) (9) Lodger
L/Lieut	Lieutenant
L1/1Lt	First Lieutenant
L2/2Lt	Second Lieutenant
L3	Third Lieutenant
la	(1) laborer (2) lane (3) letters of administration
La	(1) Laborer (2) Lancashire, England
La/Ln	Lane
LA	(1) Letters of Administration (2) Library Association (3) Los Angeles LDS Temple (4) Louisiana
LA/La	Louisiana
L-An	Lesser Antilles (Virgin Islands)
lab	(1) laborer (2) Labrador
LabM	labor master
labr	laborer
laby	laboratory
Lac	a resinous substance used in sealing wax, lacquer, etc.
La Colonials	Louisiana Colonials
lad	lad
Ladies of GAR	Ladies of the Grand Army of the Republic
lady	lady
LAGS	Livermore-Amador Genealogical Society, Pleasanton Library, 400 Old Bernal Avenue, Pleasanton, CA 94566
LAK	Lanarkshire
LAm	Latin America
LAN	Local Area Network (computer term)
LAN/ LANC/Lancs	Lancashire, England
LANA	Lanark, Great Britain
lang	language
LANGE	Los Angeles LDS Temple
LAO	Laos
LAPL	Los Angeles Public Library, History and Genealogy Department, 630 West Fifth Street, Los Angeles, CA 90071
LaSL	Louisiana State Library, Baton Rouge, LA
Lat/L(at)	Latin
LAT	Latvia
LAT-WP	*Los Angeles Times—Washington Post News Service*
lau	laundry
Lau	Launderer

LaU	Louisiana State University, Baton Rouge, LA
LAUE	Lauenburg
LAW	Letters of Administration with Will Annexed
LawP	Lawrence, Pennsylvania
Lawr	Lawrence
lb	pound
LB	(1) Bachelor of Letters (2) Brevet Lieutenant (3) London Borough
LBC	Letter Book Copy
lbr	lumber
l.c.	lower case (type)
LC	(1) Landing Craft (2) Lower Canada (i.e., Bas-Canada or Québec)
L.C./l.c.	legitimate child
LC/LtCol	Lieutenant Colonel
LC/LOC	Library of Congress, Local History and Genealogy Reading Room, Thomas Jefferson Building, 10 First Street SE, Washington, DC 20540-5554
LCC	London County Council
LCI	landing craft, infantry
lcks	locks
Lcmp	lady's companion
LCol	Lieutenant Colonel
lcor	Licking Co. Probate Records, Licking Co. Ohio Genealogical Society
LCP	landing craft, personnel
LCSH	Library of Congress Subject Headings
Lctr	lecturer
ld	(1) land (2) lawful daughter

Ld	(1) Lodger (2) Lord
LD	(1) Doctor of Letters (2) London England LDS Temple
L^d B^p	Lord Bishop
LDE	*London Daily News*
LDET	Lipp Detmold
ldg	lodge
LdgB	lodger's brother
LdgC	lodger's child
LdgD	lodger's daughter
LdgF	lodger's father
LdgH	lodger's husband
LdgK	lodge keeper
LdgM	lodger's mother
LdgN	lodger's nephew or niece
LdgS	lodger's son
LdgW	lodger's wife
LdKs	lodge keeper's son
LDMS	London Domestic Mission Society (England)
ldr	leader
lds	lords
LDS	Latter-day Saint. A member of The Church of Jesus Christ of Latter-day Saints (sometimes known as the Mormon Church).
LdyH	lady helper
LdyM	lady's maid, lady's matron
le	local elder in a church
LE	(1) Lake Erie (2) London, England
LEB	(1) Lebanon (2) Lebbe

LEC/Lei/   Leicestershire, England
LEIC/Leic

lect   lecturer

led   *ledig* (unmarried)

Lees of Va   Society of the Lees of Virginia

leg   legacy, legatee

Leg/legis   Legislation, legislative

LEG   Legacy genealogy software

legit/legt   legitimate

legn   legion

Leics/LEIC   Leicestershire (England)

Leipzg   Leipzig, Sax.

Leisureman   man of leisure

Leitr   Leitrim, Ireland

Leix   Leix, Ireland

Len   Lenan/Lennen

LenH   Lenhosk

Leon[d]   Leonard

Leonh   Leonhard, Leonhart

LetC   letter carrier

letters CTA   letters cum testamento annexed

LEXIS/   computer full-text research and informational
NEXIS   retrieval service containing current news
       information databases; legal research database of
       current federal and state appellate court
       decisions; available at many university libraries

lf   loaf

Lfd   Longford, Republic of Ireland

lg   letters of guardianship

LG   (1) *Landed Gentry* (2) Logan LDS Temple

LGAR   Ladies of the Grand Army of the Republic

LGen   Lieutenant General

LgGC   lodger's grandchild

LgGD   lodger's granddaughter

LgGS   lodger's grandson

LGL   large genealogical libraries

LgMD   lodger's maid

LGO   Land Grant Office

lgt   light

Lgt. Art.   Light Artillery (military regiment)

LgtM   lighterman

LH   local history

LH   *Louisiana History*

LHD   Litterarum Humaniorum Doctor (Doctor of
       Humanities, Doctor of Humane Letters)

LHo   Parts of Holland, Lincolnshire, England

lht   light

LHQ   *Louisiana Historical Quarterly*

li   (1) abbreviation for pound (2) lines (3) lived;
       living

LI   (1) Light Infantry (2) Long Island (New York)

lib   liber. book

LIB   (1) Libeg/Liebig/Liberia (2) Libya

lib/libr   library

Libby &   Noyes, Libby, and Davis, *Genealogical Dictionary
Noyes   of Maine and New Hampshire*

libn/libr/   librarian
librn

lic   license

Lic	Lichtenfels		litho	lithographer
Lie	(1) Liebbo/Lebbe/Liennen (2) Liepsic		liv	livery
LIE/LIEC	Liechtenstein		liv/li	lived or living
Lienh	Lienhard, Lienhart		Liv	Liverpool
Lieut/Lt	Lieutenant		liv.abt	lived about
LIHS	Long Island Historical Society, Brooklyn, NY		live/w	lives with
LiIre	Lisbon, Ireland		LivT	living together
LIJGS	Jewish Genealogical Society of Long Island, 37 Westcliff Dr., Dix Hills, NY 11746		lk/lke/lks	lake(s)
Lim/Limer/ LimI	Limerick, Ireland		Lke	Parts of Kesteven, Lincolnshire, England
LIMA	Lima, Peru LDS Temple		LkSm	locksmith
Lime brnr	lime burner		ll	(1) lines (2) local libraries
Lin	Linn/Linnen/Liennen/Lienen		Ll	Lima, Peru LDS Temple
LIN/ LINC/Lincs	Lincolnshire, England		LLB	*Legum Baccalaureus* (Bachelor of Laws)
Lincs	Lincoln, England		LLD	*Legum Doctor* (Doctor of Laws)
LinN	Lincoln, Nebraska		LLD	Lineage-linked databases
lino	linotype		LLDB	Linked Lineage Data Base
LipD	Lippe Detmold/Lippe Darmstadt		LLi	Parts of Lindsey, Lincolnshire, England
LipM	Lippemold		LLM	*Legum Magister* (Master of Laws)
Lippe	Lippe-Detmold, Germany		Llrd	landlord
Lis	Lisabeth		LlrS	landlord's son
lit	(1) literally (2) literary (3) literature		LM	lawful money
LIT	Lithuania		Lmat	laundry matron
Lit B/Litt B	(1) *Literatura* Bachelor (Bachelor of Literature) (2) *Litterarum* Bachelor (Bachelor of Letters)		lmbr mct	lumber merchant
			LMC	Library Management Committee
Lit D/Litt D	(1) *Literatura* Doctor (Doctor of Literature) (2) *Litterarum* Doctor (Doctor of Letters)		LMl	Lake Michigan
			ln	lane
LITH	Lithuania		LN	Last name

lnd	land	Lon	Londonderry, Northern Ireland
LND	Noyes, Libby, and Davis, *Genealogical Dictionary of Maine and New Hampshire*	Lond/ LOND/LonE	London, England
Lnd/Lrd	Land Lord	LONDO	London, England LDS Temple
lndg	landing	Longfd	Longford, Ireland
LndL	landlady	L.O.O.M.	Loyal Order of Moose
Lndr	laundress	loq	*loquitur* (he (she) speaks)
lndrs	laundress	Lor	Lorraine
lndry	laundry	Lorai	Loraine
Lnk	Lanarkshire, Scotland	Lord-Lieut	Lord-Lieutenant
LNL	Linlithgow/West Lothian	Lot	Lottering
Lnm	Landsman	Lou.	Louis
LnMd	laundrymaid	Louis	Louise
lo	lodge	LovC	love child
l/o	late of	Low.	Lower
loc	(1) local (2) locative	LowH	Lower Hesse/Hessen
Loc.	location of original item	lp	local preacher
LOC	Library of Congress, 10 First Street SE, Washington, D.C. 20540-5554	lr	Law Record
local hist	local history	LR	(1) land records (deeds) (2) local repositories
loc cit	*loco citato* (in the place cited)	LRC	learning resource center (a library which usually houses non-print materials, such as videotapes, etc.)
Lodg	lodger		
Loerr	Loerrach, Baden	ls	lawful son
L of C	Library of Congress, Washington, DC	LS	(1) Landing Ship (2) *locus sigilii* (the place of the seal)
LOGAN	Logan, Utah LDS Temple	l(s)s	letter(s) signed
LOL	Laughing Out Loud	LSASE	long self-addressed stamped envelope
Lom/ LOMB	Lombardy	LSCH	Lippe Schaumberg
LOM	Loyal Order of Moose	Lsd	pounds, shillings, pence

LSDa	lodger's stepdaughter
LSG	Librarians Serving Genealogists
Lsgt	lance sergeant
LSI	large-scale integration
LSis	lodger's sister
LSSn	lodger's stepson
LST	landing ship, tank
Lt/ltnt	Lieutenant (military)
LT/Lt	(1) Letters Testamentary (2) Lieutenant(military rank) (3) light (4) *Times of London*
LTA	(1) Land Tax Assessment(s) (England) (2) Letter(s) of Administrations
Lt Arty	Light Artillery
Lt Battry	Light Battery
Lt Cmdr	Lieutenant Commander
LtCmdt	Lieutenant Commandant
Lt Col/ Lt Coll	Lieutenant Colonel (military)
Lt Comm	Lieutenant Commander
ltd	limited
Lt Gen	Lieutenant General
Lth	Louth, Republic Ireland
ltl	little
ltm	liberated to marry; left at liberty to marry
Ltm	Leitrim, Republic of Ireland
LTN	Liechtenstein
Lubec/ LUEB	Luebeck, Germany
LucS	Lucerne, Switzerland

Lud	Ludbar
Ludw	Ludwig
Lumbr	Lumberer
Lung/ Comp	Lung Complaint
Lut	(1) Lutren (2) Luttenberg
Luth	Lutheran
LUX/ Luxem/ LX/LUXE	Luxembourg
lv	(1) lived (2) living
LVA	Library of Virginia
lvd	lived
lvg	living
LVEGA	Las Vegas, Nevada LDS Temple
LVPL	Las Vegas Public Library, Las Vegas, NV
LWF	Lutheran World Federation
LWG	Lexicon Working Group
lwr	lower
lwyr	lawyer
Lx	Laoighis (Leix), Republic of Ireland

M

m   (1) male form (2) man or male (3) marry; marriage; married; marrying (4) masculine (5) measure (pl. mm) (6) meter (7) mile or miles (8) mineur-minor (9) month(s); monthly (10) mother (11) noon (12) thousand

m/ma/marr (1) marriage (2) married

M   (1) Controlled Extraction number (LDS) (2) indicates marriages extracted in the Controlled Extraction Program (LDS) (3) Magister or Meister, master (either by university degree or of a craft) (4) majeur-of age (5) Male Sealing List (LDS) (6) Manufactures censuses (7) Marquess (8) marriage register (9) masculine (10) Master (of) (11) meridies (noon) (12) Microfilm/microfiche (13) Middle (14) miscellaneous (15) Monat(e), month(s) (16) Monday (17) Monsieur (18) morning (newspaper) (19) Mother (20) National Archives microfilm series (21) thousand

M/Mon   Monday

m1   (1) married first (2) mother-in-law

m/1, m/2   first marriage, second marriage, etc.

m2   married second

Ma   Malay

MA   (1) Manila Philippines LDS Temple (2) Mary Ann (3) Master of Arts (4) metropolitan area (5) Military Academy (6) Minor's Application

MA/Mass   Masssachusetts

MA Arch   Massachusetts Archives

M-A   *Mid-America*

M^a   Maria

Matie/ Matys/ Mats/majt   Majesty's, as in his Majesty's horse

Mac   Maclenburg

MAC   Members' Ancestor Charts. A collection of pedigree charts maintained by the National Genealogical Society, 4527 17th Street North, Arlington, VA 22207-2399

mach   (1) machine (2) machinist (3) macheronerie (Norman) masonry

MAD   Madagascar

MADE   Madeira

Madm/ Mdm   madam

mag   magazine

mag/magist magistrate

Mag   (1) Magistrate (2) Magnate

Magd.   (1) Magdalena (2) servant girl, maid

MAGIC   Midwest Afro-American Genealogical Interest Coalition, P.O. Box 300972, Kansas City, MO 64130-0972

MAGIC   Mohican Area Genealogists Interested in Computers (Ohio)

magist   magistrate

mag^{la}   Magdalena

Magna Charta   National Society Magna Charta Dames, P.O. Box 4222, Philadelphia, PA 19144

M Agr   Master of Agriculture

MAGS   Mid-Atlantic Germanic Society, 14710 Sherwood Drive, Greencastle, PA 17225-8403

Mah	Mahican dialect
mah^y	mahogany
mahog^y	mahogany
maid/Maid	maid, maidservant
mail cntr	mail contractor; rent conrtactor
maj/majr	major
Maj/Mj	Major (military rank)
Maj Gen/ Major-Gen	Major General
mak	making
MAL/ MALTA/ MALT	Malta
malls	measles
Malmhs	Malmohus, Sweden
malt	maltster
man/Man	(1) manager (2) manor
Man/ MAN/MB	Manitoba, Canada
Mana^a	Manuela
Man Dir	Managing Director
MANIL	Manila, Philippines LDS Temple
Man^l	Manuel
Man. List	State Register and Manual lists of villages, etc., without post offices
Mannh/ Mannhm	Mannheim, Baden
mannl.	mannlich (masculine)
mans	mansions
MANTI	Manti Utah LDS Temple

manu	(1) manumission, the act of formally freeing a slave (2) mauscript
MAPLIN	Manitoba Public Library Information Network (Canada)
mar/MAR/ marr/MARR	(1) marriage (2) married
Mar	(1) Maria (2) Marines
Mar/Mr/ mRch	March
MARA	machine-readable accessions
MarbHS	Marblehead Historical Society, 161 Washington Street, Marblehead, MA 01945
marble ctr	marble cutter
MARC	Machine-Readable Cataloging
MARCH	Montague Association for the Restoration of Community History, 320 River Road, Montague, NJ 07827
MarD	married daughter
marg	(1) margin (2)marginal
Marg/ Marg^t/Margt	Margaret
Marg^{ta}	Margarita
MarS	married son
marsh	marshall
MaSAr	Massachusetts Secretary of State, Archives Division, Boston, MA
masc	masculine
MASc	Master of Applied Science
Mass/ Mass./Massa	Massachusetts
Mass. Arch.	Massachusetts Archives Collection (Massachusetts Archives), 220 Morrissey Boulevard, Boston, MA 02125

Mass. Bay Rec.	Records of the Governor and Company of the Massachusetts Bay	MB	(1) Manitoba, Canada (2) marriages & burials (3) *Medicinae* Bachelor (Bachelor of Medicine) (4) megabyte(s) (5) municipal borough
Mass HS	Massachusetts Historical Society, 1154 Boylston Street, Boston, MA 02215	MBA	Master in, or of, Business Administration
Mass in the war	James L. Bowen, *Massachusetts in the War*, 1861-1865	MBC	Missionary Baptist Church
		MBCR	Massachusetts Bay General Court
MASSOG	*A Genealogical Magazine for the Commonwealth of Massachusetts*	MBE	Member, Order of the British Empire
Mass. Reports	*Massachusetts Reports* (published reported decisions of the Massachusetts Supreme Judicial Court)	Mbk	minute book
		mbn	marriage banns
Mass soldiers	(1) *Massachusetts Soldiers, Sailors and Marines in the Civil War, 1931-35* (2) *Massachusetts Soldiers and Sailors of the Revolutionary War*	mbr	member
		MBR	Member of the Order of the British Empire
mast	master	mbrp/ mbrshp	membership
mat/mater	(1) maternal (2) matron	MBS	Multilingual Biblioservice
Mat	(1) Matron (2) Matthew	MBUG-PC	Monterey Bay Users Group—Personal Computer (California)
MAT	Master of Arts in Teaching	MC	(1) Adams and Weis, *Magna Charta Sureties 1215* (2) Marriage certificate (3) Master of Ceremonies (4) Medical Corps (5) Member of Congress (6) Methodist Church (7) Military Cross (8) Minor's Certificate
mate	(1) mate (2) spouse (3) consort		
math	(1) mathematical (2) mathematics		
MATh	Master of Arts in Theology		
Matr	Matross	MCA	Microfilm Corporation of America
matric	matriculated (entered and recorded at college or university)	MCC	(1) Massachusetts Cultural Council (2) Microfilm Corporation of America
Matth	Matthaeus	MCC	Microfilm Card Catalog
MAU	Mauritius	mcd	married contrary to discipline
MaUA	Massachusetts University, Amherst	MCD	(1) minor civil division (2) Municipal Civil District
Maur	Maurenberg	MCE	Master of Civil Engineering
Mayflower	General Society of Mayflower Descendants, 4 Winslow St., P.O. Box 3297, Plymouth, MA 02361	MCGS	Mendocino Coast Genealogical Society, P.O. Box 762, Fort Bragg, CA 95437
mb	Minute Book	MCh	Magister Cheir (Master of Surgery)
		mcht	merchant

MCL	(1) Marietta College Library, Marietta, Ohio (2) Master of Civil Law
mcpl	municipal
MCPL	Mid-Continent Public Library, 317 West 24 Highway, Independence, MO 64050
mct	merchant
md	(1) maid (2) married
MD	(1) *Medicinae Doctor* (Doctor of Medicine) (2) Middle Dutch (3) Military District (4) *The Mayflower Descendant* (journal of the Massachusetts Society of Mayflower Descendants)
MD/Md	Maryland
MDAR	Massachusetts Daughters of the American Revolution
Md Arch	Maryland Archives (Hall of Records), 350 Rowe Blvd. Annapolis, MD 21401
MDG	*Maryland and Delaware Genealogist*
MdHi/ MdHs	Maryland Historical Society, 201 West Monument Street, Baltimore, MD 21201
M Div	Master of Divinity
mdl	middle
MDR	(1) Madeira (2) Mamorial Documents Register (British)
MDS	Master of Dental Surgery
MdSCPA	Maryland State College, Princess Ann
mdse	merchandise
MDSX	Middlesex County
mdws	meadows
Me.	Maine
ME	(1) Methodist Episcopal Church (2) Middle English
ME/Me	(1) Maine (2) Mechanical Engineer

ME/Meth	Methodist
Mec/Meck	Mecklenburg
MEC	Methodist Episcopal Church
mech	mechanics
Meck, Sc./ MSCH	Mecklenburg-Schwerin
MeckS/ Meck,St./ MSTR	Mecklenburg, Strelitz
M Econ	Master of Economics
MECS	Methodist Episcopal Church South
MecSc	Mecklenberg-Schwerin
med	(1) median (2) medical (3) medicine (4) medieval (5) medium
MEd	Master of Education
MedA	medical assistant
Medit	Mediterranean
MedO	medical officer
MedS	medical superintendent
MeHS	Maine Historical Society, 485 Congress Street, Portland, ME 04101
Mei	Meins
Mel	Melheim on Rhine
MEL	Michigan Electronic Library
Melb	Melbourne, Australia
Melch	Melchior, Melcher
MELVYL	Union catalog for the University of California library system
mem	(1) membership (2) membrane (3) memoir (4) memorandum (5) memorial(s)
mem/memb	member

MemH	member of household
memo	memorandum
MemT	Memphis, Tennessee
Mend^z	Mendez
Meng	Middlesex, England
Menn	Mennonite
ment	(1) mention (2) mentioned
mer	(1) mayor (2) meritorious
Mer/MER	Merionethshire, Wales
merc/merch	merchant
merchntclk	merchant clerk
MERI/ Merion	Merioneth, Wales
Mesg	messenger
mess	messuage
Messa	Messach
Messrs	Messieurs (plural of mister)
Messrs/ Messrs/Mssrs	Messieurs
Met	Metropolitan
Met.B	metropolitan borough
meter rdr	meter reader
Meth	Methodist
meth prchr	Methodist preacher
M.'et'L.	Maine' et' Loire
M.'et'M.	Meurthe' et' Moselle
MeVS	Maine Office of Vital Statistics, Maine Department of Human Services, State House Station II, Augusta, ME 04333-0011

MEX/ MEXI	Mexico/San
Mex.$	Mexican peso
MEXIC	Mexico City LDS Temple
Mex. S.O.	Mexican Survivors' Originals
Mex W.C.	Mexican Widows' Certificate
MeyS	Meyerstadt
mf	mulatto female
MF	*Mayflower Families* (General Society of Mayflower Descendants, 4 Winslow Street, P.O. Box 3297, Plymouth, MA 02361)
MF	(1) microfiche (2) microfilm (3) Minor's File
MFA	Master of Fine Arts
MFF	Missing Folk Finder
mfg	manufacture/manufacturing
MFIP	*Mayflower Families in Progress.* General Society of Mayflower Descendants, 4 Winslow St., P.O. Box 3297, Plymouth, MA 02361
m'form	microfilm, microfiche, microform
mfr	manufacturer
Mfrank	Mittel-Franken, Bav.
mfrs	manufactures
MG	(1) *Manchester Guardian* (2) megabyte
M.G./mg	Minister of the Gospel
MGC	Michigan Genealogical council, P.O. Box 80953, Lansing, MI 48909-0953
MGen	Major General
Mgm	Montgomeryshire, Wales
mgr	(1) manager (2) monsignor
MGS	Minnesota Genealogical Society, P.O. Box 16069, Saint Paul, MN 55116-0069

MGS	Mobile Genealogical Society, P.O. Box 6224, Mobile, AL 36660-6224	Mi	Mistress
MGS	Montgomery Genealogical Society, 3110 Highfield Drive, Montgomery, AL 36111	MI	(1) Military Intelligence (2) Monumental Inscription(s)
Mgy	Margery	MI/Mich	Michigan
MH	(1) meetinghouse; church (2) *Michigan History* (3) *Minnesota History*	MIA	missing in action
		MIBiol	Member of the Institute of Biology
MHA	Marine Historical Association, Mystic, Connecticut	Mic	Micah
MHA	Mormon History Association	Mich	Michaelmas, the Feast of St. Michael (many old dates are given as of a Saint's feast day, or days preceding or following it), Christmas
MHB	*Minnesota History Bulletin*		
MHG	Middle High German	Mich/Mi	Michigan
MHGR	*Maine Historical and Genealogical Recorder*	Mich/ Michl/Mic^ls	Michael
MHGS	Midwest Historical and Genealogical Society, 1203 North Main, P.O. Box 1121, Wichita, KS 67201	micro	(1) microfilm (2) microfiche
		Mid	(1) Middle (2) Midshipman
MHI	Military History Institute. *See also* United States Army Military History Institute, 22 Ashburn Drive, Carlisle Barracks, Carlisle, PA 17013-5008	MID/ Midd/ Middx/MidE	Middlesex, England
		Midl	Midland(s)
		MidW	midwife
MHM	*Michigan History Magazine*	Mig^l	Miguel
Mhn	Monaghan, Republic of Ireland	MiH	*Michigan History*
MHR	*Missouri Historical Review*	MiHC	*Michigan Historical Collections*
MHRAB	Massachusetts Historical Records Advisory Board	MiHM	*Michigan History Magazine*
MHS	*Maine Historical Society*	mil	(1) militia (2) military (3) mother-in-law
MHS	Massachusetts Historical Society, 1154 Boylston Street, Boston, MA 02215	mil/milit	military
MHS	Minnesota Historical Society, 345 Kellogg Blvd. West, St. Paul, MN 55102-1906	m-i-l/ M-in-l	mother-in-law
MHS Colls	*Massachusetts Historical Society Collections*		
mHZ	Mega Hertz	Mil Dis Rec	Military Discharge Records
mi	(1) mile(s) (2) monumental inscription (tombstone)	mill	(1) miller (2)milliner

Mil Ord of Crusades	Military Order of the Crusades, 014 Bladdyn Road, Ardmore, PA 19003
Mil Ord, Loyal Legion	Military Order of the Loyal Legion of the United States, 1805 Pine Street, Philadelphia, PA 19103
MilPL	Milwaukee Public Library, 814 West Wisconsin Avenue, Milwaukee, WI 53233
milt	military
MilW	Milwaukee, Wisconsin
MIME	(1) Member of Institution of Mining Engineers (2) Multipurpose Internet Mail Extensions
Mimeo	Mimeographed
min	(1) mineral (2) mineralogy (3) minister (4) ministry (5) minor (6) minority (7) minute(s)
m-in-l	mother-in-law
Minn/MN	Minnesota
minm	minimum
minr	(1) milliner (2) minor
min. ret.	minister's return
MInstCE	Member, Institute of Civil Engineers
MInstT	Member, Institute of Transport
m.int	marriage intentions
mis	missioner
misc	miscellaneous
MisD	mistress's daughter
MiSL	Michigan State Library, East Lansing, MI 48824
miss	mission
Miss/MS/MSA	Mississippi
MisS	mistress's son

MIT	Massachusetts Institute of Technology, 77 Massachusetts Avenue, Cambridge, MA 02139-4307
MiU	Michigan State Library, East Lansing, MI 48824
MJur	*Magister Juris* (Master of Law)
MkCl	Muskingum College Library, New Concord
mkr	maker
mkt	market
mktg	marketing
ml(s)	mill(s)
ML	(1) marriage license (2) marriage licence records (3) Master of Laws (4) military land (5) mother-in-law
MLA	Maine Library Association, Community Drive, Augusta, ME 04330
MLA	Member, Legislative Assembly
MLC	Member, Legislative Council
mldr	molder
mle	mile
MLE	Military Land Entry
MLG	Middle Low German
MLIS	Master of Library and Information Science
MLitt	Master of Letters
MlkC	milk carrier
MlkM	milk man, milk boy
mlle	Mademoiselle
Mll/Wgt	Millwright
MLN	Midlothian (see Edinburgh)
Mlnr	milliner
MLo	Midlothian, Scotland

M. Loth/ MLOT	Midlothian, Scotland	MnHS	Minnesota Historical Society, 345 Kellogg Blvd. West, St. Paul, MN 55102-1906
MLS	Master of Library and Information Science	MNM	Monmouthshire
MLT	Malta	MNO	Monaco
MLW	Military Land Warrant	mnr	manor
mm	(1) *matri-monium* (2) millimeter(s) (3) mulatto male (4) *mutatis mutandis* (necessary changes being made)	mns	mines
		MNS	Massachusetts News Service
MM	(1) Maelzel's metronome (tempo indication) (2) Messieurs (3) Minuteman (4) Monthly Meeting (Society of Friends, Quaker)	MnSAr	Minnesota State Archives, St. Paul, MN
		mnst	minister
MM	Mariners Museum, Newport News, VA	MNT	Montgomeryshire
M & M	Mr. and Mrs.	mntd	maintained
MMan	(1) militiaman (2) minuteman	MNTG/ Montg	Montgomery, Wales
Mme	Madam	mo	(1) microfilm of original (2) month (3) mother (4) mustered out (of military service)
MMFF	Missouri Mormon Frontier Foundation, P.O. Box 3186, Independence, MO 64055	m/o	mother of
MMGS	Mid-Michigan Genealogical Society, P.O. Box 16033, Lansing, MI 48901-6033	MO	(1) Major Ordnance (2) Medical Officer (3) Military Merit (Canada) (4) Money Order. *See also* MNO
MMM	Member, Order of Military Merit (Canada)		
mn	(1) Latin for "more novo" which means, "in the new manner" (2) man (3) minister	MO/Mo	Missouri
		MOA	Making of America (digital library)
Mn	Modern (MnI: Modern Irish, etc.)	Mobil	Mobile, Alabama
MN	(1) Merchant Navy (2) middle name	mobles	movables
MN/Minn	Minnesota	MOCA	Maine Old Cemetery Association, P.O. Box 641, Augusta, ME 04332-0641
mnd	mound		
MnE	Modern English	mod	moderator
mng	managing	MoD	Month of Death
mngr	manager, manageress	Mod E	Modern English
MNHP	Morristown National Historical Park, Morristown, NJ	Modem	Modulator/Demodulator (transmit data to and from a computer)

MOFW	Military Order of Foreign Wars of the United States
Moh	Mohegan dialect
MOH	Medical Officer of Health
MoHS	Missouri Historical Society, Research Library and Archives, Jefferson Memorial Building, Forest Park, St. Louis, MO 63112-1099
MOHS	*A Guide to Manuscripts at the Ohio Historical Society*, Andrea D. Lentz, ed.
moiety	one-half
MOLLUS	Military Order of the Loyal Legion of the United States, 1805 Pine Street, Philadelphia, PA 19103 (Headquarters, 600 S. Central Ave. Glendale, CA 91204)
MOLO	Mid-Eastern Ohio Library Association
MoLS	mother-in-law's son
mon	monument, tombstone
Mon	(1) Monday (2) Monmouthshire, England
Monagn	Monaghan, Ireland
MONM/ Monms	Monmouth, England
mono	monotype
Mons	Monsignor
Mont	Montgomery
Mont/MT	Montana
MONT	(1) Montenegro (2) Montgomeryshire
mor	mother
Mor/MOR	Morayshire (see Elgin), Scotland
Mor/ Morav/MORA	Moravia
MORA	Moray, Great Britain

Mor Arch	Moravian Archives, 4 East Bank Street, Winston-Salem, NC 27101
morg	(1) morganatic (2) morgen
morn	morning
MORO	Morrocco
mors	death, corpse
mort	(1) mortgage/mortgaged (2) mortally
mos	(1) married out of Society of Friends (2) months
MOS	Military Occupation
MoSA	Missouri State Archives, P.O. Box 778, Jefferson City, MO 65102
Mosbch	Mosbach, Baden
MoSGA	Missouri State Genealogical Association, P.O. Box 833, Columbia, MO 65205-0833
MoSHS	Missouri State Historical Society, 1020 Lowry Street, Columbia, MO 65201-7298
MoSL	Missouri State Library, P.O. Box 387, Jefferson City, MO 65102-0387
Most Rev.	Most Reverend
mot/moti/ moto	motion
MotA	mother's aunt
MotC	mother's cousin
MotD	mother's daughter
MotF	mother's father
moth	mother
MotH	mother's help
MotL	mother-in-law
MotP	mother of patient
MotS	mother's son

MotU	mother's uncle	MRIN	Marriage Record Identification Number (used in Personal Ancestral File® genealogy software program)
MOU	in Quaker records this means "married out of unity" which means that the person has married a non Quaker	mr-in-l	mother-in-law
mov	move; moved	mris	mistress
MOWW	Military Order of the World Wars, 435 North Lee Street, Alexandria, VA 22314	mrkd/ mrked	marked, branded (as in cattle)
MOZ	Mozambique	MRL	Master Repository List (The Master Genealogist genealogy program)
MP/M.P.	(1) Member of Parliament (England) (2) Military Police	M-Rmdl	More & Romsdal, Norway
MPA	Master of Public Administration	mrnr	mariner, seaman
MPCR	*Maine Province and Court Records*	M^{rs}/Mrs.	Mistress; identifying that the woman is married or an unmarried woman of high social standing
MPd	Master of Pedagogy		
MPE	Master of Physical Education	mr sgt	Master sergeant
mph	miles per hour	ms	mews
MPH	Master of Public Health	ms/mss	(1) male servant (2) *manuscriptum* (-a) (3) manuscript(s)
MPHC	*Michigan Pioneer and Historical Collections*	Ms	miss
Mplr	Montpelier Public Library, Montpelier, Vermont	MS	(1) maiden surname (2) Merchant Service (merchant navy) (3) Michigan Survey
MPR	Military Personnel Records (*see also* NPRC)	MS/M.S.	male servant
MQ	*The Mayflower Quarterly*	MS/Miss.	Mississippi
mr	(1) missionary rector (2) mother	MS/MSc	Master of Science
Mr./M^r	Mister or Master	MSA	Maine State Archives, 84 State House Station, Augusta, ME 04333-0084
MR	(1) Marriage Record (2) Miscellaneous Registers (3) Mississippi River (4) Municipal Records	MSA	Massachusetts State Archives, Columbia Point, 220 Morrissey Blvd., Boston, MA 02125
Mrbo	Maribo, Denmark		
mr cooper	master cooper	MSA	metropolitan statistical area
Mrcr	Dwyer-Mercer County Library, Mercer	MSCH	Mecklenburg (Schwerin)
MRE	Master of Religious Education	MSDa	mother's stepdaughter
mr gun	master gunner	MsDAR	Mississippi Daughters of the American Revolution

MS-DOS	Microsoft Disk Operating System		Mt	Mount
Msgr.	Monsignor		MT	early, the Michaelmas term of court, November
M/Sgt.	Master Sergeant		MT	(1) machine translation (2) Military Tract (Illinois) (3) Montana
MshU	James E. Morrow Library, Marshall University, Huntington, WV 25755			
			mtce	maintenance
MSI	medium-scale integration		mtd	mounted
MSIA	Master of Science in Industrial Administration		mt DNA	mitochondrial DNA (deoxyribonucleic acid)
Msis	mother's sister		Mte	Mate on a ship
MSL	Maine State Library, State House Station 64, Augusta, ME 04333		mtg	(1) meeting (2) mortgage
			mtge	mortgage
msn	mission		mtg hs	meeting house
MSN	Microsoft Network			
msngr	messenger		MTGS	Middle Tennessee Genealogical Society, P.O. Box 190625, Nashville, TN 37219-0625
MSOG	Massachusetts Society of Genealogists, P.O. Box 215, Ashland, MA 01721-0215		Mth	Meath, Republic of Ireland
MSPA	Master of Science in Public Administration		MTh	Master of Theology
MSPH	Master of Science in Public Health		MtHS	Montana Historical Society, Memorial Building, 225 North Roberts Street, Helena, MT 59620
mss	hand- or typewritten manuscript(s)			
MS&S	*Massachusetts Soldiers and Sailors of the Revolutionary War*		MTIMP	Mount Timpanogos, Utah LDS Temple
			Mtitck	Mattituck
MsSAr	Mississippi Department of Archives and History, 100 South State Street, Jackson, MS		MtlM	mantle maker
			mtn	mountain
MST	Mountain Standard Time		M Tn	Memphis, Tennessee
Mstr	(1) master (2) master of a ship (3) Meister		MTP	Master Title Plat(s) (General Land Office)
MSTR	Mecklenburg (Strelitz)		mtr	motorman; motor
Mstu	medical student		mtrn	matron
MsU	(1) Michigan State University (2) Mississippi University		Mtrs	mistress
			mu	musician
MSW	Master of Social Work/Welfare			
mt	(1) married to (2) mountain		MU	Mulatto

MU	Walter Havighurst Special Collections, Miami University, Oxford, OH
MUL	Marshall University Library, Huntington, WV 25775
mun/munic	municipal
Mun	Munica
Mun	Munster
mus	(1) museum (2) music (3) musical (4) musician
MUS	Muscat
MusB	Bachelor of Music
MusD	Doctor of Music
MusT/ Mus/Tch	music teacher
mut	mutual
mv	*more vetere* (in the old way)
MV	Moravia
mvd	moved
MVD	Soviet Ministry of Internal Affairs
MVHR	*Mississippi Valley Historical Review*
MVO	Member of the Royal Victorian Order
MW	*Maine Wills*
Mx	Middlesex, England
MX	(1) Mexico (2) Mexico City LDS Temple
My	(1) May (2) Montana Territory
MyB	Myersbad
MYBP	million years before the present
my/d	my daughter
Myo	Mayo, Republic of Ireland
myth	mythology

N

n   (1) name (2) natus (born) (3) nephew (4) nomen (name) (5) north (6) northern (7) note, footnote (pl.nn.) (8) noun

N   (1) census (source in IGI) (2) National News Service (3) Navy (4) Negro; Negroes (5) Nephew (6) Niece (7) Norse (8) North (9) number

N/NN   (1) *nomen* (nomina) (name(s), indicates the actual name is not known) (2) note(s)

N1, NFC   Negroes of the first age class

N2, NMC   Negroes of the second age class

N3, NLC   Negroes of the third age class

na   not attending meeting

na/nat   (1) national (2) natural (3) naturalize(d)

NA   National Archives and Records Administration, 700 Pennsylvania Ave. NW, Washington, DC 20408

NA   (1) *non allocatur* (not allowed) (2) North Africa (3) North America (4) Native American (5) naturalized citizen (e.g., an immigrant who is a naturalized citizen); this abbreviation may be listed in a U.S. census schedule

NAACP   National Association for the Advancement of Colored People, Washington Bureau, 1025 Vermont Ave NW, Suite 1120, Washington, DC 20005

NAC   National Archives of Canada, Ottawa

NAFTA   North American Free Trade Agreement

NAHA   Norwegian-American Historical Association, St. Olaf College, Northfield, MN 55057

NAI/NAIR   Nairn, Great Britain

NAIL   National Archives and Records Administration Archival Information Locator

NAILDD   North American Interlibrary Loan and Document Delivery

NAIP   North American Immigrants Project

NAM   (1) National Association of Manufacturers (2) North America

NAMA/NA   North American Manx Association

N-An   Netherlands Antilles

nany   nanny

NAP   National Archives-Mid-Atlantic Region, 900 Market St., Philadelphia, PA 19107-4292

NAPHSIS   National Association for Public Health Statistics and Information Systems, 1220 19th St. NW Ste 802, Washington, D.C. 20036

NAR   National Archives and Records Administration, 700 Pennsylvania Ave. NW, Washington, DC 20408

NARA   National Archives and Records Administration, 700 Pennsylvania Ave. NW, Washington, DC 20408

NARB   National Archives Regional Branches

narr   narrative

Narra.   Narragansett dialect

NARS   National Archives and Records Service, Washington, DC (*see* NARA)

Nas/Nassa   Nassau/Nausau

NAS   National Academy of Science

NAS	no author or compiler shown in the source listing
NAS	National Archives of Scotland (Scottish Records Office, formerly known as Old Register House)
NASSAR	National Society for Armenian Studies and Research, Inc., 6 Divinity Avenue, Cambridge, MA 02138
NasT	Nastata
nat	natural, i.e., illegitimate; a natural son or daughter is an illegitimate son or daughter
nat	(1) naturalization (2) *natus, nata* (born)
nat/natl	national
Nat Arch	National Archives and Records Administration, 700 and Pennsylvania Ave. NW, Washington, DC 20408
NAtd	night attendant
NATF	National Archives form number
Nat Gallery	National Gallery
Nath/ Nathl/Nathl/ Nathan^l	Nathaniel
Nat Hist	Natural History
Nath^n	Nathan
Nat Huguenot	National Huguenot Society, 9033 Lyndale Avenue South, Suite 108, Bloomington, MN 55420-3535
Natl	National
Natl Gen Soc Qt	*National Genealogical Society Quarterly.* National Genealogical Society, 4527 17th Street North, Arlington, VA 22207-2399
NATO	North Atlantic Treaty Organization
Nau	Nausau/Nassau
naut	nautical

NAVA	National Archives Volunteer Association
Nb	Northumberland, England
NB	(1) New Brunswick (uncommon usageSNorth Britain, i.e. Scotland), Canada (2) North Britain (3) *nota bene* (take careful note; mark well and pay particular attention to that which follows)
NB/Neb	Nebraska
Nbaye	North Bayern
NBrun/NB	New Brunswick, Canada
Nbtn	Norrbotten, Sweden
NC	(1) Civil Reference Aid (National Archives) (2) non-conformist (3) North Carolina (4) North Central
NCAC	National Capital Area Chapter, Association of Professional Genealogists, P.O. Box 11601, Washington, DC 20007
NCC	National Conference Chair, e.g., Federation of Genealogical Societies National Conference Chair
NCDAH	North Carolina Division of Archives and History, 109 East Jones Street, Raleigh, NC 27601-2807 (mailing address, 4610 Mail Service Center, Raleigh, NC 27699-4610)
nce	niece
NCES	National Center for Education Statistics, 555 New Jersey Ave NW, Washington DC 20208-5574
NCGS	North Carolina Genealogical Society, PO Box 22, Greenville, NC 27835-0022
NCHS	National Center for Health Statistics, 6525 Belorest Road, Hyattsville, MD 20782-2003
NCIC	National Cartographic Information Center
nck	neck
ncm	*non compos mentis*
NCO	non-commissioned officer

NCOD	No Code (not found on this list)
NCPC	National Personnel Records Center, Civil Personnel Records *See* NPRC.
NCPO	National Congress of Patriotic Organizations
NCRR	National Center for Research Resources, NCRR, Nat'l Institutes of Health, Bethesda, MD 20892-5662
NCSA	National Center for Supercomputing Applications, NCSA, University of Illinois at Urbana - Champaign, 152 Computing Applications Bldg, 605 East Springfield Ave., Champlaign, IL 61820-5518
NCSA	National Computer Security Association
NCU	North Carolina University, Chapel Hill, NC
NCURA	National Council of University Research Administrators, One Dupont Cir. NW Ste. 220, Washington DC 20036
NCV	North Carolina Volunteer(s)
NCy	North Country (England)
nd/n.d.	no date; no date of publication indicated (the date of the original is not known)
ND/NDak	North Dakota
NDau	natural daughter
NDHS	North Dakota Historical Society, 612 East Boulevard Avenue, Bismarck, ND 58505-0830
NDHSGR	North Dakota Historical Society of Germans from Russia, 1008 E. Central Ave., Bismarck, ND 58501
Ndlw	needlewoman
né	original, former, or legal name of a man
née	as born; precedes the maiden name of a married woman
ne(e)	born (as); used to introduce the maiden name of a wife
NE	(1) nephew (2) New England (3) North East

NE/Nebr/ Neb/Nb	Nebraska
NEA	(1) National Education Association 1201 16th St. NW, Washington DC, 20036 (2) Newspaper Enterprises Association
nebr	neighbour
NEBS	New England Business Service
NECG	*The New England Computer Genealogist*, New England Historic Genealogical Society, *The Computer Genealogist,* 101 Newbury St., Boston, MA 02116-3007
NED	*A New English Dictionary* (The Oxford English Dictionary)
neg	(1) negative (2) neglecting attendance
NEH	National Endowment for the Humanities
NEHGR/ NEH & GR	*The New England Historical and Genealogical Register,* New England Historic Genealogical Society, 101 Newbury St., Boston, MA 02116-3007
NEHGS	New England Historic Genealogical Society, 101 Newbury St., Boston, MA 02116-3007
NEI	*non est inventus*; notation by an officer or court that a person sought was not found; usually meant recently deceased
nel/ neph-i-l/ nepl	nephew-in-law
NEL	Netherlands
NENGS	Northeastern Nebraska Genealogical Society, P.O. Box 169, Lyons, NE 68038
NEO-CAG	North East Ohio-Computer Aided Genealogy Group
nepC	nephew's child
nepD	nephew's daughter
neph	(1) nephew (2) sometimes grandchild
nepS	nephew's son

nepW	nephew's wife	news	newspaper
NEQ	*The New England Quarterly*, 239 Meserve Hall, Northeastern University, Boston, MA 02115	NewZ/ NEZ	New Zealand
NERGC	New England Regional Genealogical Conference	NEXUS	bimonthly newsmagazine of the New England Historic Genealogical Society, 101 Newbury Street, Boston, MA 02116-3007
Nerv/Aff	Nervous Affection	NEYM	New England Yearly Meeting (Society of Friends)
NeSHS	Nebraska State Historical Society, Division of Library/Archives, P.O. Box 82554, Lincoln, NE 68501-2554	Nf	Norfolk, England
Net/Neth	Netherlands	NF	*Neue Folge* (New Series)
NET	No Electronic Theft Act	NF/NFD/ NFL	Newfoundland (Canada)
Neth Arch	Netherlands Archives, The Hague	nfi	no further information
Netherlands Soc of Phil	Netherlands Society of Philadelphia	nfk	nothing further known
Neur/Brain	Neuralgia of Brain	NFK/ NORF/Norf	Norfolk, Great Britain
Neust	Neustadt	Nfld	Newfoundland, including Labrador (Canada)
neut	neuter	nfr	no further reference or record found
Nev/NV	Nevada	NG	(1) National Guard (2) New England (3) no good (4) Norse-Gaelic (5) not given
new	newspaper		
NewB	New Brunswick	NGDC	National Geophysical Data Center
Newbu	Newburg, OH	nger	engineer
New Eng	National Society of New England Women, P.O. Box 367, Women Union City, TN 38261-0367	NGO	non-governmental organization
		NGRA	New Granada
New Era	*The New Era* (publication of the LDS Church, Salt Lake City, UT)	NGS	National Genealogical Society, 4527 17th Street North, Arlington, VA 22207-2399
Newf/NF	Newfoundland	NGS-BBS	National Genealogical Society—Bulletin Board System (now defunct)
NEWGS	Northeast Washington Genealogical Society, 195 South Oak, Colville, WA 99114	NGS/CIG	National Genealogical Society Computer Interest Group, 4527 17th Street North, Arlington, VA 22207-2399
NewH	New Hampton		
New M	New Mexico		
NewOr	New Orleans	NGS/CIS	National Genealogical Society Conference in the States

NGSQ	*National Genealogical Society Quarterly*, 4527 17th Street North, Arlington, VA 22207-2399	NHSL	New Hampshire State Library, 20 Park Street, Concord, NH 03301
NH/N.H.	New Hampshire	NHSOG	New Hampshire Society of Genealogists, P.O. Box 2316, Concord, NH 03302-2316
NHA	Nantucket Historical Association, P.O. Box 1016 Nantucket, MA 02554	NHSP	*New Hampshire Province and State Papers*
NHACS	Negro Historical Association of Colorado Springs, P.O. Box 16123, Colorado Springs, CO 80935	Nhumb/ NHUM/ Northumb	Northumberland, England
NHAM/ Norf/ Northants/ Northton	Northamptonshire (England)	ni	no issue
		ni/Ni	niece
Nhant	Northampton, England	NI	Native Infantry
N.H. Arch	New Hampshire Archives, 71 South Fruit Street, Concord, NH 03301-2410	NIAU	Northern Iowa University, 1227 West 27th Street, Cedar Falls, IA 50614
NHCHS	New Haven Colony Historical Society, 114 Whitney Avenue, New Haven, CT 06510	NIC/Nica	Nicaragua
NHGOS	New Hampshire Society of Genealogists, P.O. Box 2316, Concord, NH 03302-2316	Nich/Nic^s	Nicholas
		Nicl	Niklaus, Niclaus
NHGR	*New Hampshire Genealogical Record*	NIDS	National Inventory of Documentary Sources (reference source available on microfiche). Finding aids and indexes for the United States, United Kingdom, Ireland, and other countries. Published by Chadwyck-Healey. Index on CD.
NHHS	New Hampshire Historical Society, 30 Park Street, Concord, NH 03301		
NHOGA	New Hampshire Old Graveyard Association, New Hampshire Society of Genealogists, P.O. Box 2316, Concord, NH 03302-2316	niec/ni	niece
		NieC	niece's child
NHPP	Provincial Papers, Documents and Records Relating to the Province of New Hampshire from 1866 to 1722	NieD	niece's daughter
		Niedbn	Niederbayern, Bavaria
NHPRC	National Historical Publications and Records Commission, Washington DC 20408-0001	NieH	niece's husband
		NieL/Nil	niece-in-law
NHS	National Huguenot Society, 9033 Lyndale Avenue South, Suite 108, Bloomington, MN 55420-3535	NieS	niece's son
		NIGR	National Institute on Genealogical Research, P.O. Box 14274, Washington, DC 20044-4274
NHS	Newport Historical Society, 82 Touro Street, Newport, RI 02840	NIGRAA	National Institute on Genealogical Research Alumni Association
NHSG	New Hampshire Society of Genealogists, P.O. Box 2316, Concord, NH 03302-2316	Nil	niece-in-law

nil	nothing found; no information located	nmed	named
NINCH	Networked Cultural Heritage	NMGS	New Mexico Genealogical Society, P.O. Box 8283, Albuquerque, NM 87198-8330
Nip	Nipmuck dialect	nmi	no middle initial
NIPR	*National Index of Parish Registers* (British)	NMM	National Maritime Museum, Greenwich, London, England SE10 9NF
N. Ire	Northern Ireland		
NIS	Network and Information Services	nmn	no middle name
NISL	Nevis Island	NMU	New Mexico University, Alberquerque, NM
NISO	National Information Standards Organization	N.'Mul	Nordur' Mulasysla
NiSv	niece's servant	nn	(1) no name (2) notes
NJ	New Jersey	Nn	Nun
NJArRM	New Jersey Archives and Records Management,	NN	*Nomen nescio* (name not known)
NJBAr	New Jersey State Library, P.O. Box 520, Trenton, NJ 08625-0520	NNE	North Northeast
NJHS	New Jersey Historical Society, 230 Broadway, Newark, NJ 07104	NNRR	Textual Reference Branch, National Archives and Records Administration, Washington National Records Center, Washington, DC 20409
NK/N.K.	not known (may be found in census schedule)	NNS	Newhouse News Service
nl/Nl	nephew-in-law	NNW	North Northwest
NL	Netherlands	no	(1) none, no relation (2) north (3) number
NLC	National Library of Canada, 395 Wellington Street, Ottawa, Canada K1A 0N4	No.	(1) north (2) northern (3) number
NLCHS	New London County Historical Society, 11 Blinman Street, New London, CT 06320	NO	(1) New Orleans, LA (2) North
NLRB	National Labor Relations Board	NOA	North America
NLW	National Library of Wales, Aberystwyth, Ceredigion, Wales SY23 3BU	No. Brab	North Brabant
		N.'Oestr	Niederoesterreich
nm	nonmember (i.e., nonmember of a church)	No. Holl.	North Holland
nm(s)	name(s)	noia	*nomina* (names)
n/m	not married	noie	*nomine* (by name)
		nois	*nominis* (of the name)
NM	Military Reference Aid (National Archives)		
NM/NMex	New Mexico	nol. pros.	*nolle prosegui* (which see)

nom	nominative	NovS/ NovSc	Nova Scotia, Canada (*see also* N.S.)
Noncom	Non-Commissioned Officer	np	(1) no page (2) no papers in packet (3) no place of publication indicated
non copos mentis	not sound of mind	np/n.pub	(1) no publication place (2) no publisher shown
non obs	*non obstante* (notwithstanding)	NP	(1) Negro Polls (2) no protest (3) Notary Public (4) *The Ohio NISI PRIUS Reports*
non seq	*non sequitur* (it does not follow)	N. pag	no pagination
NOR/ Nor/ NORW	Norway, Norwegian	NPC	National Program Chair
Nordld	Nordland	npn	no page number
NorE/Norf	Norfolk, England	np or d	no place or date
NortA	North A.	npp	no place of publication
Norw	Norwich	NPRC	National Personnel Records Center (1) Civilian Records Facility, 111 Winnebago Street, St. Louis, MO 63118-4199 (2) Military Records Facility, 9700 Page Avenue, St. Louis, MO 63132-5100
Norw/ NRY	Norway		
NOS	not on [library] shelf	NPS	National Park Service
not	noted	N. pub	no publisher
notK	not known	N & Q	*Notes and Queries* (England)
not md	not married	NQF	*National Queries Forum*, P.O. Box 593, Santa Cruz, CA 95061-0593
notp	not of this parish		
not pub/ notry pblc	notary public	nr/NR	(1) near (2) not related (3) none recorded or not recorded (4) not reported (often found in recent U.S. census schedules, e.g., citizenship not reported; or vital records)
NOTT/ Notts	(1) Nottingham, England (2) Nottinghamshire	NR	North Riding
nov/n.o.v	notwithstanding the verdict of a jury judgment	NRA	(1) National Recovery Administration (2) National Register of Archives (British)
Nov/ Novmbr/ Novm/ Novmb/N	November	NRA(S)	National Register of Archives (Scotland), HM General Register House, 2 Princes Street, Edinburgh EH1 3YY Scotland
no.vo.	*nolens volens* (with or without consent)	NRH	New Register House, Edinburgh, Scotland
		Nrld	Nordland, Norway
		Nrn	Nairnshire, Scotland

NrsC	nursed child	NSDCH	National Society, Dames of the Court of Honor
nrsd	nursed	NSE	*New Standard Encyclopedia*
NrsG	nursegirl	NSF	National Science Foundation
nrsl	nursling	NSO	Navy Survivor's Originals
NrsM	nursemaid	NSon	natural son
Nrsy	nursery	NSP	Newbury Street Press, 101 Newbury Street, Boston, MA 02116-3007
NRY	(1) North Riding of Yorkshire, England (2) Norway	NSSAR	National Society of the Sons of the American Revolution, 1000 South Fourth Street, Louisville, KY 40203
ns/NS	(1) new series (2) new style (3) north side	NSSD Pilgrims	National Society, Sons and Daughters of the Pilgrims, 3917 Heritage Hills Drive #104, Minneapolis, MN 55437-2633
NS	(1) Naval Service (2) New Style, referring to the Gregorian calendar (in America and Great Britain since 1752) (3) Nova Scotia, Canada	NSTC	Nineteenth-century Short Title Catalogue (bibliography)
NSA	National Speakers Association, 150 South Priest Drive, Tempe, AZ 85281	NSTL	National Software Testing Laboratory
NSA	National Student Association	NStud	*Northern Studies*
NS Amer of Royal Desc	National Society of Americans of Royal Descent	NS Vrs	Nova Scotia Vital Records
NS Arch	Public Archives of Nova Scotia, Halifax, Nova Scotia	NSW	New South Wales, Australia
		Nt	Nottinghamshire, England
NSC	Navy Survivor's Certificates	NT	(1) Nebraska Territory (2) New Testament (Bible) (3) Northwest Territories, Canada
NSCD	National Society, Colonial Dames of America, Dumbarton House, 2715 Q Street NW, Washington, DC 20007	Nth/NTH	(1) Netherlands (2) Northamptonshire, England
NSCD-17	National Society, Colonial Dames of the Seventeenth Century, 1300 New Hampshire Avenue NW, Washington, DC 20036-1595	Nthbld	Northumberland
		N.'Thing	Nordur Thingeviarsysla
NSCDA/ NSCol Dames	National Society of the Colonial Dames of America, Dumbarton House, 2715 Q Street NW, Washington, DC 20007	N-Tlg	Nord-Trondelag, Norway
		NTM	Northumberland
NScot	*Northern Scotland*	N.'Tronglg	Nord Trondelag
NSDAR	National Society, Daughters of the American Revolution, 1776 D Street NW, Washington, DC 20006-5392	NTT	Nottinghamshire
		nu/Nu	nurse
NSDCGS	North San Diego County Genealogical Society, Inc., P.O. Box 581, Carlsbad, CA 92008-0581	NUCMC	*National Union Catalog of Manuscript Collections* (Library of Congress)

NUKUA	Nuku'alofa, Tonga LDS Temple
num	(1) numeral (2) numerically
numb	numbered
nunc	nuncupative (spoken an oral will)
nupt	were married
Nur	Nurenberg
NurB	nurse's baby
NurC	nurse's child
NurD	nurse's daughter
NurH	nurse's husband
nurs	nurse
NurS	nurse's son
NV	Nevada
NV	Nauvoo, Illinois LDS Temple
Nva/Sco	Nova Scotia, Canada
NvSHS	Nevada State Historical Society, 1650 North Virginia Street, Reno, NV 89503
NvU	Nevada University, Reno, NV
nw	new
NW	(1) Northwest (2) Norway
NWale	North Wales
NwB	New Brunswick
NWFP	North West Frontier Province (India)
NWMP	Northwest Mounted Police (Canada)
NWO	Navy Widow's Originals
NWOQ	North West Ohio Quarterly
NWP	North-Western Province

NWT/ NW Terr	(1) Northwest Territories, Canada (2) Northwest Territory
NXN/nxn	no Christian name
NY	New York
NY Arch	New York Archives, New York Department of Education, Cultural Education Center, Albany, NY 12230
NYC	New York City
NYCRO	North Yorkshire County Record Office
NYGB	New York Genealogical and Biographical Society, 122 - 126 East 58th Street, New York, NY 10022-1939
NYGBR	*The New York Genealogical and Biographical Record*, 122-126 East 58th Street, New York, NY 10022-1939
NYG&BS/ NYGBS	New York Genealogical and Biographical Society, 122-126 East 58th Street, New York, NY 10022-1939
NYHS	New York Historical Society, 170 Central Park West, New York, NY 10024-5194
NYPL	New York Public Library, U.S. History, Local History and Genealogy Division, Fifth Avenue and 42nd Street, New York, NY 10017
NYSA	New York State Archives, New York Department of Education, Cultural Education Center, Albany, NY 12230
NYScC	New York Public Library, Schomburg Collection, Fifth Avenue and 42nd Street, New York, NY 10017
NYSL	New York State Library, 7th floor, Cultural Education Center, Albany, NY 12230
NYT	*New York Times*
NYYM	New York Yearly Meeting (Quaker records)
NZ/NZD/ NZEA	New Zealand
NZEAL	New Zealand LDS Temple

O

o | (1) oath (2) officer (3) only

o/oe/oi/ oy/oye/oey | grandson or nephew (Scottish)

O | (1) October (2) Officer (3) Ohio (4) Old (OC: Old Celtic, etc.) (5) Oriental (6) Orthodox (7) Oxfordshire, England

O' | (1) A prefix to ancient Irish family names followed by the genitive case of the name of the ancestor, as O'Neil (nom. Niall). Before surnames of females, O' is replaced in Irish by ni, daughter. It prefixes H before a vowel, as Oh Airt, O'Hart. The apostrophe is due to the mistaken idea that O stands for *of*. (2) whatever follows

OA | Oberamt

OA | Ontario Provincial Archives, Toronto

OAH | Ohio Academy of History, Elliott Hall, Ohio Wesleyan University, Delaware, OH 43015-2398

OAHQ | *Ohio Archaeological and Historical Quarterly*

OAKLA | Oakland, California LDS Temple

OAP | Old Age Pension

OARA | Oregon Adoptive Rights Association

OAS | Organization of American States

OAU | Organization of African Unity

ob/OB | (1) *obit* (died) (2) order book(s)

ob/obit | obituary

OBA | Office of Business Analysis

OBE | Officer of the Order of the British Empire

Oberbn | Oberbayern, Bavaria

Oberfr | Oberfranken, Bavaria

Oberhn | Oberhessen, Hess-Darmstadt

ob inf | *obit infantia* (died in infancy)

ob inf set | died whilst still a minor

obit | obituary; notice of a person's death

obj | (1) object (2) objective

ob juv | *obit juventus* (died in childhood)

Obk | order book

obs | (1) observer (2) obsolete (3) obsolete name

ob. s.p. | died without issue

ob. s.p.m. | died without male issue

obt | (1) *obit* (2) obedient (e.g., "Your Obt. Servant")

ob unm | *obit* (died unmarried)

oc | (1) Old country (2) ope consilio (an accessory, usually criminal) (3) opere citato (only child)

OC | (1) Officer, Order of Canada (2) Orphan's Court

OCA | Archives, Oberlin College, Oberlin, OH

occ | (1) occasionally (2) occupation (3) occupied (4) occurs -ing

OCCGS | Orange County California Genealogical Society, Huntington Beach Public Library, 7111 Talbert Avenue, Huntington Beach, CA 92648

OCD | Office of the Civilian Defense

OCFA | Ontario Cemetery Finding Aid, Ontario, Canada

OCI | *Ohio County Index* (West Virginia)

OCLC	Online Computer Library Center, 6565 Frantz Road, Dublin, OH 43017-3395
OCP	Ohio Company Purchase
OCR	Optical Character Recognition
OCRP	Oxford Colonial Records Project (University of Oxford, Oxford, England)
OCS	Officer Candidate School
Oct/O	October
OCTA	Oregon-California Trails Association, 524 South Osage Street, Independence, MO 64050
ocup	occupant, occupier
OCWGJ	*Ohio Civil War Genealogy Journal*, Ohio Genealogical Society, 713 South Main Street, Mansfield, OH 44907-1644
OD	(1) Officer of the Day (2) olive drab (uniforms)
ODDC	Old Darlington District Genealogical Chapter of the South Carolina Genealogical Society, P.O. Box 175, Hartsville, SC 29551-0175
ODCI	Ohio Death Certificate Index (Ohio Historical Society, 1982 Velma Avenue, Columbus, Ohio 43211)
ODH	Ohio Department of Health, Division of Vital Statistics, Ohio Departments Building, Room 6-20, 65 South Front Street, Columbus, OH 43266-0333
OE	(1) Old England (2) Old English, Anglo-Saxon (3) Ordinance Index (LDS Church database)
OED	*Oxford English Dictionary*
OEMP	Ottoman Empire
OEN	Overland Emigrant Names
OEO	Office of Economic Opportunity
OES	(1) Oesterreich (Austria) (2) Order of the Eastern Star
Of	Officer (rank unknown)

off/offi	(1) office (2) official
Off	Offaly, Republic of Ireland
offc	(1) office (2) officer
offD	officer's daughter
offg	officiating
offl	official
Offnbg	Offenburg, Baden
offr	officer
OFFRI&PP	Order of First Families of Rhode Island & Providence Plantations
OffS	officer's son
OffW	officer's wife
Ofkp	office keeper
OFPA	Order of the Founders and Patriots of America, 15 Pine Street, New York, NY 10005
OFr	Old French
OFS	Orange Free State (South Africa)
OfsS	officer's sister
oft	often
OGDEN	Ogden, Utah LDS Temple
OGQ	*Ohio Genealogical Quarterly*
OGS	Ohio Genealogical Society, 713 South Main Street, Mansfield, OH 44907-1644
OGS	Oklahoma Genealogical Society, P.O. Box 12986, Oklahoma City, OK 73157-2986
OGS	Ontario Genealogical Society, 40 Orchard View Blvd., Suite 102, Toronto, Ontario, Canada M4R 1B9
OGS	Oregon Genealogical Society, P.O. Box 10306, Eugene, OR 97440-2306

OGS	Ozarks Genealogical Society, P.O. Box 3945, Springfield, MO 65808-3945	OHS	Oregon Historical Society, Oregon History Center, 1200 SW Park Avenue, Portland, OR
OGS-CIG	Computer Interest Group of the Ohio Genealogical Society, 713 South Main Street, Mansfield, OH 44907-1644	OHS	State Archives, Ohio Historical Society, Columbus, OH
OGS REP	Ohio Genealogical Society: Report, quarterly	OhU	Ohio State University, Columbus
OGSRP	*The Report*, Ohio Genealogical Society, 713 South Main Street, Mansfield, OH 44907-1644	OIEAHC	Omohundro Institute of Early American History and Culture, P.O. Box 8781, Williamsburg, VA 23187-8781
Ogtld	Ostergotland, Sweden	OI	Ordinance Index™ (duplicate of information in the International Genealogical Index, but with LDS temple ordinance dates)
OH	(1) Ohio (2) *Ohio History*		
OHG	Old High German	O.Ijsel	Overijssel (Overyssel)
OHMS	On His (or Her) Majesty's Service	OISL	Orkney Island
OHP	Ohio Historic Preservation Office, 567 East Hudson Street, Columbus, OH 43211-1030	OJ	*Overland Journal*, Oregon – California Trails Association
OHPA	Ohio Historic Preservation Office, 567 East Hudson Street, Columbus, OH 43211-1030	OK	Oakland, California LDS Temple
OHQ	(1) *Ohio Historical Quarterly* (2) *Ohio State Archaeological and Historical Quarterly*	OK/Okla	Oklahoma
		OkHS	Oklahoma Historical Society, 2100 North Lincoln Boulevard, Oklahoma City, OK 73105-4997
OHS	Ohio Historical Society, 1982 Velma Avenue, Columbus, OH 43211	OL	(1) Laws of Ohio (2) Oriental-American Indian (3) online
OHS	Oregon Historical Society, 1230 SW Park Avenue, Portland, OR 97205		
OhSHS	Ohio State Historical Society, 1982 Velma Avenue, Columbus, OH 43211	OLAP	Online Analytical Processing
OhSL	State Library of Ohio, Genealogy Division, 65 South Front Street, Columbus, OH 43266-0334	Old/Olden/ Oldnbg/OLDE	Oldenburg, Germany
OhR	Ohio River	Old Plymouth Col Desc	National Society of Old Plymouth Colony Descendants, Rt. 2, 24 Samoset Road, East Sandwich, MA 02537
OHRPF	*Ohio Records and Pioneer Families*, Ohio Genealogical Society, 713 South Main Street, Mansfield, OH 44907-1644	OLIS	Oxford Library System Online Catalog (Oxford, England)
		OLM	*Old-Lore Miscellany of Orkney, Shetland &c.*
OHS	Oklahoma Historical Society, 2100 North Lincoln Blvd., Oklahoma City, OK 73105	OLS	Online Search
OHS	Ohio Historical Society, Columbus, OH	OM	(1) Order of Merit (2) organized militia
		OMM	Officer, Order of Military Merit (Canada)

omnibusdrv omnibus driver

Oms Omssia

ON Old Norse

ON/Ont. Ontario, Canada

ONAHRC Ohio Network of American History Research Centers

ONC Office of National Statistics (England)

OneC one of a community

ONGQ *Old Northwest Genealogical Quarterly*

ONR Office of Naval Research, 800 North Quincy Street, Arlington, VA 22217-5660

ONS Office for National Statistics, General Register Office, Overseas Registration Section, Trafalgar Road, Southport England PR8 2HH

ONS Ottawa News Service

OO Order of Ontario

OOP out of print

op (1) operating (2) operator (3) opus; work (4) out of print

OPAC Online Public Access Catalog

OPC Orthodox Presbyterian Church

op. cit. *opere citato* (in the work cited; previously cited)

OPCS Office for National Statistics (British)

oper/opr/ oprtr operator

Opfalz Oberpfalz, Bavaria

OPLIN Ohio Public Library Information Network

OPM Office of Personnel Management

opp opposite

OPR Old Parochial Register(s) (Church of Scotland) parish registers. Housed at New Register House, Edinburgh, Scotland (microfilmed).

optn optician

optom optometrist

OQ Officer, National Order of Québec

Or/or (1) gold (heraldry) (2) Orphan

OR (1) Ohio Roster Soldiers of 1812 (2) Orderly

OR/Oreg/ Ore Oregon

Or^r orator

orch orchard

ord (1) ordained (2) orderly (3) ordinance (4) ordinary

ord/ordr/ ordrd order(ed)

Ord Ct Ordinary Court

ordl orderly

OrdlSgt Orderly Sergeant

Ord of Acorn Colonial Order of the Acorn

Ord of Amer Ancestry Order of Americans of Armorial Ancestry, 2700 East of Armorial Minnehaha Parkway, Minneapolis, MN 55406

Ord of Crown in Amer Order of the Crown in America

Ord of Crown in Charlemagne Order of the Crown of Charlemagne in the United States of America, 7177 Williams Creek CharlemagneDrive, Indianapolis, IN 46240

Ord of Lafayette Order of Lafayette

Ord of Stars & Bars Order of the Stars and Bars

ORes	*Ohio Researcher*, Allstates Researchers, Murray Utah, periodical (defunct)	Osn	Osnaberg
org/orgn	(1) organization (2) organizing	osp/ob.s.p.	*obiit sine prole* (died without issue)
organ	organized politically	Osrfd/Ostf	Ostfold, Norway
orgr	organizer	OSS	Office of Strategic Service
OrHS	Oregon Historical Society, 1200 SW Park Avenue, Portland, OR 97205	Ost	Ostfriesland
orig	origin; original(ly)	osteo	osteopath
Ork/ ORK/ORKN	Orkney, Scotland	ostler grd	ostler & gardner
		Ostpr	Ostpreuseen, Prussia
ORLAN	Orlando, Florida LDS Temple	OT	(1) Old Tenor (2) Old Testament (Bible)
orp	orphan	OTB	On the Bookshelf
ORPF	*Ohio Records and Pioneer Families* (publication of the Ohio Genealogical Society, 713 South Main Street, Mansfield, OH 44907-1644)	OTD	On This Day (event database genealogy software utility)
orph/ orpht/orpns	orphan(s), orphanage	oth/othr	other(s)
		Othm	Othmar
Orph Ct	Orphans Court	OTHSA	Orphan Train Heritage Society of America, 4912 Trout Farm Road, Springdale, AR 72762
orp/o	orphan of	otp	(1) of this parish (2) of this/that place
OrSAr	Oregon State Archives, 800 Summer Street NE, Salem, OR 97310	OTS	(1) Officers' Training School (2) On The Sea
ORSSAR	Oregon Society of the Sons of the American Revolution	ou	out of unity
ORULS	Oregon Union List of Serials	OU	(1) Archives and Special Collections, Alden Library, Ohio University, Athens, OH 45701-2978 (2) Oxford University (England)
os	(1) old series (2) old style (3) only son (4) original secession	OUP	Oxford University Press
		OUZn	Ohio University Library, Zanesville, OH
OS	(1) Old Saxon (2) Old Style calendar (prior to 1752) date; referring to the Julian calendar (3) Ordinate Survey (4) Ordinance Survey (5) Osthofen	OVA	Ohio Volunteer Artillery
		OVAL	Ohio Valley Area Libraries, 252 West Thirteenth Street, Wellston, OH 45692
OSL	Oregon State Library, State Library Building Winter and Court Streets NE, Salem, OR 97310-0641	OVC	Ohio Volunteer Cavalry
		over	overman
oslr	ostler	Overs	overseer(s)

OVI	Ohio Volunteer Infantry (Civil War). For example 20th OVI
OVIL	Ohio Vital Information for Libraries Center
o.v.m.	*obiit vit~a matris* (died in lifetime of mother)
OVM	Ohio Voluneer Militia (Military)
ovp	*obiit vit~a patris* (died in lifetime of father)
owb	old will book
OWI	Office of War Information
ownr	owner
Ox	Oxford
OXF/ OXFO/Oxon	Oxfordshire, England
Oxon	(1) of Oxford, England (2) Oxfordshire (3) Oxoniensis
Oy	grandchild
oz.	ounce

P

p   (1) British pound (2) LDS Controlled Extraction indicates christenings (or births) extracted in R-Tab program (Family History Department, Salt Lake City, UT) (3) pagination page(s) (4) parent(s); parentage (5) parish (6) past (7) pater (8) patient (9) pence (10) penny (11) pensioner (usually Army or Navy) (12) per (13) perch (14) poll(s) (15) Polynesian (16) populus (17) post, after (18) posted as a parent (19) pro (20) probably (21) 1840 Revolutionary War veteran census

p/pp(s)   page(s)

P   (1) Pacific News Service (2) Patient

Pa   Partner

PA   (1) papers submitted. The individual prepared first papers for naturalization (in this case, "PA" is not an abbreviation for Pennsylvania) (2) partner (3) *per annum.* (4) petition (abbreviation often found in recent U.S. census schedules) declaration of intent filed (e.g., an immigrant who has petitioned a court for citizenship) (5) Power of Attorney (6) public address (7) purchasing agent

PA/Pa   Pennsylvania

Pa Arch   Pennsylvania Archives, P.O. Box 1026, Harrisburg, PA 17108-1026

PAAS   *Proceedings of the American Antiquarian Society*

Pac/Pacif   Pacific

PAC   Public Access Catalog (library catalog)

p. adj.   participial adjective

PAF   Personal Ancestral File®, genealogy software developed by the Family History Department, Salt Lake City, Utah. The current PAF version for DOS is 3.01M, for windows PAF 4.0, and for Macintosh PAF 2.3.1.

PAK   Pakistan

PAL/PALE   Palestine

PALA   Palatinate

Pal-Am/ PALAM   Palatines to America, Capital University, Box 101, Columbus, OH 53209-2394

Palp/Heart   Palpitation of Heart

pam/pamph   pamphlet

PAN   Panama

PANS   Public Archives of Nova Scotia, 6016 University Avenue, Halifax, NS Canada B3H 1W4

PAPEE   Papeete Tahiti LDS Temple

par   (1) parade (2) paragraph (3) parallel (4) parents, parentage (5) parish (6) parson

par/pce/ps   piece

para   paramour

Para   Paraguay

Para/Epilg   Paralysis Epiglottis

Par Clk   Parish Clerk

paren   parentheses

Parl   Parliament/ Parliamentary

par reg   parish register(s)

pars   (1) parents (2) parsonage

part   (1) parliamentary (2) participant (3) participle

pas   pastor

pass	(1) passage (2) passenger (3) passim, throughout (4) passive	PCC	Parochial Church Council
pat	(1) patent(ed) (2) paternal (3) patriot (Revolutionary War Service)	PCC	Prerogative Court of Canterbury (England). The probate court of the Province of Canterbury. The senior ecclesiastical court in England.
path	(1) pathological (2) pathologist (3) pathology	pccPAU	Paraguay
Patk/Patr^k	Patrick	PCD	Kodak Photo CD
PauC	pauper's child	pce	piece
PauD	pauper's daughter	p:cells	parcels, usually of land (with or without a crossed p)
Paug	Paugassett dialect		
paup	pauper	pchd	purchased
PauS	pauper's son	PCHS	Platte County Historical Society, P.O. Box 103, Platte City, MO 64079
PauW	pauper's wife	PCLP	Presbyterian-Canada and Lower Provinces
p/b	place of birth	P-Cn	Panama Canal Zone
PB	Patriarchal Blessing Index	PCY	Prerogative Court of York (England). Probate court of the Province of York.
PB	pamphlet box		
PBA	pamphlet box, small	pd/p^d	(1) paid (2) the day after
PBC	Primitive Baptist Church	p/d	place of death
PBCGS	Palm Beach County Genealogical Society, Inc., West Palm Beach Public Library, 100 Clematis Street, P.O. Box 1746, West Palm Beach, FL 33402	PD	Police Department
		PdB	Bachelor of Pedagogy
		PdD	Doctor of Pedagogy
pbk	paperback	PDF	portable document format
Pbl	Peeblesshire, Scotland	PdM	Master of Pedagogy
PBO	Presiding Bishopric's Office	pdob	place, date of birth
PBoy	postboy/postman	pdod	place, date of death
pc	(1) personal computer (2) piece (3) precinct	pds/#	pounds of weight
p.c.	(1) per cent (2) post card	Pe/Pec	Peculiar Court
PC	(1) Panama Canal (2) parent & child on archive records (3) Police Constable (4) Privy Council (British) (5) Probate Court	PE	Presiding Elder
		PE/PEI	Prince Edward Island, Canada
PCA	Presbyterian Church in America	PEE	Peebleshire

Peeb/PEEB Peebles, Scotland

PEF Perpetual Emigration Fund (19th century LDS Church source)

PeHS Historical Society of Pennsylvania, 1300 Locust Street, Philadelphia, PA 19107-5699

PEI Prince Edward Island, Canada

PEM/Pemb Pembrokeshire

PEMB/Pembs Pembroke, Wales

Penn/Penna Pennsylvania

Penna Pennacook dialect

pens (1) pension (2) pensioned (3) pensioner

Pensr Pensioner

penult penultimate, last but one

peo people

per (1) by means of (2) periodical

PER (1) Perthshire (2) Peru

perf (1) perfect (2) perforated (3) performed

perh perhaps

period periodical

perm (1) permanent (2) permission

pers (1) peers (Norman) (2) personal; personally (3) personnel

PERS (1) Persia (2) Persian

per se by itself, in itself

PERSI *PERiodical Source Index*, Allen County Public Library, 900 Webster Street, Fort Wayne, IN 46802. An index to many current and retrospective genealogical and historical periodicals. In printed form, on compact disc, and on the Internet

pers knowl personal knowledge

person[1]/p'son[1] personal

pert pertaining

PERT Perth, Great Britain

Perths Perthshire

PERU Peru

Peruv Peruvian

PeSL Pennsylvania State Library, P.O. Box 1601, Harrisburg PA 17105

pet/petitn/petn petition

petd petitioned

petr petitioner

PEU Peru

pf printed forms

PFAL Pfalz

Pfc Private first class (Army)

PFC Presbyterian Free Church

pfect perfect

Pfr. Pfarrer (minister)

pg (1) page number (2) preacher of the gospel

Pg Portugal

PG President General

PG Professional Genealogist

PGCS Publisher's Genealogical Coding Service (system)

PGM *The Pennsylvania Genealogical Magazine*

PGP Pretty Good Privacy (computer encryption program)

PGRS	*Proceedings of the First (Second, etc.) Priesthood Genealogy Research Seminar* (held on the campus of Brigham Young University, Provo, Utah)
PGS	Pinellas Genealogical Society, P.O. Box 1614, Largo, FL 34649-1614
PGSA	Polish Genealogical Society of America, 984 North Milwaukee Avenue, Chicago, IL 60622
PGS CA	Polish Genealogical Society of California, P.O. Box 713, Midway City, CA 92655-0713
PGSM	Polish Genealogical Society of Michigan, Detroit Public Library, Burton Historical Collection, 5201 Woodward Avenue, Detroit, MI 48202
PGST	Polish Genealogical Society of Texas, 218 Beaver Bend, Houston, TX 77037
ph/Ph	(1) physician (2) telephone
ph/pish/ parsh	parish
PH	Purple Heart
PharB	Bachelor of Pharmacy
PharD/ PharmD	Doctor of Pharmacy
pharm	pharmacist
PharmM	Master of Pharmacy
PhB	Bachelor of Philosophy
PhD	Doctor of Philosophy
Ph^e	Phelipe
PhG	Graduate in Pharmacy
Phil	(1) Philemon (2) Philip (3) Philippians (4) Philippine (5) philosophy Phila/Phi/Phil Philadelphia
PhiP	Philadelphia, Pennsylvania
PHL/PHIL	Philippines
PhM	Master of Philosophy

photog	(1) photographer (2) photography
PHR	*Pacific Historical Review*
PHS	Historical Society of Pennsylvania, 1300 Locust Street, Philadelphia, PA 19107-5699
PHS	*The Publications of the Harleian Society*
Phthisis/Pul	Phthisis Pulmonales
phy/phys/ physcn	physician
PI	(1) Preliminary Inventory (e.g., National Archives preliminary inventory) (2) The Republic of the Philippines; Phillipine Islands (3) Place interred
PIC	Picton Press, P.O. Box 250, Rockport, ME 04856
PID	Parentage in doubt
PIED	Piedmont
PIHL	Publications of the Illinois State Historical [Library] Society
PILI	*Passenger and Immigration Lists Index*, edited by P. William Filby, et al. (Detroit: Gale Research)
p IL insco	President-IL Insurance Co.
Pilot	River Pilot
pish	parish
PitP	Pittsburgh, Pennsylvania
PiU	Pittsburgh University, Pennsylvania
PJK	Probate Judge of the Peace
pjp	probate justice peace
PJP	Probate Judge of the Peace
pk	(1) packet (estate file) (2) park (3) peck
pkg	package
pkr	packer
Pkwy/pky	Parkway

PKZIP   file compression utility (program)

pl   (1) place (2) plate (3) plural

PL   (1) Place (2) Poland, *see* POL (3) Public Laws

PLA   Port of London Authority

Plant/plant   Plantation

PLB   Poor Law Board

PLC   Public Library of Cincinnati

PLCH   Public Library of Cincinnati and Hamilton County, History and Genealogy Department, 800 Vine Street, Cincinnati, OH 45202-2071

PLD   Poland

Pldg   Paulding Public Library, Paulding

plen   plenipotentiary

plkroadagt   plank road agent

plmb   plumber; plumbing

plms   palms

pln(s)   plain(s)

PLOW   Palatinate. Lower

plr   pillar

plshr   polisher

plstr/plster   plasterer

plt/pltf   plaintiff

Plt   Plantation

plu/plu/plur   pluries, a 3rd or subsequent writ, warrant, or court order

PLU   poor law union(s) (British)

plum   plumber

PlwB   ploughboy

PlwM   ploughman

Ply   Plymouth

Ply Col Rec   Records of the Colony of New Plymouth

Plz   Plaza

PM   (1) Paymaster (2) Peabody Museum, Salem, MA (3) piae memoriae, of pious memory (4) Police Magistrate (5) post meridiem (afternoon) (6) Postmaster (7) Post Mortem, Latin for after death (8) Preparative Meeting

P.M.   Principal Meridian (federal township and range survey system)

Pmb   Pembrokeshire, Wales

PMC   Protestant Methodist Church

PMG   Postmaster General

PMHSM   Papers of the Military Historical Society of Massachusetts

PML   Pierpont Morgan Library, 29 E. 36th Street, New York

PM's Clk   Pay Master's Clerk

Pmst   paymaster

p Mu insco   President-Mutual Insurance Company

PN   Place-Name

PNEASISS   *PN Evidence for the Anglo-Saxon Invasion &c.*

pnes   pines

PNG   Papua New Guinea

pni   pagination not indicated

PNQ   *Pacific Northwest Quarterly*

PNRISSHS   Personal narratives Rhode Island soldiers and sailors historical society

PNSR   Soldier Pensioned

pntr   painter

pnts   pointsman

p/o	parents of	port	porter, portree
P/O	Pilot Officer	Port	(1) Portugal (2) Portuguese
PO/P.O.	(1) Pacific Ocean (2) Poland (3) Poll Book (4) Post Office (5) President's Office	PORTL	Portland, Oregon LDS Temple
poa/POA	power of attorney	Portr	portrait
POA	*Pennsylvania Oaths of Allegiance*, William Henry Egle	Ports	Portsmouth, Ohio
		Portu/ PORT	Portugal
POB	Post Office Box	PorW	porter's wife
POD	Professional and Organizational Development Network in Higher Education	pos/poss	possible/possibly
PodD	Doctor of Podiatry	POSA	Patriotic Order Sons of America
POE	(1) preponderance of the evidence (2) port of entry	POSE	Posen
		poss	possessive, posssion
POL/Polan/ PLD/Plnd/ POLA	(1) Poland (2) Polish	poss/of	possession of
		post	after
pol	political	Poth	pathologist
polc	police, police constable	PotM	potman
PolW	police officer's wife	POW	(1) prisoner of war (2) Prince of Wales
POME	Pomerania (Pommern)	powr	any power to act for another, as in power of attorney
Pomm	(1) Pommerania (2) Pommern, Prussia	pow res	power reserved
poorhsekpr	Poor House Keeper & farmer	pp	(1) pages (2) parcel post (3) parish priest (4) past participle (5) past president (6) pauper (7) post paid (8) privately printed
pop	population		
POP	(1) Point of Presence (2) Post Office Protocol	P&P	past and present
popn	population	ppa	per power of attorney
por/Por	porter	PPFA	Palatinate, Pfalz
Por	Portugal	PPGS	Pikes Peak Genealogical Society, P.O. Box 1262, Colorado Springs, CO 80901
Po.R	Puerto Rico		
PorD	porter's daughter	PPLS	pixels per line segment
PorS	porter's son		

p:pole/ p:poll	per person
ppose	propose
PPP	Point-to-Point Protocol (computer term)
P.P.propria-persona	*in propria persona* (litigant who represents himself)
PPR	Principal Probate Registry (England)
PPS	*post postscriptum* (a later postscript)
PQ/Que	Québec, Canada
P&QS	Pleas & Quarter Sessions
pr/prob/probᵗ	probate or probated
pr/prs	two or a pair, a number of pairs
PR	(1) Commonwealth of Puerto Rico (2) Parish Register (3) Physicians' Records/Returns (4) Prussia
PR/pr	(1) parish register(s) (2) prairie (3) preacher (4) prisoner (5) printed book (6) probate record(s); probated (7) proved (8) public relations (9) the day before
pʳ/p²	pair, per
Pragu	Prague
Pr Appt	Prior Appointment
Praus	Prausen (Prussia)
prbn	probationer
prc	(1) Probate Record, case number (2) proclamation (marriage) (3) produced a certificate
prcf	produced a certificate from
PrCo	Providence College, Rhode Island
Preb	Prebendary (England). Office and title of a priest.
prec/precd	preceding

Prec	Precinct
prede	precede
Pr. Edw. Isl.	Prince Edward Island
pref	(1) preface (2) prefix
p.registʳ	probate register
prep	(1) preparatory (2) preposition
prepd	prepared
pres	(1) presence (2) present (3) presented (4) president (5) presumed
Pres/Presb/Presby	Presbyterian
PREST	Preston, England LDS Temple
presv	preservation
pret	preterit
prev	previous
PRF	*Pedigree Resource File* (lineage-linked pedigrees on compact discs). Family History Department, Salt Lake City, UT.
prfrdr	proofreader
PRHE	Palatinate, Rhenish
PrHes	Prussia, Hesse
pri/Pri	(1) principal (2) price
PRIC	Puerto Rico
Pries	Prieson
prim	(1) primitive (2) Primitive Baptist
prin/princ	principal
pris	prisoner
priv	(1) private (2) privilege
priv pr	privately printed

priv pub	privately published	prom	(1) promenade (2) promontory (3) promoted
pr md	previously married	pron	pronoun
PrMd	parlormaid	PRONI	Public Record Office of Northern Ireland, Belfast
prnt	parent	prop	property
prntr	printer	prop/propr	proprietor
pro	(1) probate record (2) proprietor (3) proved (4) province (5) provost	proprhouse	proprietor of the house
pro/prob	(1) probate (2) probation (3) probationary	ProS	proprietor's son
PRO	Public Record Office, Ruskin Avenue, Kew, Richmond, Surrey, England TW9 4DU	pros. Atty.	prosecuting attorney
prob	probable/probably	prot	protector
PROB	Prerogative Court of Canterbury, England	Prot	Protestant
probal	probable	Prot. E.	Protestant Episcopal
prob. Ct.	probate court	pro tem	*pro tempore* (for the time being)
proc	(1) proceedings (2) procurator	prov	(1) proved (2) provided (3) province/provincial (4) provost
ProCD	ProPhone (national telephone directory on CD-ROM)	prov/provis	provision
procl/ procla/prol	proclamation	Prov. Laws	Acts and Resolves of the Province of the Massachusetts Bay
Proc. Mass. Soc	*Proceedings of the Massachusetts Historical Society*	PROVO	Provo, Utah LDS Temple
		prox	*proximo* (next month)
prod	produce, production	PRP	Professional Registered Parliamentarian
ProD	proprietor's daughter	Prs	Parish Registers
prof/Prof.	(1) professional (2) professor	PRS	(1) Pedigree Referral System (2) Prussia
profl	professional(s)	PRSA	Public Relations Society of America, 33 Irving Place, New York, NY 10003-2376
prog	program		
PROG NAME	program name	prsfdr	press feeder
		PRSH	Parish
proj	project	prsmn	pressman
Pro Judge	Probate Judge	prsr	presser

prst	priest
Prst	Praesto, Denmark
PRT/prt	(1) Portugal (2) priest
prt brwr	partner in brewery
prtg	protègèe, protégè
PRU	Prussia
Pruss/ PRUS/PRUSS	Prussia/Prusia
Prv/prvt/	private
prvd	proved
ps	(1) previously submitted (an LDS term). Indicates that the name of a person has been submitted for temple ordinance work. (2) pieces
PS	Pilgrim Society, Plymouth, MA
PS/ps	(1) Patriotic Service (2) postscriptum (3) postscript (4) primary sources (5) Public Services (6) Public School
PSAX	Saxony (Province of Saxony)
psd	p = pound; s = shilling; d = pence; which are denominations of English money
psentmt	a presentment, or charge, made by a grand jury
psh	parish
pshr	parishioner
psnr	pensioner
PSon	principal son
psych	psychology
PST	Pacific Standard Time
pt	(1) part (2) part of roll of film (3) partition case (4) patient (5) petition (6) point (7) port (8) pro tempore (for the time) (9) pint
pt/pts	part(s)

PT	(1) Petitioner's List (2) Portugal
p&t	plain and true
PTA	Parent-Teacher Association
pte	private
ptf/plt	Plaintiff
PTFS	Progressive Technology Federal Systems
Pth	Perthsire, Scotland
PTLDC	Provincial and Territorial Library Directors Council (Canada)
PtnD	partner's daughter
ptnr	partner
PtnS	partner's son
ptnt	patient
PtnW	partner's wife
pto	please turn over (the page)
p.t.p.	*post tribus proclamationibus* (after calling the banns 3 times)
PTS	Postal Transportation Service
PtWi	patient's wife
pty	proprietary
pu/Pu/pupl	pupil
PU	Prussia
PUASAL	*Proceedings of the Utah Academy of Sciences, Arts & Letters*
pub/publ	(1) public (2) published; publication; publisher; published by (3) published inventory, guide, directory
pubn	publication(s)
pubr	publisher
Puer/Fev	Puerperal Fever

PUL	Princeton University Library, Princeton, NJ 08540
Pul/Affec	Pulmonary Affection
Pul/Con	Pulmonary Consumption
PUPP	Palatinate, Upper
pur	purveyor
PUR	Puerto Rico
purch	purchase; purchasing
Put/So/Th	Putrid Sore Throat
PV	Provo Temple
pvd	proved
PVRL	Parish and Vital Records Listing (Family History Library, Salt Lake City, Utah)
pvt	private
Pvt	Private (military)
Pvtr	Privateer
pw	per week
PW	*The Presbyterian Witness and Evangelical Advocate* (Halifax, Nova Scotia)
PWA	Public Works Administration
PWCGS	Prince William County Genealogical Society, P.O. Box 2019, Manassas, VA 20108-0812
PWGSC	Public Works and Government Services Canada
PX	Post Exchange
py	per year/annum
pymt	payment

Q

q	(1) a query (2) qu. or qts. (3) quarterly (4) queen	QMst	quartermaster
Q	Quarto, oversized book	qrtr/qtr/qr	quarter
Q/QC/Qe/ Que/QB	Québec, Canada	qt	quart
Q & A	question(s) and answer(s)	Qt/Qtly/ qtrly	quarterly
qaly	qualifying	Qtm	Quartermaster
q c	quit claim	qs	quod sacrs
QC	Queen's Council (British)	QS	Quarter Sessions
QC	Quad Cities	qt	quart
QED	*quod erat demonstrandum* (which was to be demonstrated; which was to be proved)	Qtr Mstr	Quarter Master
		qu	qualities
qen	wherefore execution (q.v.) should not issue	QU/Que	Québec, Canada
Qkr	Quaker	quad	(1) quadrant (2) quadrennial (3) topographical map
Qld	Queensland		
Q-Link	Quantum Computers, Vienna, VA (BBS on-line service)	quar	a stone quarry
		quart	(1) quarter (2) quarterly
Qly	Quarterly	QUE/Que	Québec, Canada
QM	(1) Quarter Master (2) Quarterly Meeting (Quakers)	Quinc	Quincy
QMC	Quartermaster Corps	qv/QV	*quod vide* (refer to; which see)
QMD	Quartermaster's department	qy	query
QMG	Quartermaster General		
QMGen	Quartermaster General		
QMORC	Quartermaster Officers Reserve Corps		
Qm.Sgt/ QMSgt	Quartermaster Sergeant		

R

R/r — (1) on a Revolutionary War pension jacket, R means "rejected" (2) Rabbi (3) Range: on a Rectangular Survey map (legal land description (4) record (5) rector (6) reigns, reigned (7) *recto* (8) regina; queen (9) regular censuses (10) rejected (11) removed (12) Republican (13) resides (14) rex; king (15) right (in stage directions) (16) river (17) road (18) room(s) (19) roomer (20) Royal (21) rural (22) Rutland, England

R2aa-14 — letter preceding 2aa on a female's card; represents the letter of the alphabet in which the sheet was filed

ra — raising

RA — (1) Rear Admiral (2) Royal Academician (3) Royal Artillery (British) (4) Russia

RAC — Royal Automobile Club (British)

Rad/RAD — (1) Radnor (2) Radnorshire, Wales

RAD — Records Adjustment Department

RADN — Radnor, Great Britain

RAF — Royal Air Force

RAL — Reuss Altere Linie

RAM — (1) Random Access Memory (computer term) (2) Royal Arch Mason

Rang — Rangarvallasysla

rat — rated

Rau — Rause

rb — Record Book

RB — Rigle Brigade

RBaue — Rein Bauer

RBH — Rutherford B. Hayes Presidential Center, Spiegel Grove, Fremont, OH 43420

RC — (1) Red Cross (2) Reserve Corps (3) Roman Catholic (4) Roman Catholic Church

R&C — Ross & Cromarty, Scotland

RCAF — Royal Canadian Air Force

rcd/rec — (1) record (2) recorded

rcdr/rcor — recorder

Rcdr Deeds — Recorder of Deeds

Rcds — records, recorders

RCE — Register of Corrected Entries (Scotland)

Rch — Research

RCHM — Royal Commission on Historical Monuments (British)

Rcm — Roscommon, Republic of Ireland

R-Cn — Republic of the Congo

rcp — Roman Catholic priest

rcpt — receipt

rcut — recruit

Rd — (1) release of dower rights (2) Road

RD — (1) Registration District (2) Revolutionary Daughter (3) Rural Deaneries (British) (4) Rural Delivery

RDF — Research Data Filer (a program in Personal Ancestral File 2.31, and older versions). This program is not available in PAF 3.0 or 4.0.

rdg — ridge

rdnt	resident	reffrd	referred
rdr	reader	refgr	refrigeration; refrigerator
re	regarding	refl	reflexive
RE	Royal Engineers (British)	Ref.Pres.Ch.	Reformed Presbyterian Church
re-af	reaffirmed	reg	(1) regiment (2) region (3) register(s) (4) registration (5) regular
REAH	*Reading Early American Handwriting*, by Kip Sperry (Baltimore: Genealogical Publishing Co., 1998)	reg/reg^r/ regist^r/regt	(1) regiment (2) register
real est	real estate	Reg	Regula
realestagt	real estate agent	REG	*The New England Historical and Genealogical Register*
ReaP	Reading, Pennsylvania		
Rear Adm.	Rear Admiral	regd	registered
reb	rebellion	Reg Gen	Registrar General
rec	(1) receive; received; receiving (2) record (s) (3) recording	Reg in Chan	Register in Chancery
rec/rec^d	record(s); recorded	Regis	Registration
recd/rec'd/ rec^d/recv^d	received	Register	*The New England Historical and Genealogical Register*
rec'd by corr	received by correspondence	regn	region
rec of mem	record of members	regnal year	the date most often used in medieval documents referring to the number of the year of the reign of the monarch at the time the document was dated
recoll	recollections		
Record	*The New York Genealogical and Biographical Record*		
recpt	(1) receipt (2) receptionist	regnl	regional
recrq	received by request	Reg of Wills	Register of Wills
Recrt	(1) Recruit (2) Recruiting	regt	regiment
rect/rec	rector, rectory	regtl	regimental
rec^t	receipt	rehab	rehabilitation
ref	(1) refer (2) reference (3) reformed	ReiB	Reichenberger
refers	reference	Reinb	Reinbiern
		reinstd	reinstated

rej	rejected	res	(1) research (2) reservation (3) reserve (4) reservoir (5) residence (length of, in county; lived at) (6) resident (7) resides, resided (8) residue (9) resign (10) resolution
rel	(1) related, relative(s) (2) relations (3) relationship (4) released (5) relict (6) religion; religious		
		res. aids	research aids
rela	relative	resd	(1) reserved (2) resigned
RelC	religious condition	res leg	residuary legatee
reld	relieved	resrt	resort
relecta	widow	restr	restaurant
relectus	widower	ret	(1) retail (2) returned
relfc	released from care for	ret/retd	retired
rel/o	relict of	Ret/Far	retired farmer
rel-i-l	relative-in-law	ret mbrp	retained membership
RelO	religious order	Ret/Wvr	retired weaver
relrq	released by request	ReuO	Reuss-Olden
rem	(1) remain (2) remainder (3) reminiscences (4) remove; removed	REUS	Reuss
		rev	(1) reverend (2) reversed (3) review (4) revised (5) revision (6) revived use
Remit/Fev	Remittent Fever		
ren	(1) renatus, renata (baptized) (2) renounced, renunciation	Rev	(1) Revelation (2) Reverend (3) Revolution / Revolutionary
ren cov	renewed covenant	rev. ed.	revised edition
RENF/ Renf	Renfrew, Scotland	Revol	Revolutionary War, American Revolution
		Rev vet	Revolutionary War veteran
renun	renunciation	Rev War	Revolutionary War, American Revolution
rep	(1) repair (2) report (3) representative (4) reprint(ed)	RF	research folder
Rep	(1) Representative (2) Republican	RFC	Royal Flying Corps
repl	replacement; replaced	RFD	Rural Free Delivery
repr	(1) repair; repairman (2) reprint, reprinted	RFW	Renfrewshire
republ	republished		
repud	repudiated		
reqt	request		

RG   (1) General Register Office, Public Record Office, Kew, Surrey, England (2) Record Group (e.g., National Archives and Records Administration record group number) (3) Registered Genealogist (4) Registrar General

Rgl   Rogaland, Norway

RGRE   Reuss Griez

RGS   Rochester Genealogical Society, P.O. Box 10501, Rochester, NY 14610-0501

Rgstr   Registrar

RHA   Royal Horse Artillery (British)

Rheinh   Rheinhessen, Hess-Darmstadt

Rheinl/ Rhinel   Rheinland, Prussia

Rhi   Rhine

RhiB   Rhine Bion

RHIN   Rhineland (Rheinland, Rheinprovinz)

RhiR   Rhine Bier/Beir

RHistS   Royal Historical Society (British)

RHL   Rhodes House Library (Bodleian Library, University of Oxford), South Parks Road, Oxford, England OX1 3RG

RHO   Rhodesia

RHP   Register House Press, Scottish Record Office, HM General Register House, Princes Street, Edinburgh EH1 3YY Scotland

RHQ   Regional Headquarters

ri   rise

RI   Rhode Island

RiaB   Rian Baron

R.I. Arch.   Rhode Island Archives, Providence, RI

Ric/Rich/ Richd/ Rich^d/R^d Richard

RIC   Research Information Center (Family History Library, Salt Lake City, Utah)

RIC   Royal Irish Constabulary

Richf   Richfield, Ohio

RicV   Richmond, Virginia

RIGR   *Rhode Island Genealogical Register*, Rhode Island Families Association, P.O. Box 1414, Ashburn, VA 20146-1414

RIGS   Rhode Island Genealogical Society, 13 Countryside Drive, Cumberland, RI 02864-2601

RIHS   Rhode Island Historical Society, 110 Benevolent Street, Providence, RI 02906

RIN   Record Identification Number (used in Personal Ancestral File® genealogy software program)

rinq   relinquished

R.I.P.   *requiescat in pace* (rest in peace); frequently found on gravestones

RISL   Rhode Island State Library, Providence, RI

RIU   Research and Intelligence Unit

riv   river

RIVR,NS   *Rhode Island Vital Records,* New Series

RJUL   Reuss Jungere Linie

rk   rock

Rkbg   Ringkobing, Denmark

RL   regional libraries

RLAC   Research Libraries Advisory Committee

RLDS   Reorganized Church of Jesus Christ of Latter Day Saints, P.O. Box 1059, Independence, MO 64055

RLG   Research Libraries Group. See RLIN.

RLIN	Research Libraries Information Network; Research Libraries Group: computerized bibliographic database of over 85 million titles, including the acquisitions of the Library of Congress since 1968.	roc	received on certificate
		ROC	Ross & Company
		rocf	received on certificate form
RLL	Roots Location List	ROCR	Ross & Cromarty, Great Britain
rlnq	relinquished	Rodrig^z	Rodriguez
rly	railway	rol	received on letter
rm	(1) ream (of paper) (2) reported married	rolf	received on letter from
Rm	(1) room (2) roomer	Rom	Roman(s)
RM	Royal Marines (British)	ROM	(1) Read Only Memory (2) Romania
RMC	Royal Military College	ROMA	Romania
RMS	Royal Military Surveyor (British)	Rom.Cath.	Roman Catholics
rmt	reported married to	R–Or	Rio De Oro
RN	(1) Record Number (Family History Library Catalog computer number) (2) Registered Nurse (3) Reuters News Agency (4) Royal Navy (British)	Ros	Ross and Cromarty, Scotland
		ROST	Rostock
		Rot.	Roll; Rolls (rotalus); a term used for many types of early records
RNA	ribonucleic acid		
rnch(s)	ranch(s)	ROTC	Reserve Officers' Training Corps
Rnds	Randers, Denmark	Rox/ROX	Roxburghshire, Scotland
RNE	Register of Neglected Entries (Scotland)	ROXB/ Roxb	Roxburgh, Scotland
Rnf	Renfrewshire, Scotland		
Rngr	Ranger	ROY	Royal Navy
RNR	Royal Naval Reserve	RP	(1) Reformed Presbyterian (2) Reformed Presbyterian Church
RNVR	Royal Naval Volunteer Reserve		
RO	(1) Record Office (2) Recruiting Officer (3) Romania	rpd/rpt	reported
		rpds	rapids
road ngner	engineer on road	RPI	Research Publications, Inc., Woodbridge, CT
Rob/Robt/ Robt/Ro^t	Robert	rpm	revolutions per minute
Robt^o	Roberto	rpt	(1) reprint(ed) (2) report, reported

Rpt   respited (no accompanying inventory). Term found in Prerogative Court of York (England).

rq   request (s); requested

rqc   requested certificate

rqct   requested certificate to

rqcuc   requested to come under care (of meeting)

r.r./RR   railroad

RR   (1) railroad (2) Rent Role (3) Right Reverend (4) Rural Route

RRB   Railroad Retirement Board

rr bggmstr   railroad baggage master

rr cndctr   railroad conductor

rr ngner   railroad engineer

rrq   request; requests; requested

RS   (1) Resident's List (2) Revolutionary Soldier

RSA   Republic of South Africa

RSC   Religious Studies Center, Brigham Young University,167 Heber J. Grant Bldg., Provo, UT 84602

RSCG   Reuss Schleiz Gera

RSCH   Reuss Schleiz

rsh   research

rshr   researcher

RSL   Roots Surname List

RSL   Royal Staff Corps (British)

RSM   *Records Submission Manual* (former LDS handbook)

RSNMA   Royal Scottish Naval and Military Academy

rst   (1) reinstated in membership (2) rest

RSV   Revised Standard Version (of the Bible)

RSVP   please reply

rt   (1) right, as in a right of dower (2) route

Rt/ Rt. Honab   Right Honorable, a title

R-Tab   Records Tabulation

RTC   (1) Real Time Clock (personal computer) 2) relationship to claimant

Rte   Route; U.S. or State numbered road

RTF   Rich Text Format (computer format)

R Tkt   Reader's Ticket

RtSU   Rutgers State University, New Brunswick, New Jersey

RU   Rumania

RU/RUS/   Russia

RUSA   Reference and Users Services Association

Rud   Rudolf, Rudolph

rudimnts/ rudmnts   rudiments

Rum   Rumania(n)

Rupt   Rupture

RUS/RUSS   Russia(n)

RUT/ Rutl/Rutlds   Rutland, England

Ruther   Rutherford

RUTL   Rutlandshire, Great Britain

RVA   Richmond, Virginia

Rvr   River

Rvrhd   Riverhead

RW   (1) Red War (2) Revolutionary War

RWGR   Revolutionary War Graves Register (National
        Society of the Sons of the American Revolution)

RWR   RootsWeb Review

Ry   Railway

ry sta   railway station

S

s	(1) section (2) sepulture (burial) (3) *sepultus* (4) shilling (5) siecle (century) (6) single (7) soldier (8) son(s) (9) son of (used in Quaker records) (10) south (11) spinster (12) succeeded (13) successor (14) surveyed (15) survivor	Sac	Sachs/Sachs Weimer/Sachsen
S	(1) Saturday (2) section (3) *Selig,* (of persons) (late, deceased) (4) Sister (5) Son (6) South (7) Sunday (8) survivor (in a Revolutionary War pension jacket)	SacC	Sachs Coburg/Saxe Coburg
		Sachs	Sachson
		Sacogo	Sachsen-Coburg-Gotha, Thuringia
S/Sergt/Sgt	Sergeant	SAE	self-addressed envelope
S1	First Sergeant	SAF	South Africa
S2	Second Sergeant	SAFHS	Scottish Association of Family History Societies, 15 Victoria Terrace, Edinburgh EH1 2JL, Scotland
S3	Third Sergeant	SAG	*Swedish American Genealogist,* Swenson Swedish Immigration Research Center, Augustana College, Rock Island, IL 61201-2273
S4	Fourth Sergeant		
S5	Fifth Sergeant	SAHS	Swiss American Historical Society, 6440 North Bosworth Avenue, Chicago, IL 60626
S6	Sixth Sergeant		
S7	Seventh Sergeant	sail	sailor
S8	Eighth Sergeant	sal/Sal	saleslady
sa	(1) sailor (2) *secundum artem* (3) see also (4) *sine anno* (without year) (5) *sub anno* (under the year)	Sal	Salmon
		Salop	Shropshire
s-a	twice annually	SALT	Saxony Altenburg
Sa	(1) Saxony (2) Shropshire, England	SALT	Subject, Author, Locality, Title (catalog search)
Sa/Sat	Saturday	Saltbg	Sachsen-Altenburg, Thuringia
SA	(1) corporation (2) Sociètè Anonyme (3) South Africa (4) South America (5) Spanish America (6) Survivor's Application	Salv	El Salvador
		Salzbg	Salzburg
		Sam/Saml/ Sam¹	Samuel
S^a, S^ra	Señora (title)		
SAA	Society of American Archivists, 527 S. Wells, 5th floor, Chicago, IL 60607	SAM/ SAME	South America

Samein	Sachsen-Meiningen, Thur.
SAmer	South America
samt.	together with
san	sanitary
s and coh	son and coheir
s and h	son and heir
San Jacinto Desc	San Jancinto Descendants
SANTI	Santiago, Chile LDS Temple
SAR	National Society of the Sons of the American Revolution, 1000 South Fourth Street, Louisville, KY 40203
SAR	Sark, Channel Islands
SARA	New York State Archives and Records Administration
SARD	Sardinia
Sarum	Salisbury
SAS	Saskatchewan, Canada
SASE	self-addressed, stamped envelope
Sask	Saskatchewan
Sat	(1) Saturday (2) Saturn
sauv	savage (Indian)
sauvagesse	savage (feminine) (Indian)
Sav	(1) savings (2) Savior
Savage	James Savage, *Genealogical Dictionary of the First Settlers of New England*, 4 vols. (1860-62; reprint. Baltimore: Genealogical Publishing Co., 1981)
Saweim	Sachsenl-Weimar-Eisenach, Thur.
SAX/Sax/ SAXO	Saxe/Saxony/Saxon
SaxC	Saxe Coburg/Sachs Coburg

Saxe	Prov. Sachsen, Prussia
Saxe	Sachsen or Saxe
SAXO	Saxony-Kingdom of
SaxW/ SaxeW	Saxe Weimer
say	used with a date indicating a great degree of uncertainty
sb	(1) settlement because (2) step brother (3) still-born
s/b	should be
SB	(1) Bachelor of Science (2) source book of documents (3) Step-brother
SBA	Small Business Administration
SBC	Southern Baptist Convention
SBCGS	Santa Barbara County Genealogical Society, P.O. Box 1303, Santa Barbara, CA 93116-1303
SBCGS	South Bay Cities Genealogical Society, P.O. Box 11069, Torrance, CA 90510-1069
SBDa	stepbrother's daughter
SBHLA	Southern Baptist Historical Library and Archives, Nashville, TN 37203-3620
Sbl/SBL	step-brother-in-law
SBro	stepbrother
SBSn	stepbrother's son
SBWi	stepbrother's wife
sc	(1) scene (2) science (3) scilicet; namely (4) sculpsit; carved by (5) Supreme Court (held in each county)
Sc	Settlement Certificate
SC	(1) Schomburg Center for Research in Black Culture (2) Scotland (3) Sergeant Commissary (4) Society of the Cincinnati (5) South Carolina (6) South Central (7) Southern News Service (8) Staff Corps (9) Survivor's Certificate(s)

SCA	Leonardo Andrea Collection of South Carolina genealogies	schl	scholar, student
SCAN	Scottish Archive Network	SchL	Schaumberg Lippe
Scand/ SCAN	Scandinavia(n)	Schles	Schlesien, Prussia
		Schles'Holst	Schleswig' Holstein
Scarl/Fev	Scarlet Fever	Schlho	Schleswig-Holstein, Prussia
scatt	scattering or scattered	Sch.' Lippe	Schaumburg' Lippe
scc	sworn chain carrier	SchM	school mistress, schoolmaster
SCC	Southern California Chapter, Association of Professional Genealogists (APG), P.O. Box 9486, Brea, CA 92822-9486	scho	school
		schs	schedules (e.g., Veterans' Schedules)
SCCAPG	Southern California Chapter, Association of Professional Genealogists (APG), P.O. Box 9486, Brea, CA 92822-9486)	SCHS	Shelby County Historical Society, P.O. Box 376, Sidney, OH 45365-0376
SCCHGS	Santa Clara County Historical and Genealogical Society, Santa Clara Central Library, 2635 Homestead Road, Santa Clara, CA 95051-5387	SCHS	South Carolina Historical Society, Fireproof Building, 100 Meeting Street, Charleston, SC 29401
		Sch/Tchr	School Teacher
SCCOGS	Southern California Chapter, Ohio Genealogical Society, P.O. Box 5057, Los Alamitos, CA 90721-5057	SCHW	Schwarzburg
		Schwa	Schwabia
ScD	Doctor of Science	Schwab	Schwaben, Bavaria
SCDAH	South Carolina Department of Archives and History, 8301 Parklane Road, Columbia, SC 29223	Schwe	Schwere
		Schwru	Schwarzburg-Rudolstadt, Thur.
		Schwso	Schwarzburg-Sondershausen, Thur.
SCGS	Shelby County Genealogical Society, 17755 State Route 47, Sidney, OH 45365-9242	Schwz	Schwarzenborn
SCGS	South Carolina Genealogical Society, P.O. Box 16355, Greenville, SC 29606	Schwzw	Schwarzwald, Wuerttemberg
		sci	science
SCGS	Southern California Genealogical Society, 417 Irving Drive, Burbank, CA 91504	sci. fa.	scire facias
sch	school	scire facias	and it is ordered that
Sch	Schleswig/Schlessien/Schleweig/Schumbold	scj	Supreme Court Journal
SchB	Schalbag	Scl	step child
Schd	stepchild	scm	Supreme Court Minutes
sched	schedule		

ScM	Master of Science	SCW	(1) Society of Colonial Wars (2) South Central Wisconsin
SCMAR	*The South Carolina Magazine of Ancestral Research*, P.O. Box 21766, Columbia, SC 29221	SCWFO	Society of Civil War Families of Ohio (Ohio Genealogical Society, 713 South Main Street, Mansfield, Ohio 44907-1644)
ScMd	scullery maid		
Sco/Scot	Scotland, Scottish	sd/s^d	(1) said (2) *sine die* (without setting a day for reconvening)
SCOB	Supreme Court Order Book		
SCOG	Saxony Coburg Gotha	s'd	scribes abbreviation for "said," found in legal documents
SCOT	Scotland	Sd	Sohn des, Sohn der (son of)
Scou	stepcousin	Sd/SDau	stepdaughter
SCP	Suffolk County, Massachusetts, probate records	SD	(1) Doctor of Science (2) Spirit of Democracy, Woodsfield, Monroe Co. (3) Sydney Australia LDS Temple
scr	scrivener		
SCR	Scottish Church Records (FamilySearch)	SD/SDak	South Dakota
SCRE	Scottish Council for Research in Education	SDA	Seventh Day Adventist
script	scriptor	SDaL/Sdl	stepdaughter-in-law
SCRO	Staffordshire County Record Office, Stafford, England	SDC	State Data Center
		SDDa	stepdaughter's daughter
SCRO	St. Croix	SDFH	Society of the Descendants of the Founders of Hartford
Scro/Dysp	Scrofula Dysipales		
scru	scruple	sdg	siding
SCRU	Santa Cruz	SDGS	San Diego Genealogical Society, 1050 Pioneer Way, Suite E, El Cajon, CA 92020-1943
SCSAr	South Carolina State Archives, Columbia, SC		
SCSI	small computer system interface [a parallel interface standard]	SDI	Signer of the Declaration of Independence
		SDIEG	San Diego, California LDS Temple
scst grind	scissor grinder	Sdl	stepdaughter-in-law
sct	secretariat(s)	Sd/o	stepdaughter of
SCT	Scotland	SDOM	Santo Domingo
scts	scouts	SDOP	Sons and Daughters of Oregon Pioneers, P.O. Box 6685, Portland, OR 97228
SCU	South Carolina University, Columbia, SC		
SCV	Sons of Confederate Veterans	SDRAM	Synchronous Dynamic Memory (computer term)

SDS	Students for a Democratic Society	SEL	Selkirkshire
SDSHS	South Dakota State Historical Society, South Dakota Archives, Cultural Heritage Center, 900 Governors Drive, Pierre, SD 57501-2217	Seli	Silesia
		SELK/Selk	Selkirk, Scotland
SDSn	stepdaughter's son	sell	seller
se/Se	servant	sen/senr/sr/ sen^r/s^r	senior
SE	(1) Sea (2) Seattle, Washington LDS Temple (3) Settlement (4) Settlement Examination (5) Southeast	Sen	(1) senate (2) Senator
		SEN	Senegal
SEA	At Sea	sent	(1) sentence (2) sentry
SeaCap	Sea Captain	SEOUL	Seoul, Korea LDS Temple
SEAGS	Southeast Alabama Genealogical Society, P.O. Box 143, Dothan, AL 36302	sep	(1) Latin form used as separate Christian name from date shown (2) separate(d)
seal	sealing (an LDS temple term)	Sep/Sept/S	September
SEATT	Seattle, Washington LDS Temple	seqq	sequentia
SeaW	seaman's wife	ser	(1) series (2) servant
Sebast	Sebastian	SerB	servant's baby
sec	(1) second (2) secretary (3) section (4) sector (5) *secundum* (according to) (6) security	SERB	Serbia
		SerC	servant's child
Sec	Secklendorf	SerD	servant's daughter
sec IL ins	Sect. IL for insurance	serg/sergt	sergeant
SeCl	servant's child	SerH	servant's husband
Secr/Secy	secretary	SerM	servant's mother
secs	securities	SerN	servant's nephew or niece
sec state	secretary of state	ser no	serial number
sect	section	SerS	servant's son
sectn boss	section boss	sert/serv/ servt	servant
secty/secy	secretary		
sel	(1) selected (2) *selig* (of persons) (late, deceased)	serv	serve -ice,-ant
Sel	Sellmont	serW	servant's wife

ses/sess	session
Sess. Clk.	Session Clerk (Presbyterian)
set	settled
set/sett	settlement, settlement record
settl	(1) settled (2) settler
sev/sevl	several
sevt	servant
SEY	Seychelles
Sf/SF	(1) step-father (2) Suffolk, England
SF	Survivor's File
SFal	servant's father-in-law
SFat	stepfather
SFBA JGS	San Francisco Bay Area Jewish Genealogical Society, 4430 School Way, Castro Valley, CA 94546-1331
S-Fj	Sogn & Fjordane, Norway
Sfl/SFL	step-father-in-law
SFPL	San Francisco Public Library, San Francisco, CA 94102
sg	singular
SG	Society of Genealogists, 14 Charterhouse Buildings, Goswell Road, London, England EC1M 7BA
SG	St. George, Utah LDS Temple
SG/Surg	Surgeon (or Assistant)
SGCh	step grandchild
sgd	signed
Sgd/SGD	step-granddaughter
SGDL	step granddaughter-in-law
SGEOR	St. George, Utah LDS Temple
SGML	Standard Generalized Markup Language
SGMo	step grandmother
Sgs/SGSn	step-grandson
SGS	*Scottish Gaelic Studies*
SGS	Scottish Genealogical Society, 15 Victoria Terrace, Edinburgh EH1 2JL Scotland
SGS	Seattle Genealogical Society, 8511 15th Avenue, NE, P.O. Box 1708, Seattle, WA 98111
Sgt	Sergeant (military)
Sgt. Maj.	Sergeant Major
sh	(1) share (2) ship (3) shortly
SH	Schkeswig
s & h/ s. & h.	son and heir
Sha	Shanbry
SHAEF	Supreme Headquarters, Allied Expeditionary Forces
Shak	Shakespeare
SHAN	Shanghai, China
Sh/Bt/Mk	shoe and boot maker
shd	shode
shef	sheriff
shep	shepherd
SHET/Shet	Shetland Isles, (Zetland) Scotland
shgs	shillings
SHHAR	Society of Hispanic Historical and Ancestral Research, P.O. Box 490, Midway City, CA 92655-0490
ship	shipping
shl(s)	shoal(s)

Shn	Shanburgh	sib	sibling(s)
SHNA	Scripps-Howard Newspaper Alliance	Sib.	Siberia(n)
Shoe/Mkr	Shoemaker	sic	written thus; as copied; as shown in original: often inserted after an obvious error
ShoL	shoplad		
SHOL	Schleswig Holstein (Rudolstadt)	SIC	standard industrial classification
SHols	South Holstein	SICI/SIC	Sicily
ShoM	shoemaker master	SIE	Sierra Leone
shop	(1) shopman (2) shopping (3) shopwoman	sig	(1) signal (2) signature (3) signed (4) Signor
ShpA	shop assistant	SIG	Special Interest Group(s)
Shp/Cptr	ship carpenter	SiGD	sister's granddaughter
ShpG	shop girl	SIGG	Society of Indexers Genealogical Group, The RidgeWay, Kenton, Newcastle-upon-Tyne, England NE3 4LP
ShpK	shopkeeper		
ShpW	shop walker		
shr(s)	(1) sheriff (2) shore(s)	Signmaker	Lincomatic Banner Maker
SHR	*Scottish Historical Review*	SiGs	sister's grandson
shrff dept	sheriff deputy	sil/SIL	(1) sister-in-law (2) sometimes means stepson (3) son-in-law
SHRO/ SHR	Shropshire, Great Britain		
		SiLD	sister-in-law's daughter
Shrops	Salop (Shropshire, England)	SILE	Silesia (Schlesien)
sh. sh.	sharpshooters	Silic	Silicia
SHSM	State Historical Society of Missouri, 1020 Lowry Street, Columbia, MO 65201-7298	SilM	sailmaker
		sin	sine
		SIN	Singapore
SHSW	State Historical Society of Wisconsin, 816 State Street, Madison, WI 53706	*sine die*	without delay, indefinitely
		sing	singular
sht mtl	sheet metal	SInm	special inmate
si/sis	(1) sister (2)sister (of)	sis/sist	sister
SI	(1) Sand Island (2) Sandwich Islands (3) Sister (4) Smithsonian Institution, Washington, DC (5) Staten Island (New York)	SIS	Supplementary Information Services
		SisC	sister's child
SIAM	Siam		

SisD	sister's daughter	SldC	soldier's child
SisH	sister's husband	SldD	soldier's daughter
SisL/Sis-i-l/ Sis-il	sister-in-law	SldN	soldier's niece
sis/o	sister of	Sldr	soldier
SisN	sister's niece	S/Ldr	Squadron Leader
SisR	sister in religion	SldS	soldier's son
SisS	sister's son	SldW	soldier's wife
SJ	Society of Jesus	Sle	Sleswick
SJD	Doctor of Juridical Science	SLEIF	Statue of Liberty Ellis Island Foundation
SK/Sask	Saskatchewan, Canada	slg	(1) sealing (2) sine legit (without legitimate issue)
Skarab	Skaraborg, Sweden	Sli	Sligo, Republic of Ireland
Skbg	Skanderborg, Denmark	SLI/SLIG	Salt Lake Institute of Genealogy, Utah Genealogical Association, P.O. Box 1144, Salt Lake City, UT 84110
SKIT	St. Kitts		
sl/SL	(1) *sine loco* (without place) (2) slain (3) son-in-law	SliI	Sligo County, Ireland
SL	Savitz Library, Glassboro State College, Glassboro, NJ	SLIP	Serial Line Internet Protocol (Computer term)
		Slippe	Schaumburg-Lippe, Germany
SL	Scotland	Slk	Selkirkshire, Scotland
SL	Select List (e.g., National Archives select list)	SLK	Slovakia
		SLMn	slaughter man
SL/SLT	Salt Lake City, Utah LDS Temple	Sln/Kpr	saloon keeper
Sla/Slav	(1) Slavic (2) Slavonia (3) Slavonian	sl/o	slave of
SLAKE	Salt Lake City, Utah LDS Temple	SLO	Slovakia
s.l.a.n.	*sine loco, anno, vel nomine*	SLO	State Library of Ohio, 65 South Front Street, Columbus, OH 43215-4163
SLC	Family History Library, 35 North West Temple Street, Salt Lake City, UT 84150	SLOUI	St. Louis, Missouri LDS Temple
SLC	Salt Lake City, Utah	s.l.p.	*sine legitima prole*
SLCL	St. Louis County Library	slphr	sulphur
sld	sealed (LDS Church term)	SLPL	Saint Louis Public Library, St. Louis, MO

slr	sailor		smstrs	seamstress
sls	sales		Smstrss	Seamstress
SlSn	sister-in-law's son		smt	summit
SLT	*Salt Lake Tribune*, Salt Lake City, Utah		Smth	smith
s-m	twice monthly		SMtr	sub-matron
sm/sma	small		SMU	Southern Methodist University, Dallas, TX 75275
Sm/SMot	stepmother		S.'Mul	Suder' Mulasysla
SM	(1) Master of Science (2) Samoa LDS Temple (3) schoolmaster (4) Sergeant Major (5) service mark of the Board for Certification of Genealogists (6) South America (7) Step-mother		sn	(1) san (2) *santa* (3) *santo* (4) *sine* (5) stranger
			SN	(1) Santo Domingo (2) Santiago Chile LDS Temple (3) Sweden
SMan	salesman		Snaef	Snaefellsnessysla
S.'Manld	Sodermanland		SNCA	Society of North Carolina Archivists, P.O. Box 20448, Raleigh, NC 27619
SMAR	St. Martins			
S.'Marit	Seine' Maritime		SNep	step-nephew
SMCGS	San Mateo County Genealogical Society, 25 Tower Road, P.O. Box 5083, San Mateo, CA 94402		sngl	single
			SNI	Step-niece
			SNie	step-niece
SMD	General Society of Mayflower Descendants, 4 Winslow Street, Plymouth, MA 02360		SnLD	son-in-law's daughter
			SnLS	son-in-law's son
SMEI	Saxony Meiningen		SnLW	son-in-law's wife
SMGd	granddaughter's stepmother		SnML	son's mother-in-law
SMjr	sgt. major		snr	senior
Sml/SMoL	stepmother-in-law		SnSi	son's siter
Smmr/Comp	Summer Complaint		SNur	sick nurse
			SnWS	son's wife's sister
Smn	Seaman		s/o	son of
smnry	seminary		So	(1) soldier (2) Somerset, England (3) South (4) Southern
Smoa	Samoa Islands			
SMTP	Simple Mail Transfer Protocol (computer term)			
SMSA	Standard Metropolitan Statistical Area			

SO	(1) Seoul, Korea LDS Temple (2) Sergeant Ordnance (3) Son (4) South (Dixie) (5) Survivors' Originals	SOLINET	Southeastern Library Network
SOA	Society of Ohio Archivists, 10825 East Boulevard, Cleveland, OH 44106	solr	solicitor
SOA	South America	Som/Soms	Somerset, England
soc/socs	society, societies	SOM/ SOME/Somst	Somersetshire, England
Soc, Cincinnati	The Society of Cincinnati	SoMsU	Southern Mississippi University, Hattiesburg, MS
Soc Gen	Society of Genealogists, 14 Charterhouse Buildings, Goswell Road, London, England EC1M 7BA	son	son
		SonC	son's child
sociol	sociology	SonD	son's daughter
socl	social	SonF	son's father
Soc of Col Wars	General Society of Colonial Wars, 840 Woodbine Avenue, Glendale, OH 45246	SonL/ son-i-l	son-in-law
		SonS	son's son
Soc of Whiskey Rebellion	Society of the Whiskey Rebellion of 1794, 3311 Columbia Pike, Lancaster, PA 17603	Sons & Dau	National Society Sons and Daughters of the Pilgrims of Pilgrims
		Sons of Rep	Sons of the Republic of Texas
Soc Sec	Social Security		
SOcu	sole occupant	Sons Union	Sons of the Union Veterans of the Civil War, 411 Bartlett Veterans Street, Lansing, MI 48915
Soc, War of	General Society of the War of 1812, P.O. Box 106, Mendenhall, PA 19337	SonW	Son's wife
Sodmld	Sodermanland, Sweden	Source Guide	Family History SourceGuide™
SOF/S.Af	South Africa	SOS	(1) Secretary of State (2) international distress signal
SOG/SoG	Society of Genealogists, 14 Charterhouse Buildings, Goswell Road, London, England EC1M 7BA	SOT	Spirit of the Times, Batavia, Clermont County
SoHCUNC	Southern Historical Collection, University of North Carolina, Chapel Hill, NC	Southern Dames of Amer	National Society Southern Dames of America, 414 North Walnut Street, P.O. Box 43, Florence, AL 35631
Sok	jurisdiction (Scotland)	Southton	Hampshire
sol/sold/ soldr	soldier	Sov Col Soc Amer of Royal Desc	Sovereign Colonial Society, Americans of Royal Descent, P.O. Box 27112, Philadelphia, PA 19118
Sol	Solomon		

sp	(1) *sine prole; sans progeny* (without issue; childless) (2) spinster (3) spouse(s) (4) spring	SPNEA	Society for the Preservation of New England Antiquities, 141 Cambridge Street, Boston, MA 02114
SP	(1) James Balfour Paul, *Scots Peerage*, 9 vols. (1904-1914) (2) São Paulo Brazil LDS Temple (3) sealing to parents (an LDS term). A child is sealed to his/her parents in an LDS temple (4) Shore Patrol (5) signed photograph (6) South Pacific (7) Spanish (8) spring (9) State Papers (10) Symmes Purchase	Spnl Dis	Spinal Disease
		spnr	spinner
		SpPL	Spokane Public Library, West 906 Main Avenue, P.O. Box 1826, Spokane, WA 99210-1826
SP/Spa/ SPN/SPAI	Spain	spr	(1) spinster (2) sponsor
sp?	spelling is questionable	sprs.	springs
SPAM	unsolicited junk e-mail	sps	*sine prole supersite* (without surviving issue)
SPAR	Women's Coast Guard Reserves	spur	*spurius, spuria* (illegitimate)
SPAUL	São Paulo, Brazil LDS Temple	spy	spy
SPCK	Society for the Propagating (Promoting) of Christian Knowledge (British), Holy Trinity Church, Marylebone Road, London, England NW1 4DU	sq/sqr	square
		Sq	(1) Squadron (2) St. Helena
SP Dom	State Papers, Domestic	SQ	Sergeant Quartermaster
spec	(1) special (2) specialist	sqd	squad
spell	(1) spelling (2) spelled	sqdn	squadron
spg(s)	spring(s)	SQL	Stuctured Query Language
		sq. mi.	square mile(s)
SPG	Society for the Propagation of the Gospel (British), Partnership House, 157 Waterloo Road, London, England SE1 8XA	Sr/Sr/Sor	(1) Senior (2) Señor (3) servant (4) Sir (5) sister (6) soror (7) Surrey, England
SPHQ	*Swedish Pioneer Historical Quarterly*	SR	General Society Sons of the Revolution, 600 South Central Avenue, Glendale, CA 91204
spin	spinster	SR	(1) Scholarly Resources (2) Senior (3) Seven Ranges (4) son of the Revolution (5) Supplementary (or Special) Reserve
spkr	speaker		
spl	(1) *sine prole legitima* (without legitimate issue) (2) special	Sra	Señora
SPL	Seattle Public Library, 1000 Fourth Avenue, Seattle, WA 98104	SRAM	Static Random-Access Memory
		SRB	Serbia
spm	*sine prole mascula* (without male issue)	src	source
SPN	Spain	SRD	Superintendent Registrar's District (British)

SrgnMte	Surgeon's Mate	SSDMF	Social Security Death Master File
SrgO	surgical officer	SSE	South Southeast
SrgS	sergeant's son	Ssgt	staff sergeant
Srgt	sergeant	SSHRCC	Social Sciences and Humanities Research Council of Canada, University of Ottawa, Ontario, Canada KIN 6N5
sr-in-l	sister-in-law		
srnms	surnames	Ssi/SSi	step-sister
sr/o	sister of	SSI	Social Security Index (available through FamilySearch, the Internet, and on compact discs)
SRO	Scottish Record Office, HM General Register House, Princes Street, Edinburgh EH1 3YY Scotland		
		Ssil/SSiL	step-sister-in-law
SRO	standing room only	SSis	step-sister
srs	seniors	SSL	step-son-in-law
SRT	Sons of the Republic of Texas, SRT Office, 1717 Eighth Street, Bay City, Texas 77414	SSN	Social Security number (Social Security Administration, Baltimore, MD)
		SSnC	stepson's child
srtr	sorter	SSnD	stepson's daughter
SRUD	Schwarzberg Rudolstadt	SSnL	stepson-in-law
srv	(1) served (2) service	SSnS	stepson's son
ss/SS	(1) scilicet (2) south side (3) steamship (4) supra scriptum (as written above, that is to say; a form of greeting used to open charters, etc.)	SSnW	stepson's wife
		Ss/o	stepson of
SS	(1) Saints (2) *Scottish Studies* (3) sealing to spouse (an LDS temple ordinance of uniting a couple for time and eternity) (4) stepson	SSon	stepson
		SSON	Schwarzburg Sondershausen
		SSR	Soviet Socialist Republic
SSA	Social Security Administration, Baltimore, MD 21201	SST	supersonic transport
		SSW	South Southwest
SSAN	Social Security account number (Social Security Administration, Baltimore, MD 21201)	st	(1) stanza (2) state (3) street (4) student
SSC	Solicitor in the Supreme Court (British)	St	(1) non-Biblical saints (2) Saint (when used as a prefix; for example, St. Peter's Church) (3) sainte (4) street
SSDB	Social Security Death Benefits (Social Security Administration, Baltimore, MD 21201)		
SSDI	U.S. Social Security Death Index (available through FamilySearch, the Internet, and on compact disc)	St	Staffordshire, England

St/Bt/Plt	steamboat pilot	stepdau	stepdaughter
ST	(1) Scotland (2) stock in trade (3) State (4) Stockholm Sweden LDS Temple	Steph/ Steph[n]	Stephen
sta	(1) station (2) status	stereo	stereotyper
sta eng	stationary engineer	stew/stewd	steward
Staf	staff	STF	Staffordshire
STAF/Staff	Staffordshire, Great Britain	STG	Scholarly Technology Group
StaffOf	staff officer	stge	storage
Staffordsh[e]	Staffordshire	STH	St. Helena Crown Colony
Staffs	Stafford (England)	Sthld	Southold
Stand. Dict.	standard dictionary	Sthmptn	Southampton
Star	*The Latter-day Saints' Millennial Star*	STHO	St. Thomas
Stat	(1) statistical (2) statistician (3) statute	STI	Stirlingshire
STB	*Sacrae Theologiae Baccalaureus* (Bachelor of Sacred Theology)	STIR/Stirl	Stirling, Scotland
StbB	stableboy	StkH	Stockhausen
StbH	stable help	Stkhm	Stockholm, Sweden
StBL	stepbrother-in-law	stkp	storekeeper
StbM	stableman	stkr	stoker
St Chm	state chairman	Stl	(1) Sentinel (2) Stirlingshire, Scotland
std	standard	StL	St. Louis, Missouri
STD	*Sacrae Theologiae Doctore* (Doctor of Sacred Theology)	S-Tlg	Sor-Trondelag, Norway
St David's Soc of NY	Saint David's Society of the State of New York, 71 West 23rd Street, New York, NY 10010	StLGS	St. Louis Genealogical Society
		StLPL	St. Louis Public Library, 1301 Olive Street, St. Louis, MO 63103
Ste	(1) Saint (Sainte-feminine) (2) Suite	STM	Master of Sacred Theology
SteB	Steinsberg/burg	stmboatman	steam boatman
sten	stenographer	stmbtngner	steamboat engineer
step	step	stmbtpilot	steam boat pilot

stmftr	steamfitter
STMP	Simple Mail Tansfer Protocol
stn	(1) station (2) *stilo novo* (new style of dating a document)
stn cutter	stone cutter
St Nicholas	The Saint Nicholas Society of the City of New York, Soc of NY 122 East 58th Street, New York, NY 10022
Stn/Msn	Stone Mason
stnqurier	stone querrier
STOCK	Stockholm, Sweden LDS Temple
stovetnmct	stove & tin merchant
STP	Professor of Sacred Theology
str	setter
Strel	Strelitz
strg	stranger
Strkbg	Starkenburg, Hess-Dermstadt
strm	(1) storeroom (2) stream
strs	seamstress
st sprnkl	street sprinkler
StSL	stepsister-in-law
STT	St. Thomas Isl.
stud	study
Student mn	student for ministry
studt	student
Stu law	student of law
stu med	student of medicine
STUT	Stuttgart
STV	St. Vincent Isl.

stvdr	stevedore
Su	superintendent
Su/Sun	Sunday
SU	(1) Soviet Union (USSR) (2) Sturo Branch of the California State Library, San Francisco
sub	(1) as in sub-Sheriff, a deputy or chief assistant (2) subsistence (3) substitute (4) suburb
subj	subject, subjective
subp	subpoena
subst	substantive; substantial
suc	succeeded
succ	successively
sud	sudden
SUD	Sudan
suf	suffix
SUF/ SUFF/Suf/ Suff	Suffolk, Great Britain
suff/sufft/ sufftly	sufficient, sufficiently
Suic/by/L	Suicide by Loderium
suite	suit, as at law
Sul	Sultzburg
sum	summer
summ	summoned
Sun	(1) step-uncle (2) Sunday
suo juris	in his (or her) right
sup	(1) superior (2) supply (3) supra; above
superl	superlative

SUP News | *Sons of Utah Pioneers News*, 3301 E 2920 S, Salt Lake City, UT 84109-4260

supp/suppl | supplement

Supr | superintendent

supra | above

Supss | superioress

supt | superintendent

suptcoalco | Supt. Madison County Coal Co.

supt gaswk | Supt. Gas works

SupV | supervisor

supvr | supervisor

sur | survived

SUR/ SURR/Surr | Surrey, Great Britain

SurA | surgical assistant

surg | surgeon

SurGen | The Surgeon General

SURI | Surinam

sur mate | surgeon's mate

surr | (1) superior (2) surrender

Surr | (1) Surrey, England (2) surrogate

surv | survived

surv/svg | survived, surviving

sus | Suspended

Sus | Susanna

SUS/SUSS/ Suss | Sussex, England

Sut | Sutherland, Scotland

SUT/ SUTH/Suth | Sutherland, Scotland

SUV | Sons of Union Veterans, 411 Bartlett Street, Lansing, MI 48915

SUVCW | Sons of Union Veterans of the Civil War, 411 Bartlett Street, Lansing, MI 48915

sv | *sub verbo, sub voce* (under the word)

Sv | Sohn von (son of)

SV | Sons of Veterans, 411 Bartlett Street, Lansing, MI 48915

Svbg | Svendborg, Denmark

SVGA | Super Video Graphics Adapter (Super VGA)

SVIN | St. Vincent

SV-PAF-UG | Silicon Valley PAF Users Group, P.O. Box 23670, San Jose, CA 95153-3670

svt | servant

sw | (1) semi-weekly (2) southwest (3) swear, swore

SW | (1) Southwest (2) Swiss LDS Temple (3) Switzerland

Sw.A | Southwest Africa

SWA | Swaziland

Swab | Swabia

Swal/SWale | South Wales

swch | switch

SWD/ SWE/SWED/ Swed/Swede | Sweden

Swedish Col Soc | The Swedish Colonial Society, 916 Swanson Street, Philadelphia, PA 19147

SWEE | Saxony Weimar Elisenach

Swei | South Weimer

swep | sweep

SWH	Swarthmore/Haverford
Swi/SWIT/ SWT	Switzerland
SwiD	son's wife's daughter
SWiS	son's wife's son
SWISS	Swiss LDS Temple
switchtndr	switch tender
Switz/Swtz/ Swit	Switzerland
swmchnagt	sawing machine agent
swmm	saleswoman
SWOGS	Southwest Oklahoma Genealogical Society, P.O. Box 148, Lawton, OK 73502-0148
SWT	Switzerland
swtchmn	switchman
swth	sweetheart
SWZ/Switz	Switzerland
Sx	Sussex, England
SX	Saxony, Germany
SXL	step-sister-in-law
Sxw	Saxe Wissnar
syn	(1) his (2) synonym, -ous
SYR/SYRI	Syria
sys	system
SYSOP	system operator
Sz	Santa Cruz

T

t   (1) testamentary (2) tomus (3) turns of microfilm handle (4) teaspoon (5) *tempore* (in the time of)

T   (1) card already at LDS temple (2) National Archives microfilm series (3) tablespoon (4) Tag(e), day(s) (5) tax substitutes for censuses (6) Thursday (7) township (legal land description) (8) Treasury, Public Record Office, Kew, England (9) Tuesday

T/   temporary

T9   LDS temple originated family group

T99   Special handling, LDS temple code

T000001   110 year file (manual) used with Family History Library, Salt Lake City, Utah

T000011   TIB Conversion number, Family History Library, Salt Lake City, Utah

TA   Papeete, Tahiti LDS Temple

T/A   trading as; under the name of

Tafel   nickname for a short version of an Ahnentafel chart

tag   label used in PAF notes (Personal Ancestral File)

TAG   *The American Genealogist.* David L. Greene, P.O. Box 398, Demorest, GA 30535-0398

TAI   Taiwan

TAIPE   Taipei, Taiwan LDS Temple

tak   taken

talr   tailor

Tanstaafl   (1) There ain't no such thing as a free lunch (2) BBS name in Akron

TAst   trade assistant

TAT   Tatnall tombstone Collection

tb   tuberculosis

TBA   The Bible Archives

tbsp   tablespoon

TC   Technology Center

TC   The Constitutionalist, Newark, Licking Co.

TCHA   Tippecanoe County Historical Association, Wetherill Historical Resource Center, Alameda McCollough Library, 909 South Street, Lafayette, IN 47901

t&c mct   tin & copper merchant

tchr   teacher

tchr bkkg   teacher-book keeping

tchr lang   teacher of languages

tchr rhet   rhetoric teacher

TchS   teacher's son

TClk   telegraph clerk

TCP/IP   Transmission Control Protocol/Internet Protocol

T/C/Sch   Tr. Of Com. School

TCWAAS   *Trans. Cumberland and Westmorland Antiq. Arch. Soc.*

Td   *Tochter des, Tochter der* (daughter of)

TD   Territorial Decoration

TDGNHAS   *Trans. Dumfries. & Galloway Nat. Hist. Arch. Soc.*

Teachings   *Teachings of the Prophet Joseph Smith*, comp. by Joseph Fielding Smith

tech	(1) technical (2) technician (3) technology
techn	technology
TEI	Text Encoded Initiative
tel	telephone
teleg	telegraph
telegr opr	telegraph operator
telev	television
TelG	telegraphist
Telm	Telemark, Norway
temp	(1) temporary (2) tempore (living in time of) (3) temporarily
temp lctr	temperance lecturer
ten	(1) tenant (2) tenure
Tenn/TN	Tennessee
tent	tenant
tent/ten^t	tenement
ter/terr	(1) terrace (2) territorial (3) territory
Ter	Teroll
TERR	Territory
term	terminal
TeSL	Tennessee State Library and Archives, 403 Seventh Avenue North, Nashville, TN 37243-0312
test	testified
test/ testam^t/testa	testament
testr	testator
Tex/TX	Texas
TFE	The Family Edge (genealogy software program)

Tffn	Tiffin-Seneca Public Library, Tiffin
TFGS	The Fairbanks Genealogical Society, P.O. Box 60534, Fairbanks, AK 99706-0534
TFT	Thin Film Translator
TG	Nuku Alofa, Tonga Temple
TG	*The Genealogist*, American Society of Genealogists, Picton Press, P.O. Box 250, Rockport, ME 04856-0250
TGC	The Genealogical Companion (freeware Windows print utility)
Tgph/Op	Telegraph Operator
TGS	Topeka Genealogical Society, P.O. Box 4048, Topeka, KS 66604-0048
TGS	Tulsa Genealogical Society, P.O. Box 585, Tulsa, OK 74101-0585
TGSI	*Trans. Gaelic Society of Inverness*
Th/Thurs	Thursday
TH	(1) Territory of Hawaii (2) Town History
THA	Thailand
THAGS	Humble Texas Area Genealogical Society
ThD	Doctor of Theology
Theo	(1) Theodore (2) Theodosia
theol	(1) theology (2) theological (3) theologian
THI	Thailand
Thist	Thisted, Denmark
tho	though
Tho/Thos/ Tho^{s}Th^s	Thomas
thot	thought
thro	through

Thu/ THURSoc	(1) Thueringia (2) Thursday
Thur	(1) Thueringen (not Germ.) (2) Thursday
TI	Taiwan
TIARA	The Irish Ancestral Research Association, Dept. W, P.O. Box 619, Sudbury, MA 01776
TIB	Temple Index Bureau (card index available at the Family History Library and Brigham Young University, on microfilm), also known as the Temple Records Index Bureau. *See* TRIB.
TIF	Tagged Image File Format (graphic file format)
TIFF	graphics file (graphical format)
til	until
Tip	Tipperary, Republic of Ireland
TIPCOA	Tippecanoe County Area Genealogical Society, Wetherill Historical Resource Center, Alameda McCollough Library, 909 South Street, Lafayette, IN 47901
Tipp	Tipperary, Ireland
TK	Tokyo LDS Temple
TKep	tent keeper
TKey	turnkey
TKHS	Transactions Kansas Historical Society
TLC	The Learning Company, One Athenaeum Street, Cambridge, MA 02142
TM	Teamster (military)
TMG	The Master Genealogist (genealogy software program produced by Wholly Genes, Inc., 5144 Flowertuft Court, Columbia, MD 21044)
TMGW	The Master Genealogist for Windows
TMH	N.B. Lundwall, comp., *Temples of the Most High* (Salt Lake City: Bookcraft, 1968)
tmkpr	timekeeper

Tm. Off	Trademarks Office
tmpl	temple
Tms	Teamster
TMS	(1) Tafel Matching System (e.g., tiny tafels) (2) Tiger Map Service (US Bureau of the Census)
tn	(1) tenant (2) ton (3) town (4) township
TN	(1) Tennessee (2) Trade Name
tndr	tender
Tng	Tonga Islands
TNP	Temple Names Preparation (LDS feature in AncestralQuest)
tnry	tannery
to/to-w	to-wit, e.g., "He addressed the petition to the richest residents of the precinct, to., the Parkeses, the Harrisons, and others."
T.O.	telegraph office
tob/tobo	tobacco
TOB	Tobago, West Indies
TOKYO	Tokyo LDS Temple
TON	Tonga
top	topographical
TOPA	*Transactions of the Oregon Pioneer Association*
Topo. quad	U.S. topographical quadrangle maps
Toro	Toronto, Canada
TORON	Toronto, Ontario LDS Temple
tot	total
Tot/Parals	Total Paralysis
tp	(1) this parish (2) title page
tp/twp	township

TP	Taipei, Taiwan LDS Temple		TRIP	Tripoli
t & p	true and perfect		TRK	Turkey
TPJS	Joseph Fielding Smith, comp., *Teachings of the Prophet Joseph Smith* (Salt Lake City: Deseret Book Co., 1976)		trl	trail
			TRLN	Triangle Research Libraries Network
tpk/tpke	turnpike		trlr	trailer
tpm	title page mutilated		Trm	Trumpeter
tpw	title page wanting		trmp	tramp
tr	(1) town record(s) (2) transferred (3) translated (4) translation (5) troop		trmr	trimmer
			trnmn	trainman
Tr.	Trinitatis, Trinity (8th Sunday after Easter)		trnr	trainer
TR	(1) Town Records (2) traditional (3) transcribed will record		trop	tropical
			trp	troop
TRAM	The Texas Research Administrators Group		trps	troops
tran	transactions		trpt	trumpeter
trans	(1) transcription (2) transfer/-red (3) transitive, translated (4) transport (5) transportation		ts	(1) tombstone (2) typescript
			TS	Treasury Solicitor, Public Record Office, Kew, Richmond, Surrey, England TW9 4DU
trans/transl	translator			
transcr	(1) transcribed (2) transcriber (3) transcript (-ion)		TSEL	Texas State Electronic Library
Transcript	*The Boston Evening Transcript*		TSGS	Texas State Genealogical Society, 2507 Tannehill, Houston, TX 77008-3052
transfrd	transferred			
trav	traveler; traveling		TSHA	Texas State Historical Association, Sid Richardson Hall, University Station, Austin, TX 78712
trd	trading			
tres/treas	treasurer/-y		TskM	taskmaster
TRI	Trinidad		TSLA	Tennessee State Library and Archives, 403 Seventh Avenue North, Nashville, TN 37243-0312
trib	tribune			
TRIB	Temple Records Index Bureau (at Family History Library, on microfilm). *See* TIB.		tsp	teaspoon
			tss	typescript
Trin	Trinity		tstr	tester
TRIN	Trinidad		TTYL	Talk to you Later

Tu/Tue/Tues	Tuesday
TUN	Tunisia
tunl	tunnel
tunr	tuner
Tuon	tuition
Tur.	Turnpike
TUR/Trky/TURK	Turkey
Tusc	Tuscarawas County Ohio OGS chapter, newsletter, P.O. Box 141, New Philadelphia, OH 44663-0141
TUSC	Tuscany
tutr	tutor
Tunx	Tunxis dialect
TVA	Tennessee Valley Authority, 400 West Summit Hill Drive, Knoxville, TN 37902
tvrn	tavern
tw	tri-weekly
Twif	traveler's wife
twin	twin
twn	town
Twn Clk	Town Clerk
twp	township
twr	tower
TX	(1) Tax List (2) Texas
TxSL	Texas State Library, P.O. Box 12927, Austin, TX 78711-2927
TXSSAR	Texas Society of the Sons of the American Revolution
Ty	territory

typ	typist
Typh Fev	Typhoid Fever
typo	typographical
Tyr	(1) Tyrol (Austria) (2) Tyrone, Northern Ireland

U

u.	*und* (and)
U	(1) ultimo (last) (2) uncle (3) unstated
UALC	Utah Academic Library Consortium
UAP	(1) Universal Access to Publications (2) Universal Availability of Publications
UB	United Brethren
UBC	Universal Bibliographic Control
uc	(1) under care (Quaker meeting) (2) upper-case
UC	Upper Canada (i.e., Haut-Canada or Ontario)
UCC	United Church of Christ
UCGA	Upper Cumberland Genealogical Association, P.O. Box 575, Cookeville, TN 38501-0575
UCLA	University of California at Los Angeles
UCS	Utah Computer Society
u.d.	(1) *ultimo die* (final day) (2) *und des, und der* (and of)
U.D.	(1) University of Delaware Morris Library, South College Avenue, Newark, DE 19717-5267 (2) urban district
UDC	United Daughters of the Confederacy, UDC Memorial Building, 328 North Boulevard, Richmond, VA 23220-4057
UDC	(1) Universal Decimal Classification (2) Urban District Council
UDE	Universal Data Entry (a computer program used by the Family History Department, Salt Lake City, Utah)
UEL	United Empire Loyalists
UELAC	United Empire Loyalists Association of Canada, 50 Baldwin ST. Suite 202, Toronto, Ontario, Canada M5T 1L4
UF	United Free Church (Scotland)
UFDL	Ultimate Family Data Library
UFL	P.K. Yonge Library, University of Florida, Gainesville, FL
Ufrank	Unterfranken, Bavaria
UFT	Ultimate Family Tree (genealogy software program)
UGA	Utah Genealogical Association, P.O. Box 1144, Salt Lake City, UT 84110
UGGS	Utah Germanic Genealogy Society, P.O. Box 510898, Salt Lake City, UT 84151-0898
UGHM	*Utah Genealogical and Historical Magazine*
UGRR	Underground Railroad (used by slaves in antebellum America to escape to Canada)
UGS	Utah Genealogical Society. See GSU/Genealogical Society of Utah
UHF	Ulster Historical Foundation, 12 College Square East, Belfast, BT1 6DD, Northern Ireland
Uhl	Uhlenburg
UHQ	*Utah Historical Quarterly*
UJA	United Jewish Appeal
UK	(1) United Kingdom (2) Unknown
UKOLN	United Kingdom Office of Library Networking
UKOP	United Kingdom Official Publications
UKR	Ukraine

UKRA   Ukraine

Ul/uncL/   uncle-in-law
uncle-i-l

ULA   Utah Library Association

Ulc/Bowels   Ulcerated Bowels

Uli   Ulrich

ult   *ultimo* (last; a date last month; used in letters–as "in your letter of the 13th ult.", ultimate; last month, last week, etc.)

UM   University of Michigan, Ann Arbor, MI

umar/unmar unmarried

UMC   United Methodist Church

UMGBI   *Upper Midwest German Biographical Index*, by Don Heinrich Tolzmann (Bowie, Md.: Heritage Books, 1993)

UMI   University Microfilms, Inc.

UMW   United Mine Workers

un   (1) union (2) unknown

UN   (1) Unknown (2) United Nations

UN/unc/   uncle
uncl

UNBL   University of New Brunswick Library, Fredericton, New Brunswick, Canada

UNCL   University of North Carolina Library, Chapel Hill, NC

UnCr   under care

und/undr   under

undwrtr   underwriter

UnGr   undergraduate

unident   unidentified

unin   union

Unincorp.   Unincorporated

unit   united; uniting

univ   universal

univ/Univ.   university

Univ. Libr.   University Library, West Road, Cambridge, England CB3 9DR

unk/unkn   unknown

UNK   (1) United Kingdom (2) Unknown

un m/   unmarried
unm/unmd

UnNr   undernurse

UNO   United Nations Organization

unorg   unorganized

unp   (1) unpaged (2) unpublished field notes, draft reports

unpub   unpublished

U of A/UA   University of Akron, Akron, OH

U of C/UC   University of Cincinnati, Cincinnati, OH 45221-0113

UOS   United Original Secession

Up.   Upper

UP   (1) United Presbyterian Church (Scotland) (2) United Press (3) United Provinces (India)

UPA   University Publications of America, 4520 East-West Highway, Bethesda, MD 20814-3389

UPC   Universal Product Code

UPER   UMI Periodical Abstracts

UPGS   United Polish Genealogical Society

uphol   upholsterer

UPI   United Press International

upl	using profane language	USCB	United States Census Bureau
UPL	University of Pennsylvania Library, 3420 Walnut Street, Philadelphia, PA 19104	USCC	United States Chamber of Commerce
UPM	United Presbyterian Minister	USC Cav	United States Colored Calvary
Upps	Uppsala, Sweden	USCG	United States Coast Guard
upr	upper	USCGR	United States Coast Guard Reserve
U^{ra}	Ursula	USC Inf	United States Colored Infantry
URAG	Uruguay	USCL	US Congress Lands
urb	urban	USCT	United States Colored Troop(s)
URC	United Reformed Church (Great Britain; mostly Congregational and Presbyterian)	USD 1812	National Society, U.S. Daughters of 1812, 1461 Rhode Island NW, Washington, DC 20005
URL	Uniform Resource Locator (an electronic address for Web pages on the Internet)	us dp mrsh	US Deputy Marshall
URN	Uniform Resource Names	USES	United States Employment Service
URU/ UUG/ URUG	Uruguay	USF	University of South Florida
		USG	United States Government
		USGS	United States Geological Survey
US	United States	USGW	US GenWeb Project
USA	(1) Union of South Africa (2) United States Army (3) United States of America	Ushr	usher
		Usi	Usingen
USAAC	United States Army Air Corps	USIA	United States Information Agency
USAAF	United States Army Air Force	USIGS	United States Internet Genealogical Society
USAC	United States Air Corps	USM	United States Marines
USAF	United States Air Force	USMA	United States Military Academy
USA Inf	United States Army Infantry	USMC	United States Marine Corps
USAMHI	United States Army Military History Institute, Carlisle Barracks, PA 17013-5008	USMCR	United States Marine Corps Reserve
USAR	United States Army Reserve	USMD	United States Military District
USC	United States census	USN	United States Navy
USCA	United States Code Annotated	USNA	United States Naval Academy
USC Art	United States Colored Artillery	USNAC	United States Naval Air Corps

USNAM   United States Naval Academy Museum, 118
            Maryland Avenue, Annapolis, MD 21402-5034

USNG   United States National Guard

USNR   United States Naval Reserve

USO   United Service Organization, 901 M Street SE
            Building 198, Washington, DC 20374

USPG   United Society for the Propagation of the
            Gospel (British), Partnership House, 157
            Waterloo Road, London, England SE1 8XA

USPS   United States Postal Service

USS   United States Ship or Steamer

USSR   Union of Soviet Socialist Republic

USV   United States Volunteers

usw   und so weiter, and so forth

USWPA   United States Works Progress Administration

UT   (1) University of Toledo, Toledo, OH (2) Utah

Utah   early Utah LDS sealing (Pre-Endowment House)

UTL   University of Texas Library, Austin, TX, 78712

Utr/Hem.   Uterine Hemorrhage

UTSCAR   Utah Society, Children of the American
            Revolution

UTSDAR   Utah Society, Daughters of the American
            Revolution

UTSSAR   Utah Society, Sons of the American
            Revolution

ut sup   *ut supra* (as above)

UVL   University of Virginia Library, Charlottesville,
            VA 22903

UV-PAF-   Utah Valley PAF Users Group
UG

UVRFHC   Utah Valley Regional Family History Center,
            Brigham Young University, Provo, UT 84602

ux/uxor/uz (1) Mrs. (2) uxor or uxoris (wife)

V

v	(1) verse (2) *verso* (the back [of a page]) (3) vessel/ship (4) vide, see (5) vidi; see (6) volume(s) (7) von (from)
v/vb	verb
v/vs	versus (against)
V	(1) Vicar (2) Vice (3) Viscount
va	*vixit*
VA	(1) Department of Veterans Affairs (2) U.S. Veterans Administration (3) Vagrancy Arrival
VA/Va	Virginia
V-Ag	Vest–Agder, Norway
val	value, valuation
Val	Valdeck/Waldeck
VALE	Virtual Academic Library Environment
valt	valet
var	variant, variation, various, variously spelled
VARMC	Veterans Affairs Records Management Center
Varmld	Varmland, Sweden
VASSAR	Virginia Society, Sons of the American Revolution
VAT	Value Added Tax (British)
V.'Bard	Vestur' Bardastrandarsysla
VBCL	Virginia Beach Central Library, 4100 Virginia Beach Blvd., Virginia Beach, VA 23452-1767
VBGS	Virginia Beach Genealogical Society, P.O. Box 62901, Virginia Beach, VA 23466-2901
V.'bottn	Vasterbotten
Vbth	Vasterbotten, Sweden
VC	Victoria Cross
VCH	Victoria History of the Counties of England, *Victoria County Histories*
vCnc	virtual Canadian Union Catalogue
VCRP	Virginia Colonial Records Project, The Library of Virginia, 11th Street at Capitol Square, Richmond, VA 23219
vctr	victor
vCuc	Virtual Canadian Union Catalogue
v.d.	various dates
VDM	*Verbi Dei Minister* (minister of the word of God); Voluns Dei Minister
VDT	Visual Display Terminal
VDU	Visual Display Unit
ve/vve	widow
VE	Vagrancy Examination
VEN/ VENE/Venez.	Venezuela
ver	version
verch	daughter
verh.	*verheiratet* (married)
verl.	*verlobt* (engaged)
vet(s)	veteran(s), veterinary

Vet Corps of Artillery, NY	Veteran Corps of Artillery, State of New York Constituting the Military Society of the War of 1812, Seventh Regiment Armory, 643 Park Avenue, New York, NY 10021
vf	(1) vertical file (2) *veuf* (widower)
VFW	Veterans of Foreign Wars, 406 West 34th Street, Kansas City, MO 64111
VG	*The Virginia Genealogist*
VGA	Video Graphics Adapter (array)
VgrD	vagrant's daughter
VgrS	vagrant's son
Vgrt	vagrant
VgrW	vagrant's wife
VGS	Virginia Genealogical Society, 5001 West Broad Street, Suite 115, Richmond, VA 23230-3023
VHS	Virginia Historical Society, P.O. Box 7311, Richmond, VA 23211-0311
V./Hun	Vestur/Hunavatnssysla
vi	(1) verb intransitive (2) visitor
Vi	Vancouver Island, CA
VI	Virgin Islands
via	viaduct
vic	vicinity
vic/vicr	(1) vicar (2) vicarage
VicG	vicegerent
VicP	vice principal
vid.	*viduus, vidua* (widower, widow)
vide	see
VIE	Vietnam
VIGR	Virginia Institute of Genealogical Research

vil	village
Villgn	Villengen, Baden
vills	villas
Vinct/t Vincn	Vincent
Vinzt	Vincent
VIP	very important person
VIR	St. Thomas, Virgin Islands
virdt/verd	verdict, usually of a jury
Virg/Virga	Virginia (woman's name)
Virga	Virginia (the state)
vis	vista
Vis., Visit.	Visitations (of various English counties)
Vis/Visc/ Visct	viscount, viscountess
VisC	visitor's child
VisD	visitor's daughter
ViSL	Virginia State Library, 11th Street at Capitol Square, Richmond, VA 23219-3491
VISL/VI	Virgin Islands
visn	visitation
VisN	visitor's nephew or niece
VisS	visitor's son
vist	visitor
VisW	visitor's wife
vit	vital
Vit Stat	vital statistics
ViU	Virginia University, Charlottesville, VA

VIVA	Virtual Library of Virginia	VR	(1) Vagrancy Removal (2) Village Register, West Union, Adams Co. (3) vital record(s); as an example, Dedham, Mass. VR (town vital records)
vix	lived, also *vixit*		
viz.	*videlicet* (namely)	VRA	Virginia Records Award (Virginia Genealogical Society)
viz't	namely, to wit, that is to say	VRI	Virgin Islands
VL	(1) ville (2) Vulgar Latin	vs./v.	*versus* (against)
vlg	village	VS	Vital statistics
vlt	vault	VSer	visitor's servant
vly	valley	VSis	visitor's sister
v.m.	*vita matris* (during mother's life)	V.Skaft	Vestur' Skaftafellssysla
Vmanld	Vastmanland, Sweden	VSnL	visitor's son-in-law
VMD	(1) Doctor of Veterinary Medicine (2) Virginia Military District (located in Ohio)	Vstf	Vestfold, Norway
		v.t.	verb transitive
Vmst	vice-master	VT	Vermont
VN	Vietnam	VtSL	Vermont State Library, 135 Main Street, Montpelier, VT 05602
V'Norld	Vasternorrland, Sweden		
VNZ	Venezuela	Vt Soc of Col Dames	The Vermont Society of Colonial Dames
VOAA	Veterans of America Association		
voc.	vocative	VtU	Vermont University and State College, Burlington, VT
VOCA	Vermont Old Cemetery Association, P.O. Box 132, Townshend, VT 05353		
		vulc	vulcanizer
vol(s)	(1) volume(s) (2) volunteer(s)	vv	*vice versa* (as used between a first and a middle name which are reversed in some records)
VOM	*Voluns Deus Minister* (minister by the will of God)		
		Vw	view
voters/reg	voter and voter registration records		
vp	*vita patris* (in the father's lifetime)		
VP	Vagrancy Pass		
VP/Vpre	vice president		
VPG	vice president general		

W

w	(1) weekly (2) west (3) when found in a Revolutionary War pension jacket it means widow (4) widow; widowed; widower (5) wife (6) will (source in IGI) (7) with
w/	with
w/1, w/2, w/3	wife no. 1, 2, 3
W	(1) Ward (2) West (3) white (whites); Caucasian (4) wife (5) Wiltshire, England
W/Wed	Wednesday
W3C	World Wide Web Consortium
W12	War of 1812
wa	(1) Ward (2) warden
Wa	(1) Warden (2) Warwickshire, England
WA	(1) Wales (2) Washington (D.C.) LDS Temple (3) Western Australia (4) Widow's Application
WA/Wash	Washington
WAAC	Women's Auxiliary Army Corps
WAAF	Women's Auxiliary Air Force
wab	will and administration record
WAC	(1) washings, annointings, and confirmations (LDS temple ordinances) (2) Women's Army Corps
WAF	Women in the Air Force
wag	wagoner
WagB	wagon boy
wagnmaster	wagon master

WAGS	Waseca Area Genealogy Society, Waseca County Historical Society Museum, Second Avenue and Fourth Street, NE, Waseca, MN 56093
WAGS	Whittier Area Genealogy Society, P.O. Box 4367, Whittier, CA 90607-4367
wai/wait	(1) waiter (2) waitress
WAI	Web Accessibility Initiative
WAIS	Wide Area Information Server (Service)
Wal/Wald/ WalD/Walde/ Waldck	Waldeck, Germany
WAL	Wales
WALD	Waldeck Hesse Nassau
Waldsh	Waldshut, Baden
WALE	Wales
WalNY	Wales, New York
Wapp	Wappinger dialect
WAR/ WARW/ Warw	Warwickshire, Great Britain
ward	ward, reared
warden pen	warden penitentiary
WarH	warehouseman
warrt	warrant
War Ser	war service
Warws/ WARW	(1) Warwick, England (2) Warwickshire

WasDC	Washington, DC
Wash/Wa	Washington
Wash. C.H.	Washington Court House
WASHI	Washington LDS Temple
Washington Fam Desc	Washington Family Descendants
WaSHS	Washington State Historical Society, 315 North Stadium Way, Tacoma, WA 98403
WaSL	Washington State Library, P.O. Box 2475, Olympia, WA 98504-2475
WASP	Women's Air Force Service Pilots
Wat	Waterford, Republic of Ireland
Water	Waterford, Ireland
Waters	Henry F. Waters, *Genealogical Gleanings in England*, 2 vols. 1883-99. Reprint. Baltimore: Genealogical Publishing Co., 1981
Watm	watchman
Wau	Wauldig
WAVES	Women Appointed for Volunteer Emergency Service (US Navy)
WBI	*World Biographical Index* (University Publications of America)
Wbk/WB	will book (probate record)
WbrL	wife's brother-in-law
wc	with costs
w/c	in Quaker records, this means "with consent of"
WC	(1) West Central (2) Widow's Certificate
wch/w^ch	which
WChd	wife's child
WCLAR	Washington Crossing Library of the American Revolution, Washington Crossing, PA

Wclev	West Cleveland, Ohio
W/Cmdr	Wing Commander
WCTU	Women's Christian Temperance Union, Meade, KS 67864
wd/WD	(1) the widow of (2) widow; widowed (3) will dated
Wd/WD	ward
WD	(1) War Department (2) Warranty Deed (3) West Indies
wdr	widower
wds	wounds
We	Westmoreland, England
WE	(1) Wales (2) West (3) West Indies
Wed	Wednesday
Wei	Weimer/Weighains
weibl	weiblich (feminine)
weil	weiland (deceased)
WEIS	Weisenberg
WEL/ WLOT	West Lothian (see *Linlithgow*), Great Britain
Welcome Soc of Pa	The Welcome Society of Pennsylvania, 415 South Croskey Street, Philadelphia, PA 19146
Welsh Soc of Phila	The Welsh Society of Philadelphia, 450 Broadway, Camden, NJ 08103
Wer	Wertenberg/Wurtemburg
Wes	(1) Wessem (2) Westfall (3) Westphalia
WES	Westmoreland
WesD/ WestD	West Darmstadt
WesF	Westfall
WesP/Wesp	Westphalia

west	western	whls boots	wholesale dlr boots & shoe
WEST	Westphalia (Wesfalen)	whlsdrygds	wholesale dry goods merchandise
Westf	Westfalen, Prussia	whls gro	wholesale grocer
Westm/ Westmd/ WMOR	Westmorland, England	whls mct	wholesale merchant
		WHM	*Wisconsin Magazine of History*
Westph	Westfalen	whn	when
Westpr	Westpreussen, Prussia	whol	wholesale
Wex	Wexford, Republic of Ireland	WHOM	Women Historians of the Midwest, Minnesota Women's Bldg., 550 Rice Street, Suite 101, St. Paul, MN 55103
Wexfd	Wexford, Ireland		
wf	(1) the wife of (2) wharf (3) white female (4) wife	Whoop/ Cgh	Whooping Cough
WF	Widow's File	WHR	*Western Humanities Review*
W.Fland	West Vlaanderen	whsemn	warehouseman
wf/o	wife of	wht	white
WFPI	Welfare Fraud Prevention Initiative	WI	(1) West Indies (2) Wife
WFT	World Family Tree (Brøderbund, P.O. Box 760, Fremont, CA 94537-9824)	WI/Wisc	Wisconsin
		Wic	Wicklow, Republic of Ireland
WGAt	wife's grandaunt	Wiccia	Worcestershire
Wgm	wagon master	Wick	Wicklow, Ireland
WGmc	West Germanic	Wickl	Wicklow
Wgn	wagoneer	wid/widw/ wido	(1) widow (of) (2) widowed (3) widower
Wgn/Mkr	Wagon Maker		
Wgnr	waggoner	wid necs	widow's necessaries
WGW	WorldGenWeb (www.worldgenweb.org)	wid/o	widow of
wh	(1) where (2) which (3) who (4) with	widr	widower
WHC	Wisconsin State Historical Society *Collections*, 816 State Street, Madison, WI 53706	WifA	wife's aunt
		WifB	wife's brother
Whi	Whitenburg/Wittenburgh/Whesterburg	WifC	wife's cousin
Whit. Col.	Whitaker Collection		

WifD	wife's daughter		WIND/ WIN	West Indies
wife	wife		Winton	Winchester
WifF	wife's father		WinZip	Windows file compression program
WifM	wife's mother		WIP	Washington International Report
WifN	wife's nephew or niece		WIPO	World Intellectual Property Organization
WifP	wife's parent		Wir/Wirt/ WIRT/WERT	Wirtemburg/Wertenberg
WifS	wife's sister		WiSB	wife's stepbrother
WifU	wife's uncle		Wis/Wisc	Wisconsin
Wig	Wigtownshire, Scotland		WiSD	wife's stepdaughter
WIG	Wigtownshire		WISE	Wales, Ireland, Scotland, England
WiGD	wife's granddaughter		WiSHS	Wisconsin State Historical Society, 816 State Street, Madison, WI 53706
WiGF	wife's grandfather		WiSL	wife's son-in-law
WiGS	wife's grandson		WiSM	wife's stepmother
WIGT/ Wigtwn	Wigtown, Scotland		WiSn	wife's son
WIL/ WILT/Wilts	Wiltshire, Great Britain		WiSS	wife's stepson
WiID	wife's illegitimate daughter		WISU	Wichita State University Library, 1845 Fairmount, Wichita, KS 67260-0068
Wilf/Wilf^d	Wilford		WiSv	wife's servant
Wilh	Wilhelm		wit/wtn	(1) witness (2) witnessed (3) witnesses
Will/ Willm/Willm/ Wm/Wm/ Guliel/Gul	William		Wit	Wittenberg
will pr	will proved		wits	witness(es)
WiIS	wife's illegitimate son		Witt	Wittemberg
Wilts	Wiltshire (England)		Wittl	Wittlage
WIN/WIn	West Indies		Wittn	Wittenberg
WinC	Winthrop College, Rock Hill, SC		WiU	Wisconsin University, Madison, WI
wind	winder			

WJ	John Winthrop, *The History of New England from 1630 to 1649*, ed. James Savage, 2 vols. (Boston, 1853).
wk	(1) walk (2) week (3) work
wk(s)	(1) week(s) (2) works
WK	Waldeck
wkm/Wkm	workman
wkr	worker
WL	(1) Wales (2) Wilmington Institute Library
Wld	Waldic
wldr	welder
Wlo/ W.Loth/ WLOT	West Lothian, Scotland
wls	wells
WLS	Wales
wm	white male
Wm	William
WM	Wesleyan Methodist
Wmak	watchmaker
Wme/ W.Meath	Westmeath, Republic of Ireland
WMF	Windows Metafile
WMG	*Western Maryland Genealogy*
WmGS	Williams County Genealogical Society, Bryan, OH 43506
WMH	*Wisconsin Magazine of History*
WmHS	Williams County Historical Society, 13660 Country Home Road, Bowling Green, OH 43401
WMOR	Westmoreland

WMQ	*William and Mary Quarterly*
Wmst	workmistress
W.Mth	West Meath, Ireland
WN	(1) Caucasian-Negro (2) World News
Wndr	wanderer
W. Nian	West Niantic dialect
WNRC	Washington National Records Center, National Archives and Records Administration, 4205 Suitland Road, Suitland, MD 20746-8001
WNS	Women's News Service
wnt	wants
WNT	Winterthur Museum Library
WNW	West Northwest
WNYGS	Western New York Genealogical Society
w/o	(1) wife of (2) without
Wo	Worcestershire, England
WO	(1) presumed to mean white oak when found in old records (2) War Office (England) (3) Warrant Officer (4) widow's original
Women Desc Anc & Hon Artillery Co	National Society, Women Descendants of the Ancient and Honorable Artillery Company
womn	woman
Wood	Wood County Public Library, 251 North Main Street, Bowling Green, OH 43402
WOR/ WORC/ Worc/Worcs	Worcestershire, England
Worcs	Worcester
WorldCat	OCLC Online Union Catalog
Wort/Ger	Wortenberg, Germany
WOW	Woodmen of the World

WP/wp   (1) white poll(s), e.g., white poll tax (2) will probated (3) will proved or proven

w/pwr   with power

WPA   Works Progress Administration

WPB   War Production Board

WPG   WordPerfect Graphic format

WPGS   Western Pennsylvania Genealogical Society; Historical Society of Western Pennsylvania, 4338 Bigelow Boulevard, Pittsburgh, PA 15213-2695

WPI   Worcester Polytechnic Institute

WPL   Westminster Public Libraries (Archives Dept), Victoria Library, Buckingham Palace Road, London, England SW1

WPL   (1) Public Library, Whitehaven, England (2) Worcester Public Library

wpm   words per minute

WPNS   Widow Pensioned

Wprus/ WPRU   West Prussia

WR   (1) West Riding (2) Wurttemberg

WRA   War Relocation Authority (World War II, U.S. Department of War)

WrdM   wardsman

wrdn   warden

wrd/o   ward of

wrdr   warder

WrdW   wardswoman

WRENS   Women's Royal Naval Service

WRHS   Western Reserve Historical Society, 10825 East Boulevard, Cleveland, OH 44106-1788

wrkd   worked

Wrs   Wrappers (paper binding)

W-Rs   White Russia

WrSt   Wright State University Archives, 3640 Colonel Glenn Highway, Dayton, OH 45431

WRsv   Western Reserve Historical Society, 10825 East Boulevard, Cleveland, OH 44106-1788

WRY   West Riding of Yorkshire, England

ws   west side

w(s)s   warrant(s) signed

WS/W.S.   (1) Writer to the Signet; a solicitor (2) West Saxon

WSC   Worcester State College

WSDa   wife's sister's daughter

WSGS   Washington State Genealogical Society, P.O. Box 1422, Olympia, WA 98507

WSGS   Wisconsin State Genealogical Society, P.O. Box 5106, Madison, WI 53705-0106

wshr wmn   washer woman

WSI   West Indies

WSis   wife's step sister

wsky drnkr   whisky drinker

WSL   William Salt Library, Stafford, England

WSSn   wife's sister's son

Wsthmptn   Westhampton

Wstmld   Westmorland

WSU   Wright State University, Special Collections and Archives, Paul Laurence Dunbar Library, Dayton, OH 45435-0001

WSW   West Southwest

wt/Wt   waiter

wt/wth/w[th]   with

Wt   Isle of Wight, England

wtchmn	watchman
wtn	witness
Wtr	(1) waiter (2) water
Wu/Wur/Wurt	Wurtemberg, Germany
Wuertt/WUR/Wurt	Wuerttemberg
WURT	Wurtemberg
Wut	Wuttenberg
Wuv	Wustenberg/Wistenburg
WV/W VA	West Virginia
WVAr	West Virginia Department of Archives and History, 1900 Kanawha Blvd East, Charleston, WV 23505-0300
WVGS	Willamette Valley Genealogical Society, Oregon State Library, P.O. Box 2083, Salem, OR 97308
ww	(1) widow (2) will written
WW	World War
WW1/WW2	World War 1; World War 2
WWI-L	World War I Document Archive (Brigham Young University)
Wwe	Witwe (widow)
Wwer	Witwer (widower)
WWJ	*Wilford Woodruff's Journal*, Scott G. Kenney, ed., 9 vols. (Midvale, Utah: Signature books, 1983)
ww/o	widow of
wwr	widower
WWrt	wheelwright
WWW	World Wide Web (a network of documents and files on the Internet)
WY/Wyo	Wyoming

WyAR	Wyoming State Archives and History Department, 2301 Central Avenue, Cheyenne, WY 82002
WYSI-WYG	what you see is what you get

X

X   (1) a person who signed a document with an "X" (e.g., a groom signed a bond with an "X") (2) by, in dimensions (3) Christ (4) Christian (5) cross (6) equivalent to Xp (q.v.) (7) unknown (8) was not married

xch   exchange

X-cut   cross-cut

Xena   Green County District Library, Xenia, OH

Xing   crossing

XL   Sister-in-law

Xmas   Christmas

XML   Extensible Markup Language (computer term)

x/mo.   times per month

XMS   Extended Memory System

Xn   Christian

Xnty   Christianity

Xp   (Actually the Greek letters chi and rho), Chr(ist), often used as a part of someone's name as in Xpmann = Christmann or Xpian—Christian; sometimes found without the rho as is Xtopher = Christopher

Xped   christened

Xper/Xr   Christopher

Xpofer   Christopher

Xr   Christian

XSL   Extensible Stylesheet Language (computer term)

xt   next, as in next friend

Xt   Christ

xt.court/ xt.crt   next term of court

Xtian/xtian   Christian

Xty   Christianity

x/wk   times per week

x/yr   times per year

Y

y	(1) th, as in y^e (2) year (s) (3) yearly (4) young
Y	Young Men's Christian Association
Y2K	year 2000 computer issue, often known as the "Millennium Bug"
YAS	Yorkshire Archaeological Society, Claremont, 23 Clarendon Road, Leeds, England LS2 9NZ
YC	Yacht Club
YCGSJ	*York County Genealogical Society Journal*
yd	(1) graveyard (2) yard
YD	*York Deeds*
ydmn	yardman
ydmstr	yardmaster
yds	yards
ye/y^e	(1) the (2) you (3) your
YEM	People's Republic of Yemen
yeo/yeom	yeoman/yeomanry
y^{ere}	there
YG/YUG	Yugoslavia
YGC	Your Genealogy Conference, Provo, Utah
YHCIL	Youngstown Historical Center of Labor and Industry, P.O. Box 533, 151 West Word Street, Youngstown, OH 44501
y^{is}	this
YKS	Yorkshire
ym	them

YM	Yearly Meeting (Quaker)
YMCA	Young Men's Christian Association
-y-m-d	years, months, days
YMHA	Young Men's Hebrew Association
YN	Yukon
yngr	younger
yngs/yngst/ yngste/young	youngest
Yo Pub Lib	Youngstown Ohio Public Library, 305 Wick Avenue, Youngstown, OH 44503
yor/yr	younger
YORK/ Yorks/YRKS	Yorkshire, England
yr.	(1) year(s) (2) younger (3) your
yrbk	yearbook
YrdB	yard boy
YrdM	yardman
yre/yr(s)	year(s)
yrly	yearly
yrs	yours
YS	York State
y^s	this
yst	youngest
yt/y^t	(1) that (2) yet
YT/YUK	Yukon Territory, Canada

ytd	year to date
YU/YUL	Yale University Library, New Haven, CT
YU/YUG/ YUGO	Yugoslavia
Yuc	Yucatan
YWCA	Young Women's Christian Association
YWHA	Young Women's Hebrew Association

Z

Zach/ Zach^a/ Zachar^a	Zachariah
ZAN	Zanzibar
Zech.	Zechariah
Zeph	Zephaniah
Zet/ZET	Zetland/Shetland, Scotland
ZIP	Zone Improvement Plan
ZLL	Zion Lutheran Church
Znvl	John McIntire Public Library, Zanesville
Zur	Zurich, Canton of
Zwick	Zwickau, Saxony

Appendix

SYMBOLS

[ ]	original record illegible or missing	$/dol	dollar
---	no information given	¢/c/ct	cent
~	ca, circa, approximately	©	copyright
...	information illegible	£	pound sterling
★	(1) date of birth/born (2) name omitted	I£	Isreali pound
(★)	born illegitimate	%	percent
=	date of marriage	c/o	in care of
+	(1) date of death (2) information in note field (3) or later	&	and
:	commonly used to end an abbreviation	&c/& ca/ etc.	and so forth (etcetera)
★	TIB (upper left) typed from an old-style LDS temple record	(feet)	feet on microfilm spool
★★	TIB (upper left) typed from a family group record, but no copy was made at that time (archive record)	1st	first
		2nd	second
★★★	TIB (upper left) there is a question as to the correct parentage of the person described on the card	3rd	third
		4th	fourth
★★★	indicates that the LDS ordinance dates are listed in the computer parish print-out	1:57	refers to research notebook or volume number 1, p. 57
''	ditto (the same); same as above	47t	refers to the # of turns equivalent to the 87 ft. or the "F" on the take up reel of the microfilm reading machine
@	(1) at (2) individual and the principal name on the card appear as husband and wife on an archive record	(50673, pt 57)	50673 is the old Family History Library microfilm number, and pt 57 is the part number (use the new six or seven digit film numbers)
?	questionable interpretation		
X	killed	2aa-6	Family Group Record Sheets (no. following hyphen is no. of binder for that letter of the alphabet)
X	baptized or christened		
>	after	2ab-542	second thousand sheets of a large surname in 2aa
<	before	2B-414-17	same as form 2, but arranged by locality
#	number, pound		

2BA-103-17-295	bound LDS temple records; these records have been returned to the contributing families	2HuD	second husband's daughter
2BC	old lineage books - probably filed in 2aa	1Lt	1st Lieutenant
7/	7 shillings	2Lt	2nd Lieutenant
7BA-149-6	three generation pedigree charts	2Mst	second master
7R-44-6	No. 7 indicates pedigree charts. The letter represents the book; the number of the chart; & the last number, the number of the individual on the chart	2nep	second nephew
		2nie	second niece
		2sgt	second sergeant
51t	refers to the number of turns equivalent to 51 ft. on the take-up spool of microfilm reading machine	2son	second son
		2WiD	second wife's daughter
97'	refers to 97 feet of film on take-up spool of microfilm reading machine	2wif	second wife
		2WiM	second wife's mother
725	Controlled Extraction Eng-Gibson marriage Index	2WiS	second wife's son
		3/m.	three times a month
710481251	batch processed in 1971 on the 48th day of the year, 12th batch that day, page 51	3/yr.	three times a year
		3cou	third cousin
1cou	first cousin	3son	third son
1c 1r	first cousin once removed	/m	married
2c 1r	second cousin once removed	/w	widow/widower
2c 2r	second cousin twice removed	/d	divorced
2 gg dau	second great-granddaughter	/m★	married within the year
2 gg son	second great-grandson	7br	7ber ' viibr ' viiber ' September
3 gg neph il	third great-grandnephew-in-law	7bris	viibris ' Septembris (of September)
2-6-7	Form 2; family group records with four	8br	8ber ' viiibr ' viiiber ' October
1HuD	first husband's daughter	8bris	viiibris ' Octobris (of October)
1HuS	first husband's son	9br	9ber ' ixbr ' ixber ' November
1wif	first wife	9bris	ixbris ' Novembris (of November)
1WiS	first wife's son	10br	10ber ' xbr ' xber ' December
2Coh	second coachman	10bris	xbris ' Decembris (of December)
2Cou	second cousin		
2Crp	second corporal		

LENGTH

in. *or* "	inch
ft. *or* '	foot
yd.	yard
rd.	rod
mi.	mile

AREA

sq. in	square inch
sq. ft	square foot
sq. yd	square yard
sq. rd	square rod
sq. mi	square mile
a.	acre

VOLUME

cu. in	cubic inch
cu. ft	cubic foot
cu. yd	cubic yard

WEIGHT

gr.	grain
s. *or* Ə	scruple
dr. *or* ℨ	dram
dwt.	pennyweight
oz.	ounce
lb. *or* #	pound
cwt.	hundredweight
tn.	ton

DRY MEASURE

pt.	pint
qt.	quart
pk.	peck
bu.	bushel
gi..	gill
bbl.	barrel

LIQUID MEASURE

min.	minimum
fl. dr. or f.ℨ	fluid dram
fl. oz.	fluid ounce
pt.	pint
qt.	quart
gal.	gallon

BASE UNITS

m	meter
kg	kilogram
s	second
A	ampere
K	kelvin
mol	mole
cd	candela

ROMAN NUMERALS

I	one
II	two
III	three
IV	four
V	five
VI	six
VII	seven
VIII	eight
IX	nine
X	ten
XI	eleven
XII	twelve
XIII	thirteen
XIV	fourteen
XV	fifteen
XVI	sixteen
XVII	seventeen
XVIII	eighteen
XIX	nineteen
XX	twenty
XXI	twenty-one
XXII	twenty-two
XXIII	twenty-three
XXIV	twenty-four
XXV	twenty-five
XXVI	twenty-six
XXVII	twenty-seven
XXVIII	twenty-eight
XXIX	twenty-nine
XXX	thirty
XXXI	thirty-one
XL	fourty
L	fifty
LX	sixty
LXX	seventy
LXXX	eighty
XC	ninety
C	one hundred
CI	one-hundred-one
CL	one-hundred-fifty
CCC	three hundred
CD	four hundred
D	five hundred
DC	six hundred
DCC	seven hundred
DCCC	eight hundred
CM	nine hundred
M	one thousand
MDC	sixteen hundred
MDCC	seventeen hundred
MDCCC	eighteen hundred
MCM	nineteen hundred

CARDINAL NUMBER

1	unus
2	duo, duae
3	tres, tres, tria
4	quattuor
5	quinque
6	sex
7	septem
8	octo
9	novem
10	decem
11	undecim
12	duodecim
13	tredecim
14	quattuordecim
15	quindecim
16	sedecim
17	septemdecim
18	odeviginti
19	undeviginti
20	viginti
20	viginti unus
22	viginti duo
23	viginti tres
24	viginti quattuor
25	viginti quinque
26	viginti sex
27	viginit septem
28	viginti octo
29	viginti novem
30	trigenta
40	quadraginta
50	quinquaginta
60	sexaginta
70	septuaginta
80	octoginta
90	nonaginta
100	centum
101	centum unus
150	centum quinquaginta
200	ducenti
300	trecenti
400	quadringenti
500	quingenti
600	sescenti
700	septigenti
800	octingenti
900	nongenti
1000	mille

ORDINAL NUMBERS

1st	primus
2nd	secundus
3rd	tertius
4th	quartus
5th	quintus
6th	sextus
7th	septimus
8th	octavus
9th	nonus
10th	decimus
11th	undecimus
12th	duodecimus
13th	tertius decimus
14th	quartus decimus
15th	quintus decimus
16th	sextus decimus
17th	septimus decimus
18th	duodevicesimus
19th	undevicesimus
20th	vicesimus, vigesimus
21st	vicesimus primus
22nd	vicesimus secundus
23rd	vicesimus tertius
24th	vicesimus quartus
25th	vicesimus quintus
26th	vicesimus sextus
27th	vecesimus septimus
28th	vicesimus octavus
29th	vicesimus nonus
30th	tricesimus
40th	quadragesimus
50th	quinquagesimus
60th	sexagesimus
70th	septuagesimus
80th	octogesimus
90th	nonagesimus
100th	centesimus
101th	centesimus primus
150th	centesimus quinquagesimus
200th	ducentesimus
300th	trecentesimus
400th	quadrigentesimus
500th	quingentesimus
600th	sescentesimus
700th	septingentesimus
800th	octingentesimus
900th	nongentesimus
1000th	millesimus

BIBLIOGRAPHY

Abbreviations (from James Savage, *A Genealogical Dictionary of the First Settlers of New England*). Online. Available: www.qni.com/~anderson/SavageAbbrev.html

Abbreviations Found in Genealogy. Online. Available: www.rootsweb.com/~rigenweb/abbrev.html

Abbreviations Used in Genealogy. Online. Available: www.uq.net.au/~zzmgrinl/abbrev.html

Abbreviations Used in Genealogy. Online. Available: www.rootsweb.com/roots-l/abbrevs.html

Acronym Finder. Online. Available: www.acronymfinder.com

Acronyms and Abbreviations. Online. Available: mel.lib.mi.us/reference/REF-acronym.html

Acronyms Used in the Computer Community. Online. Available: www.freewarehof.org/acronyms.html

Association of Professional Genealogists. *Directory of Professional Genealogists, 20th Anniversary Edition, 1999-2000.* Compiled by Kathleen W. Hinckley. Denver: The Association, 1999, pp. 11-12.

British Genealogy Abbreviations and Acronyms. Online. Available: www.gendocs.demon.co.uk/abbr.html

Census Abbreviations. Online. Available: www.seark.net/~sabra/abbrev.txt

Census Abbreviations. Online. Available: webpub.com/~jhagee/cens-abr.html

Census Abbreviations Used in Soundex. Online. Available: www.seark.net/~sabra/sxabbrev.txt

Census and Soundex Abbreviations. Online. Available: www.genrecords.com/library/abbreviations.htm

The Chicago Manual of Style. 14th ed. Chicago: University of Chicago Press, 1993.

Cyndi's List of Genealogy Sites on the Internet: Dictionaries & Glossaries. Online. Available: www.cyndislist.com/diction.htm

DeSola, Ralph. *Abbreviations Dictionary.* 6th ed. New York: Elsevier North Holland, 1981.

DOD Dictionary of Military Terms. Online. Available: www.dtic.mil/doctrine/jel/doddict

Edmonds, David, ed. *Dictionary of Abbreviations.* Edinburgh, Scotland: Chambers, 1995.

Evans, Barbara Jean. *A to Zax: A Comprehensive Dictionary for Genealogists & Historians.* 3rd ed. Alexandria, Va.: Hearthside Press, 1995.

Family History Jargon. Online. Available: www.vellum.demon.co.uk/guide/fh11.htm

Genealogical Abbreviations. Online. Available: www.pcola.gulf.net/~llscott/abbrevia.htm

Genealogy Abbreviation List. Online. Available: www.niagara.com/~hanam/abbreviations/abbreviations.txt

Genealogy Abbreviations. Online. Available: homepages.rootsweb.com/~sam/abbr.html

Genealogy Abbreviations. Online. Available: www.hoosierlines.cqc.com/abbrev.htm

Genealogy Abbreviations. Online. Available: www.netscope.net/~tchs/hist/gene.html

Genealogy Dictionary. Online. Available: home.att.net/~dottsr/diction.html

Genealogy Dictionary. Online. Available: w3g.med.uni-giessen.de/CGB/genetxt/buzzwords

Genealogy Quest. Online. Available: www.genealogy-quest.com/glossaries/abbrev.html

Glossary of Internet Terms. Online. Available: www.matisse.net/files/glossary.html

Glossary of Terms. Online. Available: www.jpl.nasa.gov/tours/glossary.html

Harris, Maurine and Glen Harris, comps. *Ancestry's Concise Genealogical Dictionary.* Salt Lake City: Ancestry Publishing, 1989.

Hinckley, Kathleen W. *Alphabet Soup: Understanding the Genealogical Community.* Online. Available: www.genealogy.com/33_kathy.html

Mayberry, George, comp. *A Concise Dictionary of Abbreviations.* New York: Tudor Publishing Co., 1961.

Netlingo. Online. Available: www.netlingo.com

Other Genealogical Resources. Online. Available: www.scruz.net/~elias/hnoh/OTHERRESOURCES8.html

Schwartz, Robert J. *The Complete Dictionary of Abbreviations.* New York: Thomas Y. Crowell Co., 1955.

Sperry, Kip. *Reading Early American Handwriting.* Baltimore: Genealogical Publishing Co., 1998.

UK Genealogy: Common Acronyms & Jargon. Online. Available: www.oz.net/~markhow/acronym-uk.htm

United States Postal Service. *Official Abbreviations.* Online. Available: www.usps.gov/ncsc/lookups/abbrev.html

The World Wide Web Acronym and Abbreviation Server. Online. Available: www.ucc.ie/info/net/acronyms

Kip Sperry is an Associate Professor of family history at Brigham Young University, Provo, Utah, where he teaches American genealogical research methods and sources, American paleography, and computer genealogy. He is both a Certified Genealogist and an Accredited Genealogist.

Kip is a Fellow of three organizations: American Society of Genealogists, National Genealogical Society, and Utah Genealogical Association. He has received the NGS President's Citation, NGS Distinguished Service Award, NGS Award of Merit, Utah Genealogical Association Annual Award and Distinguished Service Award, and GENTECH 2000 Certificate of Appreciation.

He is the author of "Published Indexes" (Chapter 6) in *Printed Sources: A Guide to Published Genealogical Records* (Ancestry, 1998), *Reading Early American Handwriting*, *Genealogical Research in Ohio*, and other works. He is a contributing editor to *The American Genealogist* and *National Genealogical Society Quarterly*. His articles have appeared in *Ancestry* (Magazine), *The American Genealogist*, *The Genealogist* (American Society of Genealogists), *National Genealogical Society Quarterly*, *The New England Historical and Genealogical Register*, and other publications.

Kip is a lecturer at national, state, and local family history conferences and seminars, including Brigham Young University, Laie, Hawaii; BYU Campus Education Weeks, Provo, Utah; BYU Annual Genealogy and Family History conferences; National Genealogical Society annual Conferences in the States; Federation of Genealogical Societies annual conferences; 1980 World Conference on Records, Salt Lake City; National Institute on Genealogical Research at the National Archives; Salt Lake Institute of Genealogy, Salt Lake City; and others.

He has served as a trustee for Board for Certification of Genealogists, National Conference Chair for GENTECH 2000 conference in San Diego, National Genealogical Society council member, National Conference Chair of four NGS national conferences, and director of five BYU annual genealogy and family history conferences.

Biographical sketches appear in *Who's Who in the West*, 23rd edition (1992-93), *Who's Who in Genealogy and Heraldry*, 2nd edition (1990), *Contemporary Authors, New Revision Series* (Gale Research Co.), and other works. He was a content advisor for Ancestors II PBS family history television series.